FINANCIAL DECISION-MAKING IN THE FOODSERVICE INDUSTRY

Economic Costs and Benefits

FINANCIAL DECISION-MAKING IN THE FOODSERVICE INDUSTRY

Economic Costs and Benefits

Edited by
Amit Sharma, PhD

Apple Academic Press Inc.
4164 Lakeshore Road
Burlington ON L7L 1A4
Canada

Apple Academic Press Inc.
1265 Goldenrod Circle NE
Palm Bay, Florida 32905
USA

© 2020 by Apple Academic Press, Inc.

First issued in paperback 2021

Exclusive worldwide distribution by CRC Press, a member of Taylor & Francis Group

No claim to original U.S. Government works

ISBN 13: 978-1-77463-516-2 (pbk)
ISBN 13: 978-1-77188-825-7 (hbk)

Library and Archives Canada Cataloguing in Publication

Title: Financial decision-making in the foodservice industry : economic costs and benefits / edited by Amit Sharma, PhD.

Other titles: Financial decision-making in the food service industry

Names: Sharma, Amit (Professor of hospitality finance), editor.

Description: Includes bibliographical references and index.

Identifiers: Canadiana (print) 20190170069 | Canadiana (ebook) 20190170123 | ISBN 9781771888257 (hardcover) | ISBN 9780429292712 (ebook)

Subjects: LCSH: Food service—Finance. | LCSH: Food service management—Decision making.

Classification: LCC TX911.3.F5 F56 2020 | DDC 647.95068/1—dc23

Library of Congress Cataloging-in-Publication Data

Names: Sharma, Amit, editor.

Title: Financial decision-making in the foodservice industry : economic costs and benefits / edited by Amit Sharma, PhD.

Other titles: Financial decisionmaking in the food service industry

Description: Oakville, ON ; Palm Bay, Florida : Apple Academic Press, [2020] | Includes bibliographical references and index. | Summary: "The study of decision-making in foodservice is still a relatively new area of scholarly interest. The application of cost-benefit analysis and behavioral finance and economics in the foodservice context is rare. This volume, Financial Decision-Making in the Foodservice Industry: Economic Costs and Benefits, fills that gap and focuses on cost-benefit analysis, decision-making, behavioral finance, economic theories, and their application in foodservice and restaurant industry. The volume synthesizes these major themes by developing new theoretical foundations and presenting findings from the investigation of managerial practice. The authors cover an abundance of topical issues, including ethical obligations in foodservice, sustainability issues in the foodservice/restaurant industry, farm-to-school and local food expenditures in school foodservice settings, managerial traits and behavior in the foodservice industry, and more. The volume comprehensively analyzes the foodservice value chain, providing a unique perspective for not only hospitality researchers but also for those in such diverse (though related) fields as agricultural economics, food science, food nutrition, consumer behavior, decision-making, and finance and economics"-- Provided by publisher.

Identifiers: LCCN 2019035652 (print) | LCCN 2019035653 (ebook) | ISBN 9781771888257 (hardcover) | ISBN 9780429292712 (ebook)

Subjects: LCSH: Food service--Cost control. | Food service--Finance.

Classification: LCC TX911.3.C65 F56 2020 (print) | LCC TX911.3.C65 (ebook) | DDC 647.95068--dc23

LC record available at https://lccn.loc.gov/2019035652

LC ebook record available at https://lccn.loc.gov/2019035653

Apple Academic Press also publishes its books in a variety of electronic formats. Some content that appears in print may not be available in electronic format. For information about Apple Academic Press products, visit our website at **www.appleacademicpress.com** and the CRC Press website at **www.crcpress.com**

About the Editor

Amit Sharma, PhD

Amit Sharma is Professor of Hospitality Finance in the School of Hospitality Management at Pennsylvania State University (since 2006), and prior to that he was Assistant Professor at Iowa State University since 2002. He is the Director of the Food Decisions Research Laboratory and an Affiliate Faculty at the Teaching and Learning with Technologies and the Rock Ethics Institute at Penn State University. He also has an appointment as the Senior Research Associate at the University of Johannesburg in South Africa.

Dr. Sharma teaches finance and economics at the School of Hospitality Management. His interdisciplinary research focuses on Decision-Making and Cost–Benefit Analysis, and Small Business Financing, in food system contexts. He is specially interested in how individuals make food choices and decisions along the food systems continuum. The US Department of Agriculture and the World Bank have funded his research here in the United States and in southern Africa. His research has been published in leading disciplinary, and mainstream journals such as: *Journal of Hospitality and Tourism Research, International Journal of Contemporary Hospitality Management, Food Policy, Annals of Tourism Research, Tourism Management*, and others.

Dr. Sharma is also founding editor of the *ICHRIE Research Reports*, a publication focused on translational research. He also serves on the editorial boards of several leading journals. Dr. Sharma is also a Visiting Professor and Research Scholar at the Institut Paul Bocuse (Lyon, France), and was a Visiting Scholar at Kyung Hee University (Seoul, South Korea) (2013–2014). Dr. Sharma has been an advisory board member of the African Research Center at PSU, and is an Advisory Board Member of the Research Center at the Institut Paul Bocuse. He is also the past President (2017–2018) of International Council of Hotel, Restaurant, and Institutional Education, and pat president (2018–2020) of the International Association of Hospitality Financial Management Educators (iAHFME).

His education includes: PhD, Virginia Tech.; Masters, Institut de Management Hotelier International (IMHI) (France); Higher National Diploma in Hospitality Management, University of Salford (England); Bachelor in Economics (Honors), University of Delhi (India).

Contents

Dedication

Dedicated to

Michael D. Olsen,
mentor, adviser, and guide.

Contributors

Frode Alfnes
UMB School of Economics and Business, Norwegian University of Life Sciences, P.O. Box 5003, N-1432 Ås, Norway

Robert M. Chiles
Pennsylvania State University

Robin B. DiPietro
School of Hotel, Restaurant and Tourism Management, College of Hospitality, Retail and Sport Management, University of South Carolina, Columbia, SC 29208, USA

Maurice Doyon
Département d'économie agroalimentaire et des Sciences de la consommation, Université Laval, Québec, Canada

Mrudula Holkar
Interdisciplinary School of Health Sciences, Savitribai Phule Pune University, Maharashtra, India

Angeline Jeyakumar
Interdisciplinary School of Health Sciences, Savitribai Phule Pune University, Maharashtra, India

H. Kesa
School of Tourism and Hospitality, College of Business and Economics, University of Johannesburg

Naiqing Lin
Department of Hospitality Management, Kansas State University, USA

Camille Massey
Département d'économie agroalimentaire et des Sciences de la consommation, Université Laval, Québec, Canada

A. N. Melani
School of Tourism and Hospitality, College of Business and Economics, University of Johannesburg

Victor Motta
Sao Paulo School of Business Administration, Fundação Getúlio Vargas

Yuxia Ouyang
School of Hospitality Management, Pennsylvania State University, University Park, Pennsylvania, USA

Kevin R. Roberts
Department of Hospitality Management, Kansas State University, USA

Laure Saulais
Centre for Food and Hospitality Research, Institut Paul Bocuse, Ecully, France INRA - Université Grenoble Alpes, UMR 1215 GAEL, Grenoble, France

Kwanglim Seo
University of Hawaii, Manoa

Jungtae Soh
Pennsylvania State University

Amit Sharma
School of Hospitality Management, College of Health and Human Development,
the Pennsylvania State University, 201 Mateer Building, University Park, PA 16802, USA

Abbreviations

AFH	away-from-home
BMI	body mass index
CBA	cost–benefit analysis
DCF	discounted cash flow analysis
DDS	diversity scores
ELM	elaboration likelihood model
FAFH	food-away-from-home
FTS	farm to school
FVS	food variety scores
GDP	gross domestic product
HAZ	height for age
HBM	health belief model
LNED	low-nutrient, energy-dense
OH	out-of-home
RM	relationship marketing
SLR	self-regulation theory
TC	transaction cost
TCB	transaction cost and benefit
TPB	theory of planned behavior
TRA	theory of reasoned action
WAZ	weight for age
WHZ	weight for height
WTP	willingness to pay

Abbreviations

Preface

The study of decision-making in the foodservice system is still a relatively new area of scholarly interest. In fact, in many ways this area remains loosely defined, transcending disciplinary boundaries. In this collection of scholarly papers, we present an economic viewpoint to this discussion. Cost–benefit analysis (CBA) remains a critical framework of decision-making. This collection of papers presents a novel point of view of the CBA from the microeconomic perspective, with an essential overarching argument: costs and benefits, whether observable or perceived, could also impact individual decision-making. While several issues are raised in these papers, we hope future investigations will build on these perspectives to bring more in-depth understanding of CBA in individual decision-making.

More so, the impacts of the decisions in context of such costs and benefits have broader societal consequences. For instance, individual food choices impact health and nutrition. As a result, there is a growing awareness of knowing where our food originates, whether it be within the local food system, or through the use of sustainable and ethical practices. As the consumers' interest grows to become more aware and knowledgeable about the food they consume, so does the need for the business managers to be more responsible in making better decisions. Behavior change is always a challenge. Therefore, there is a growing awareness on the validity and reliability of approaches to encourage and motivate individuals to make better choices. There is much more work that needs to be done in this area of behavior change as we have only begun to scratch the surface of these issues. Given the boundary spanning nature of these discussions we believe this collection of scholarly articles is timely to present the multitude of perspectives relevant to moving forward the research agenda and therefore our understanding of the foodservice system. The purpose of this collection is therefore to stimulate thought amongst scholars.

The food-away-from-home phenomenon that essentially drives the foodservice system continues to increase in scale and scope of its activity. As a consequence, there is also a rich cross-section of economic activities that is happening within the foodservice system. While in this collection of papers we are unable to touch on each of such activities, we present frames of references, and the trade-off decision-making model that we hope could be referred to in future such investigations within the foodservice system.

I am most grateful to each of the collaborators in this collection for agreeing to be part of this project: Robin DiPietro, Kevin Roberts, Robert Chiles, Laure Saulais, Angeline Jeyakumar, Hema Kesa, Frode Alfnes, Kwanglim Seo, Victor Motta, Jungtae Soh, Yuxia Ouyang, Naiqing Lin, Maurice Doyon, Camille Massey, Mrudula Holkar, and A. N. Melani. It is our hope that these papers will create the stimulus for a deeper discussion on each of those aspects of the foodservice system, and more.

PART I

Eating Away from Home Decisions

CHAPTER 1

The ACE Trade-Off Model: A Cost–Benefit Perspective to Understanding the Process of Everyday Food Choice Transactions

AMIT SHARMA[*]

School of Hospitality Management, College of Health and Human Development, the Pennsylvania State University, 201 Mateer Building, University Park, PA 16802, USA

[*]*Corresponding author. E-mail: aus22@psu.edu*

ABSTRACT

Everyday food choices in the foodservice system continue to be investigated extensively from varied perspectives. Economics of food decisions, one such perspective, can benefit from a guiding framework to enhance a deeper understanding of the principles guiding food choice decisions. An underlying unit of food choice analysis is the transaction of buying or selling food. Such transactions present the decision maker with choices. Therefore, food decisions are the result of tradeoffs that appear within such choices. These tradeoffs are based on the costs and benefits associated with transactions. In this paper, we present a framework that describes food decisions as a tradeoff of cost and benefits that the decision-maker must resolve. The framework also incorporates the approach decision-makers take for information processing. In doing so, we draw upon the theories of informed choice and bounded rationality. How we evaluate the food choice transaction can help us better understand food decision dynamics. The adoption of this framework in studies of food decision processes and outcomes can be informative to optimize individual outcomes (such as health, utility) and consequences that will impact the broader market.

1.1   INTRODUCTION

Food choice decisions are complex and consequential to well-being of individuals and families and profitability of businesses in the foodservice system.[1] For individuals, the complexity of food choices, particularly when eating away from home, have increased manifolds given the alternatives available, invariably the high speed of such transactions, and the continuously increasing expenditure on food away from home. Similarly, businesses operating in the complex foodservice system must constantly make choices that involve the supply chain and demand side stakeholders. The question is how do individuals make these decisions?

Theories of decision-making and choice processes are abundant, both from a positivist and a normative point of view. The normative analysis in the domain of food choices and decisions has received some focus, particularly in Frost et al. (1996). However, for the most part the analysis of foodservice system choices and decisions has happened on the crossroads of the larger decision analysis context. That is, decision analysis has largely focused on longer-term decisions such as retirement planning, fixed and financial asset investment analysis, and others. We could enhance our understanding of the shorter-term decisions, particularly those that involve day to day choices, and at a high frequency. Foodservice decisions fall in this category—as individual consumers; food choice decisions are frequent, over a shorter period of time. Similarly, businesses in the foodservice system need to make choices that are frequent. However, similar to less frequent decisions, consequences of food choices could be felt over the short and the long term. Therefore, while the day-to-day decisions involve higher frequency, they also inherently lead to both long and short-term consequences.

The seminal works of Daniel Kahneman and Amos Treversky in the analysis of decisions under uncertainty have enhanced our understanding of how the System 1 processes contribute to our decision making. While System 1 is reactive and less mindful, System 2 is deliberate and thoughtful. Given the consequences of food choices and decisions, System 2 ought to be the process that could help guide our actions. System 2 requires individuals to be deliberate with seeking and obtaining information, processing it, and

---

[1]Here the foodservice system broadly refers to the various segments of the foodservice industry, the associated industries along its supply chain, and the consumer behavior in food away from home environments.

then using it to make decisions. Not everyone is prepared or even trained for such processes. One of the significant challenges for enhancing our decision making is to gain a deeper understanding of how can individuals be better trained and educated to use the System 2 processes that would help guide more deliberate decisions, particularly in the context of food. Given the growing emphasis in eating away from home environments, we believe the System 2 impact on food choices would be of critical consequence to enhance individual well-being.

Indeed, the philosophical approach in this paper needs to be recognized. While there is value in the role of our reactive and less mindful actions play in decision making, there is also a need to balance these reactive approaches with the more methodical and systematic analysis of information. If the two proposed systems (Systems 1 and 2) were to be taken on face value to exist, then there is a reason for the two to exist: Each plays a role in our choices. Both together would likely enhance our decisions and choices more so than either of the two actings alone. There is, however, an imbalance in the way we allow the two systems to evolve over time. While System 1 benefits from repetitive reactive and responsive actions, System 2 may not necessarily benefit for such repeated actions. If anything, due to lack of use System 2 could stand the risk of deteriorating over time.

There are no straightforward answers on how we can enhance System 2 (Evans, 2003; Sinayev and Peters, 2015; Frederick, 2005; Sadler-Smith and Shefy, 2007; Samson and Voyer, 2012). One that most researchers agree upon is that System 2 needs to be constantly educated so that we become more aware of our decisions and choices (Viswanathan and Jain, 2013; Dansereau et al., 2013). While this sounds simple in a statement, acting upon it is another matter. We now also have this challenge of "scaling up" that has emerged in the recent past—how can we scale up our intervention for maximum impact. This further complicates the challenges of strengthening our System 2. However, that should not lessen our efforts to do so, in fact, it should increase our efforts to find ways that would enhance System 2, and help balance the synergies between these two Systems.

Food decisions are amongst the most essential, day to day choices we make on a repeated basis. Given the recent trends, we are also eating far more away from home than ever since such observable behavior has been recorded. Therefore, foodservice choice analysis could benefit from a more focused and systematic assessment of the manner in which individuals make such decisions, and also help guide individual decision making to be more systematic and analytic, than just being reactive and responsive. In this paper, we present an approach to achieving this end and propose an analytical framework to understand the decision process within the domain of foodservice choices. The approach we take is that of a an transaction, one that involves an exchange of a good or service for cash or a promise to pay (credit). Defining such decisions as a transaction can help us systematically unfold the complex aspects involved in food decisions. Such a systematic approach would thereby help guide individuals' analytical decision making, to complement it with the more intuitive and reactive System 1 approach.

1.2   THE FOODSERVICE SYSTEM

What is the food choice system? It could be defined as the system within which an individual would make food choices. From a microeconomic perspective, and with the consumer at the center of this discussion, one way to define the food choice system could be to divide it into two key components: food at home, and food away from home. The foodservice system can be defined as the food away from home environment. This includes, and is not limited to, a supply of food for production and preparation in foodservice businesses, and the consumption of food by consumers either in these environments or in the extended foodservice environment that often includes their own homes.

The foodservice segments that could be classified in this system are varied and with a diverse set of goals (Reynolds and McClusky, 2013). Foodservice segments have traditionally been divided into commercial and noncommercial/nonprofit. That said, the lines a blurring along these traditional boundaries. For instance, corporate dining services are an interesting example of foodservice operations; while the corporation providing the foodservice is not intending to make a profit from selling that food to its employees, the foodservice company managing that unit on behalf of the corporation would have a profit objective.

Another way of segmenting the foodservice industry has been to place it distinctly different from food retail businesses. That boundary too is now increasingly blurring as grocery stores have developed their own foodservice outlets within the grocery store environment. The food delivery segment traditionally used to be an extension of the restaurants so that their physical location would not be a constraint. However, now with the advent businesses offering 'ingredient and recipe' tool kits, the line separating delivery service from restaurants has become more distinct.

There also used to be a clear distinction between food away from home versus food at home. As one can imagine, that line too has significantly blurred in the recent past; largely because food prepared away from home can more conveniently be consumed at home. In fact, food away from home can be prepared at home for home consumption, despite not being from your own pantry. These are interesting trends shaping the foodservice system, and the phenomenon we have called food away from home.

As the context of the foodservice system evolves over time, the constant aspects of this system have been the stakeholders in the system, activities that create value and establish interaction between these stakeholders, and the inputs to generate these activities, and the outputs as the outcomes of these activities. While we will restrain from dwelling into the details of this systematic view, we highlight the key elements of each of these system components, through a transactional perspective. Stakeholders in the foodservice system include the growers and producers, wholesalers, and retailer markets both physical and virtual, suppliers and transporters, storage facilities, producers, servers, consumers, associations of each stakeholder, local, state and federal governments, and the global dimension of the foodservice system. The key activities that generate value across these stakeholders could be identified as follows: Growing and producing food, harvesting, packaging and marketing, supplying, transporting, storage, production, service, and consumption. While these activities mirror the stakeholders and are sequential, they could also be repeated along the chain. The inputs of the system could be classified into monetary and nonmonetary inputs, as follows: land for growing, seeds for producing, water, climate, fuel for production and transportation, markets and information sharing, storage facilities, production expertise, menu planning and offering, service acumen, and financial capital for organizations to create the food offerings. It also involves time and money for consumption. Finally, the association and government stakeholders require information for policy advice and development, and financial resources for funding and supporting the foodservice system. The outcomes of making choices in the foodservice system can be classified as decisions by foodservice providers, consumers, and government (policy makers); furthermore the outcome measures can also be classified as monetary or non-monetary.

While there has been an extensive reporting of classifying the foodservice segments, the linkages of these segments to the extended foodservice system have been less reported. The above-stated description of the foodservice system allows us to assess and evaluate these linkages, and therefore also inform us on how decisions might be made in establishing those linkages.

1.3 FOOD DECISIONS

Food is an essential aspect of our lives. What is so unique about choosing what to eat, whether it is at home or away from home? When this act of eating occurs several times in a day, it tends to lose the attention this topic may deserve. Similarly, what is the relevance and significance of understanding the food system decisions when the consequences are not always apparent and appear consequential in the near future.

This is to state that indeed food choice decisions are complex, and consequential to well-being of individuals and families, even though these consequences are not always apparent in the short term. Therefore, it is no surprise that the inquiry on food choices has received extensive attention from researchers from varied fields of studies, including but not limited to nutrition (Cowburn and Stockley, 2005; Worsley, 2002), food science (Wilcock et al., 2004; Lytle, 2009; Jensen and Sandøe, 2002), food technology (Siegrist, 2008; Cardello et al., 2007), economics (Drewnowski and Darmon, 2005; French, 2003), psychology (Köster, 2003, 2009; Shepherd and Raats, 2006), biological sciences (Drewnowski and Kawachi, 2015; Prescottand Logan, 2017), neuropsychology (Roitman et al., 2004; Volkow et al., 2003; DiLeone et al., 2012; Lepping et al., 2015; Doucerain and Fellows, 2012), and many others. In diverse ways, this literature has investigated the core question of how do individuals make food choices? As one would expect, the answer is not a simple one. In fact, the response to this question is context-specific, and furthermore, involves both individual and environmental traits of particular food choices. We do not see this negatively, or as a challenge. On the contrary, this wide breadth and depth of investigations have begun to paint a colorful picture of food choices. However, pushing forward the research agenda to comprehensively understand food choice aspect, now more than ever, requires a cohesive and directed approach.

The purpose of this paper is to attempt to build on these findings from the literature into a food choice decisions model that could provide a cohesive approach to understanding how we make food choices. As in any other research endeavor, there is bound to incompleteness in our approach. We, therefore, hope future research will build on these initial attempts.

Integrating ideas requires identification of a common link across them. This is no trivial task, and certainly not one without the risks of alienating certain other perspectives. Therefore, even though this effort aspires to integrate ideas of our current understanding of how individuals make food choices, there is a risk of marginalizing certain others, simply by the approach selected for this purpose. However, we would propose that this by itself would be an invitation to the reader to contribute to this discussion, by further enhancing its cohesiveness.

In identifying the common links across our current understanding of food choices, we refer to the anatomy of the concept of inquiry: Food choices. In essence, choices assume the presence of alternatives. Therefore, choices also involve selecting from these alternatives. The presence of alternatives can be the function of factors that are within an individual's control, and others that are not. Selecting from these alternatives assumes that individuals would adopt criteria to select and evaluate or assess that criterion. Food then simply becomes the overarching context across these constructs linking our current understanding of how individuals make food choices.

In the rest of this paper, we will develop this idea of an integrated approach to understanding food choices. We propose the following as a normative model of food choice decisions and one based on our current and existing understanding from studies on food choices. The hope is that this model will provide direction for enhancing this understanding of this phenomenon. The gains to theoretical understanding of human choices and ways to inform practice and policy discussions can be significant through a cohesive approach. Overall, the mission is still to enhance the well-being of individuals and families through better food choices.

1.4 ECONOMIC ANALYSIS OF FOOD CHOICES AND INDIVIDUAL REASONING

The construct of food choice has been extensively studied. One of the early models describing the food choices process was by Frost et al.

(1996). In this model, the authors articulated a constructionist's perspective. Frost et al. (1996) described the process of influences in food choices as those from ideals, personal factors, resources, social framework, and food contexts. These influences were then described to be acting on the personal system. Through this personal system, the decision-maker would make value negotiations. These value negotiations were based on sensory perceptions, monetary considerations, convenience, health and nutrition, managing relationships, and quality. Eventually, these negotiations would lead to strategies that would inform food choices. This early work has been beneficial in articulating a set of influences and a process to guide food choices. Other food choice processes have been recommended (for instance see, Furst et al., 1996; Marcum et al., 2018). One of the challenges of process models is to balance the complexity of underlying relationships, while still being descriptive of the sequential interactions. Greater clarity in these sequential relationships could enhance understanding of the process and also allow for these sequential relationships to be explicitly investigated. What binds these sequential relationships, then becomes an important component of the process thinking. Can the process being described be contextualized in an argument? Or is the process being governed by an overarching principle that would guide the successive or sequential relationships?

The idea of food choices is strongly embedded within the social context of individuals. Food is a strong element/component of our day-to-day lives. Often times, studying food choices can present challenges. First, food is a life necessity, and therefore almost taken for granted. Not eating is not an option. Therefore, the study of food choice cannot be between the presence and absence of food. The choice is between a better or a worse option. Second, the ideas that define a better or a worse option, or preferences, can be influenced by numerous factors. Many of these are in the social context of an individual. Sociology of food choices is a critical element of studying food, its history, trends that have led to its current evolution and future anticipated changes in the production, distribution, and consumption of food (Devine, 2005; Marty et al., 2018). While the sociology of food provides an important perspective on our understanding of the broader forces driving change of this phenomenon, the research so far has focused more on the broader and macrolevel analysis. Microlevel, individual social analysis, or also called microsociology, focuses on studying individual social interaction, and social behaviors (King et al., 2004; Cruwys et al., 2015). Such interpretive analysis using phenomenological and grounded theory approaches have much opportunities to contribute to our understanding of food choices at the individual level.

A supplementary approach to understanding food choices is through the lens of microeconomic theory. Here our interest is in understanding the procedural aspect of food choices and decisions. The microeconomic theory focuses on the choices that individuals and households make in the process of utility maximization (Taylor and Adelman, 2003). Particular emphasis is placed on the allocation of scarce resources in this utility maximization process (Birch and Gafni, 1992; Frederiks et al., 2015). Allocation of scarce resources is a central element of choices and decisions that individuals and households make. However, an underlying assumption for the need for resource allocation is the existence of a transaction (Becher, 2007; Macher and Richman, 2008). The logic here is that in the absence of a transaction (due to a need for the demand and supply of goods/services) the necessity for resource allocation would not arise.

The transactional focus of economic thinking goes back to the early part of the 20th century. John R. Commons (1931) elaborates on the essential aspects of the transaction; how a transaction represents the "smallest unit" of economic activity from an institutionalist perspective. A transaction is further described as the precedents of any exchange of commodities "before labor can produce, or consumers can consume, or commodities be physically exchanged." Given its origins in institutional economics, the theories and investigations of a transaction have been developed in the context of the firm as the basis of these transactions. Amongst the most well recognized and extensively studied aspects of institutional transaction is transaction costs (Williamson, 1981), a termed that was originally coined by Coarse (1937), and formally studied in the latter part of the last century.

However, individual-level transaction analysis could also present opportunities to understand individual choices and decisions (Delgado, 1999). Our approach in this paper is based on the individual level transaction analysis to understand the process of food choices and decisions, an approach that is deeply rooted in the theories of economic transactions. The perspective of this analysis is that individuals engage in a transaction that eventually leads to a choice, or usually a tradeoff. Understanding this transaction could better help us understand the choice and the decision process. Based on transaction theories, we could begin with the assumption that a transaction involve costs (Williamson, 1981). These could be categorized into search and information, bargaining, and policing and enforcement costs. Conversely, transactions also represent potential benefits. The framework for analyzing transaction benefits remains incomplete. Further, there is recognition that transaction cost–benefit analysis has the potential for us to better understand the choice and decision processes (Boudreau et al., 2007).

Our approach and proposed model leverage the idea that transaction costs also have associated benefits. The eventual choices made by individuals are based on tradeoffs between these costs and benefits in the decision transaction. The process of conducting these transactional tradeoffs is the focal interest of our approach. Therefore, the core element of the proposed approach is to understand the tradeoffs that individuals make in balancing the costs and benefits of the underlying transaction. In the following section, we review the cost–benefit analysis process, as this would be able to enhance our perspective of the proposed model.

1.5   THE PROCESS OF COST–BENEFIT ANALYSIS

Cost–benefit analysis (CBA) is grounded in the theory of welfare economics (Boadway, 1974; Birch and Donaldson, 1987), and has mostly been used as a decision process for public investment projects. While there are generally agreed principles of conducting CBA, certain variations exist (Kornhauser, 2000; Coates IV, 2014). Still, there continue to exist methodological challenges in this process. Traditionally, CBA has been extensively used for policy decision purposes, that involve large public utility projects (Damart and Roy, 2009; Feuillette et al., 2016). Often times the idea of CBA is also used in private businesses, with the objective of selecting projects that have the maximum net benefit (Birch and Donaldson, 1987; Nickel et al., 2009, June). The general process of conducting CBA can be identified as follows (Cellini and Kee, 2010; King and Schrems, 1978):

1.   Identification of alternatives, and stakeholders
2.   Assessment of cost–benefit measures
3.   Predicting cost–benefit outcomes

4. Discounting future cost–benefits
5. Assessment of net benefits
6. Sensitivity or with/without project analysis
7. Making choices

1.5.1 Governing Principles of the CBA

The cost–benefit approach provides the key elements of the ACE (Alternatives, Criteria, Evaluate) model later introduced in this paper. However, the process is also guided by certain principles or guidelines for conducting the CBA process. Here are the eight principles identified by Griffin (1998):

Principle 1: Economically acceptable projects are defined as those that have benefits exceeding their costs.

Principle 2: Changes in welfare are evaluated as differences between scenarios with and without the project.

Principle 3: Measurement of costs are based on the idea of social opportunity costs.

Principle 4: Benefits to the producer are measured as changes in producer surplus.

Principle 5: Benefits to the consumer is measured as consumer surplus.

Principle 6: Zero-sum transfers of costs or benefits need to be ignored (Griffin, 1998, pp 2067).

Principle 7: Cost or benefits occurring over time in the future that require aggregation would need to employ time discounting.

Principle 8: Welfare changes that cannot be monetarized need to be disclosed.

The ACE choice model proposed in this paper is motivated by these key elements of the cost and benefit assessment process. The other motivation for the ACE remains the early work for Frost et al. (1997). The choice influences of the Frost et al. (1997) model stresses the availability of alternatives. These alternatives can emerge from various stimuli. The alternatives then must be evaluated. This overall evaluation system has been conceptualized as the personal system of the decision-maker that conducted structured analysis. However, in our view, this personal System 2 remains a black box of sorts. Eventually, the negotiations through the personal systems would lead to food choices.

While the context and purposes of the C-B framework and food choice model of Frost et al. (1997) are distinct, the motivational elements are observably similar. The presence of alternatives is critical in both approaches. Being based on personal factors and evaluations, the food choice model is less richer in its description of the particular factors that would lead to these alternatives. On the other hand, the personal system in the food choice model, while proposes an interaction of various components from varied domains, this interaction is not explicitly defined. From that perspective, the C–B framework tends to provide more specificity of elements that might be involved in the negotiation process, as proposed by the food choice model. Similarly, the selection of strategies in the food choice model does not provide explicit processes that might be involved in developing these strategies. While the C–B framework suggests ways in which this might be achieved, we believe even the C–B approach falls short in this area.

The merging of these approaches provides several benefits. We are able to draw from the richer description of factors in the food choice model that might provide choices for the decision-maker. On the other hand, we are able to draw upon the C–B framework for the specificity of factors that might be involved in the value negotiation processes, and the strategy selection process of the decision-maker. In the merging of these two approaches, one from the notion of food choice processes, and another from the institutional economic idea of decision making, the overview of the ACE model can be presented as follows:

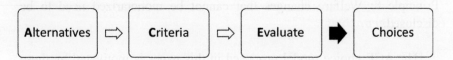

We build on those previous efforts to further elaborate on the process that individuals may or may not be accessed in food decisions. In particular, we hope that the ACE model will enhance our understanding of the food choice decisions individuals make through the lens of balancing the costs and benefits. This approach also highlights the importance of referring to these decisions as discrete transactions. Therefore, the underlying unit of analysis in the proposed model is the transaction.

Given that any transaction would have associated costs and benefits, the proposed model could enhance our understanding of how individuals would make these tradeoffs associated with costs and benefits. Given these tradeoffs, how would individuals' choices be impacted? The proposed linearity and sequence of the model elements bring together the anticipated structure of the transaction. We do not expect this structure to be stable, or even exist in its entirety. However, the model provides a basis to begin understanding various permutations and combinations of transactional analyses that individuals engage in, while making food choices. Stability of choice over time and/or the impact on choices over time would be of central interest as the potential outcomes of understanding the choice process.

1.5.2   The ACE Model

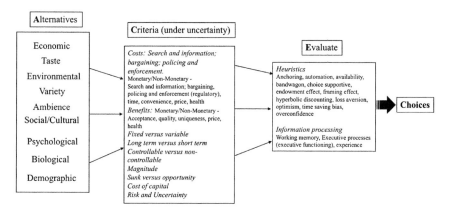

1.5.3   Alternatives

The presence of food in several aspects of our lives means that food also has a different meaning for us, from each of these perspectives. This is particularly true in the foodservice context. As discussed earlier, the foodservice environment where we usually have several choices or alternatives to pick what to eat, when to eat, with whom, for what purpose, and most importantly where to eat. All these alternatives to food are what make the food decision process unique, and yet complex. The following is a discussion of the factors that stimulate the motivations of our food choices. While some are individual-focused, others are in our environment, whether physically observable or policy and regulation-driven.

1.5.3.1 Economic

There are several potential economic motivations that influence the food choice alternatives we are faced with. Food prices are amongst the most critical economic influences on food choices (Dimitri & Rogus, 2014). In general, the law of demand and supply will also impact food choices in foodservice environments. However, in certain cases though price levels can also act as quality signals, whereby the consumers' decisions are impacted if certain preferences are evoked (Alfnes & Sharma, 2010). For the most part though, income plays an important role in context of price levels – prices become a key determinant in food choice decisions when faced with income constraints (Burns, Cook, & Mavoa, 2013). That said, economic factors need to be considered from a broader perspective, one that goes beyond monetary factors (such as income and prices) to one that also incorporates cost, accessibility, education, skills, time, and other non-monetary indicators of economic status (Firoozzare & Kohansal, 2018).

Do economic factors simply indicate how much food we will choose to purchase? Research suggest that even the quality of our food choices and decisions can be influenced by monetary factors (Lazaridis & Drichoutis, 2005). In fact, if budgetary factors are relaxed, then sensory appeal can become the more prominent determinant of food choices (Birkenhead & Slater, 2015). In other words, under budgetary constraint, the quality of food chosen is different than if the budgetary constraints are removed. How are costs and benefits assessed when budgetary constraints are changed or are different from one time period to another? Do choices continue to be made on the previous decision-process path even when the context defining factors (such as income, access, or time available) change? Can information pertaining to costs and benefits influence incremental changes in the choice structure? These are others are some of the questions that emerge and can help us better understand how we view food choices in context of economic factors. For the reasons already noted in extant literature, and additional questions that continue to emerge related to the role of economic factors on food choices, economic influences also play a significant role in the overall wellbeing associated with the idea of food choice decisions (Bublitz, Peracchio, Andreasen, Kees, Kidwell, Miller, & Vallen, 2013). A clearer understanding on how food wellbeing can be promoted from the economic context will likely yield positive individual health and wellbeing, and environmental sustainability outcomes.

1.5.3.2 Taste

Food taste can be seen both as a precursor to food choices based on preferences, but can also be viewed as post hoc validation of food choices. As a precursor, it is worthwhile to note that food taste can be motivated by a variety of social, economic, and political contexts. The idea of taste being impacted by cultural norms, and social class status has been extensively explored by Bourdieu (1984), and since then has inspired several investigations in this area of research. For instance, food taste can be motivated by sociological and historical perspectives. While culture and social norms can impact taste, so can other life contexts whether macro or micro, such as religion, globalization, and economic status of the individual (Wright et al., 2001).

For instance, Prasad (2006), describes an example of focus on gastronomy for community in the Eastern state of India (Bengal) to recognize its social dominance. The Bhadra Lok community is threatened in its social significance due to the evolving cultural, social, and economic climate. Slowly their social and economic significance is marginalized in comparison to other demographic shifts in one of the largest urban centers, Calcutta. At that point, and in order to regain their social dominance and create social capital, the community focuses on its gastronomic roots as a central method to identify formation. The author argues that food taste is not simply need-based, but also strongly driven by the historical perspectives of social and cultural life.

Taste can be leveraged as a precursor to food choices. Food companies have perfected the science of stimulating consumers by adding subtle

taste-related information on food items. Taste and healthfulness perceptions of individuals can influence their food choice decisions (Howlett
et al., 2009; Raghunathan et al., 2006). Therefore, when consumers are
made to believe that food is healthy and tastier, then it does influence
their consumption experiences. Therefore, there is a reason to believe that
such messaging would impact their food choice decisions. On the other
hand, there is also evidence to suggest that such subtle messaging can also
impact postconsumption experience. In a study, Vadiveloo et al. (2013)
found that post taste consumption of foods is impacted that are marked
as "heaty" and 'healthy,' and that the level of satiety is influenced by the
respondents' importance for taste.

Taste as an attribute in food choice has also been pitted against nutrition fact seeking. Food choices and exposure can though also modify
and hence determine taste (Pilner, 1982; Birch & Marlin, 1982). Mai and
Hoffman (2012), in their study, found that individuals who prefer taste
and price of food, care less about nutrition facts. On the other hand, those
individuals more concerned about health consciousness, care more about
nutritional facts when making food choice decisions. In fact, this latter
group of individuals seems to be exerting more cognitive effort than do
consumers who prefer taste and price attributes. The health-conscious
individuals consider more health-related attributes than consumers that
had lover self-efficacy scores for nutrition.

1.5.3.3   Environmental Factors

There is extensive literature on the impact of environmental factors on
food choice. While certain environmental conditions are directly aimed
at influencing food choices, for instance, variety and the amount/portion
of food offered, others are less explicit, such as the ambiance. In either
case, though, there is increasing evidence to suggest that individual's food
choice decisions are impacted by environmental influences. Therefore, the
environment could alter the composition of food alternatives, or at least as
perceived by the decision-maker.

Food portion sizes can be an influence on food choice decisions. In
fact, as Rils (2014) points out, portion options can be leveraged to influence food choices, given how such decisions can be challenging for
consumers. While several strategies can be implemented in leveraging

portion sizes, such efforts could impact the profitability of foodservice businesses, both from the revenue and from the cost perspectives. These are important considerations for the businesses to ensure portioning of food remains a sustainable approach to support individual efforts to make more responsible food choices.

While there remain barriers for businesses to implement food portioning strategies, individuals themselves need to be enticed to make appropriate portion size decisions. In their experimental study, Reimann et al. (2015) found that offering small, uncertain, nonfood incentives could motivate individuals to choose smaller portion sizes. Such influences on choice decisions have been argued as emerging from the theory of reasoned choice, and from the motivational determinants to the choice decisions. Reimann et al. (2015) also argue that food choice motivations could be replaced with nonfood incentives such as money. Therefore, assess how food and money substitute for each other is a fruitful area of future investigations. Furthermore, it is also interesting to note that food choice decisions could encapsulate the cost and benefit motivations for the individual. Therefore, understanding these mechanisms and correlations between them could be beneficial in assessing food choice processes.

One of the first challenges to consider in portioning of food is whether individuals understand portion sizes. In their study, Rizk and Treat (2015) found that individuals' sensitivity to food portion sizes varies.

The sensitivity is higher when presented with low to medium portion sizes. However, this sensitivity decreases as the portion sizes increase to larger levels. Furthermore, their study also found that individuals who already consume healthier foods such as fruits and vegetables tend to be more sensitive to portion sizes than those that do not. The effect of portion sizes, though, could be altered or manipulated as suggested by the study conducted by Davis et al. (2016). The researchers found that smaller portion sizes were less noticeable when presented on a relatively larger table size than when presented on smaller table size. In essence, the contrasting effect of the table size impacts the food choice decision of individuals. Even though in general studies have found support for offering small unit sizes, contrasting effect on small unit sizes could further reduce consumption thereby reducing the calorie intake. However, these results have not been conclusive in the literature. In fact, Reily and Vartanian (2016) were unable to show that contextual reference could be effective in impacting consumption through portion size manipulation. While the impact of portion sizes on food choice decision is less in question, it is unclear how we might mitigate these effects (Steenhuis and Poleman, 2017). One thing is for certain, more education is needed for all types of consumers across demographic categories (Guthrie, 2017), so that individuals are more aware of the impact of portion sizes on their food choice decisions.

1.5.3.4   Variety

Research suggests that food variety impacts food choices in often complex ways. The influence of food variety begins from a very young age of individuals and likely changes over the course of the lifetime. For instance, research shows that variety in food choices can be observed as early as in children aged 2–3 years old (Nicklaus et al., 2005). In this particular age group, the research found that while variety varied during the study period, certain factors, such as breastfeeding, month of the year, and gender, impacted the preference for variety. The study also found that while there may exist an optimal point in time during early years to expose children to variety, over time there appeared to be an observable decrease in preference for variety. Other research also suggests how variety might be stimulated amongst individuals, particularly children (Epstein et al., 2010). The emphasis on variety is due to the potentially positive benefits it has on individuals' diets. For instance, research shows that indicators such as food variety scores (FVS) and diet diversity scores (DDS) can be used to measure the impact of food variety on individual health (Steyn et al., 2006). The research also found that higher FVS and DDS scores were associated with more adequate nutrition among children ages 1–8 years of age. However, while there are clear benefits of increasing food variety in the individual diet, the concern is that increased variety could also stimulate food consumption thereby increasing the risk of obesity, particu- larly among children (Nicklaus, 2009). There is a need for us to better understand the tradeoffs between these two aspects of food variety—the cost–benefit tradeoffs. However, this requires a better observation of food variety preferences at the individual levels. Despite the importance of this issue, there is relatively less research in this area, and could primarily be attributed to the lack of individual-level observations (Weiss, 2010). While the actual food consumption data is restricted, researchers have been also interested in investigating the food choice process leading to variety from the perspective of food sourcing in the eating away from home activity (Jung et al., 2015). In their research, the authors found a stronger preference for food quality than other dimensions of the food consumption experience such as service. Food quality might also be a leverage point to incentivize consumers to reduce their preference for greater variety of foods (Loh, 2014) given that increased variety, as pointed out earlier, may not be a positive influence on nutritional well-being, and may also lead to other externalities such as food waste, and food sourcing pressures on the food system.

1.5.3.5   Ambience

Sensory, physiological, and psychological stimulation is an intrinsic aspect of food choices (Gibson, 2006). The physical, physiological, and psychological components of food are essential elements of the experience food choices, decisions, and the ultimate consumption of food hinges upon. As a matter of fact, research suggests that aligning these aspects could encourage individuals to improve their food choice decisions. Therefore, the sensory aspects of food choice have been extensively discussed in the literature. There are also approaches that researchers are utilizing to create interventions that would enhance food decisions by focusing on the sensory aspects. For instance, Terzimehic´ et al. (2018) propose four situations when interventions focusing on the sensory aspects of food could be introduced to enhance food choices: (1) lack of alternatives, (2) unawareness of alternatives, (3) evening cravings, and (4) social pressure. In fact, the sensory food aspects have developed sufficiently that an interdisciplinary approach would like to yield a more holistic understanding of this phenomenon and its impact on food choices than doing so in disciplinary compartments (Giboreau, 2017). We note the extensive literature on sensory aspects of food and its impact on food choice decisions and restrain from attempting a comprehensive literature review in this section.

1.5.3.6   Social and Cultural Factors

The social aspects of food cannot be ignored when discussing food choices and decisions. Despite the changes in or lifestyle, where we live, and work, the occasional determinants of food choice and decisions remain an important influence of what and how we choose to eat (Marshall, 1993). To the extent, the structure of our meals, what is offered and eaten at these meals, how we consume the meals, and what those meals mean to us are highly driven by the social occasion. Emotion and food choices have also shown to be associated, where positive and negative emotions may be associated by certain and different types of food-choice responses (Dube et al., 2006). There would also be associations between social elements and emotional responses. Therefore, the social and emotional impacts on food choice and decisions remains an interesting area to study so that we may better understand our motivations for food decisions. The cultural aspects of food choice have also been explored in the literature though we are only beginning to understand these relationships and how they come to exist (Rozin, 2006). The complex set of influences through social and cultural norms are several, and we are only now beginning to unfold these to understand food choice behavior.

1.5.3.7 Psychological Factors

The formation of preferences is a function of several aspects such as experiences, social and cultural background, and evolutionary development. The study of these in the context of food choices continues to be of importance as we learn how and why we eat what we do (Rozin, 2006). Preferences may not be stable over time, and as they change it could impact food choices. The changing aspect of preferences also implies that individuals need to understand how to manage their own preferences. Self-control, therefore, becomes an important aspect of food choice behavior (Sharma, 2017). As we uncover the increasing diversity of preferences, the motivations behind those preferences, and the limitations in behavioral mechanisms to manage these preferences, the associated links of these ideas to food choice, we believe, is becoming increasingly meaningful for the health and well-being of individuals. For a more detailed and comprehensive link for the psychology perspectives in food choice, see Sheperd and Raats (2006).

1.5.3.8 Biological Factors

The biological aspects of food choices have been discussed in two ways: The first aspect is the physiological mechanisms of food and energy intake. The second biological aspect in the context of food choices is the understanding of how the brain receives information on the metabolic aspects of food and how that impacts food choice (Rozin, 2006). In more recent literature, there is growing evidence related to how the human gut microbiome could play a critical role in the physiological and the "brain impulse" connectivity of food choice behavior (Perez-Burgos et al., 2014).

1.5.4 Criteria to Evaluate Associated Benefits and Costs

The approach being proposed here through the ACE model is that of treating our food choice decisions as discrete transactions, albeit with a dependence structure. Then, from a transactional perspective, the choice and decision process is being articulated as one that would require identification of transactional costs and benefits, and an evaluation of these costs–benefits to eventually make choices. We began with a discussion of the various factors that would provide alternatives for such transactions. See earlier sections. In the following sections we discuss how the various costs and benefits could be identified, observed, and potentially measured. This provides the basis for the next stage of the process, that is, evaluation.

Williamson (1981) articulated the transaction cost (TC) approach to understanding the economics of business organizations. The transaction cost theory and analysis of such costs are a field of study in microeconomics literature, however from the perspective of an organization. We believe there is potential to leverage the underlying principles of this theory into individual and household decisions as well. Therefore, the first contribution that the ACE model proposes is to leverage the TC approach into understanding the economics of individual and household food decisions. Another aspect that has received relatively less attention in the literature is to evaluate transactional costs and benefits as a balanced approach to understanding decisions. Therefore, another contribution we propose of the ACE model is to take the approach of transactional analysis by evaluating the tradeoffs that may exist between costs and benefits. We further argue that benefit structure at the individual and household level provide opportunities for us to enhance choice and decision-making processes and eventual actions.

1.5.4.1   Uncertainty in Cost–Benefits

Cost and benefits are not always certain, in fact, there is sufficient evidence to suggest that uncertainties surround such measures of to the extent that even the traditional use of cost–benefit analysis needs to incorporate bounds to rational assessment (Cuéllar and Mashaw, 2017). Deterministic nature of cost–benefits measures, therefore, is a strong assumption in such analyses. Relaxing those assumptions presents opportunities to explore how individuals perceive such costs and benefits and incorporate them in choices and decision making. In the event, such deterministic assumptions of cost and benefit estimates are relaxed, or in other words, we can incorporate the possibility of uncertain estimates, individuals' risk preferences would also need to be included in our analytical framework.

1.5.4.2   Monetary and Nonmonetary

The reference to costs and benefits usually are associated with monetary measures of these constructs. However, the monetary measures usually imply that the underlying construct is observable, and therefore potentially measurable. Furthermore, it implies the measures have a market-based value and, therefore, can be translated into monetary values. See figure below.

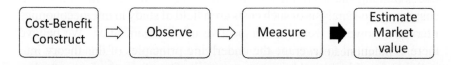

A break in this sequence would imply that even though the cost–benefit construct exists, it may not have a market-based measure. Therefore, we propose that the absence of market-based measures (such as in market-based monetary currencies) should not be deterrence from incorporating those in our analyses of choice and decision-making. Despite, and possibly due to, the omnipresence of food in our lives, the attention on the non-monetary aspects of costs and benefits remains nascent. Meanwhile, there is sufficient discussion in the literature of the existence of such monetary costs and benefits (Dinsmore et al., 2016). Incorporating these into our analytical approach, we believe, would be of value in enhancing food choices and decision-making.

The more observable and measurable costs and benefits have been extensively discussed in the literature, although from a business perspective. The individual and household level perspectives on these costs and benefits still allude us. We propose that understanding those perspectives, and incorporating them in the proposed ACE model could enhance our understanding of the analytical aspects of choice and decisions, particularly from in context of food. In the following section, we provide a brief overview of several such perspectives that have the potential of being reformulated and reframed.

1.5.4.3   Transaction Costs and Benefits

From the perspective of business economics, transaction cost and benefit (TCB) has received much attention. Erramilli and Rao (1993) investigated the transaction costs in context of the company's choice of entry mode into foreign markets. Brouthers (2002) also investigated foreign entry modes based on transaction costs of businesses, and also how the various approaches impacted firm performance. From a broader point of view, Leiblein (2003) incorporated the transaction cost approach with the resource-based view and the real options analysis to understand the impact of organizational governance structure on the creation and appropriateness of economic value. In context of the food supply chain, Boger (2001) investigated the marketing arrangements between hog producers and buyers in context of transaction costs.

As mentioned earlier, much of the literature on TCB resides in the sphere of business decision-making. There have been however relatively scattered attempts to incorporate TC at the individual or the household level. For instance, Ekehammar (1978) applied cost–benefit analytical constructs to understand how individuals make career choices. Amongst other findings, this study also found a possible gender difference in how the TCB was incorporated into career choice by men and women respondents. Ratchford (1982) proposed an economic framework for the assessment of cost and benefits in the context of consumers' information seeking for decision making. The framework this study proposed focuses on consumers' information gathering and its impact on choice. In a follow-up study, Moorthy et al. (1997) further investigated the implications of such costs on consumer decision making and also how various factors interacted with each other to impact consumer choices. In another influential study, Larrick et al. (1993) articulated three underlying principles to guide individual cost–benefit analytical thinking: (1) The net-benefit principle. The action that has the greatest expected net-benefit should be chosen from a set of possible actions. (2) The sunk cost principle. Only future benefits and costs should be considered in current decisions. Past costs and benefits are not relevant unless they predict future benefits and costs. (3) The opportunity cost principle. The cost of engaging in a given course of action is the loss of the benefits of the next-best course of action. The approach to analyze cost and benefits has been discussed by McIntosh (2006) by proposing the incorporation of these tradeoffs in choice experimental designs. This is a valuable perspective in enhancing our understanding of CBA in the food context given the relatively underdeveloped dimensions and measures of costs and benefits. The flexibility of the proposed approach and incorporation of sensitivity analysis should be encouraging for our future research efforts.

An important aspect of cost and benefits is the information, a topic addressed later in our discussion, reflective of these constructs. In an interesting study of this aspect, Marette et al. (2008) investigated how consumers respond to the costs and benefits associated with the choice of fish species. What they found was that consumer preferences were dependent on the sequencing of information presented to them. In other words, value of information provided for making choices was perceived differently when the order of this information presentation was modified. Risk and benefit assessment have been investigated relatively more frequently in context of individuals' medical decisions.

The value associated with costs and benefits could also impact choices. In their study, Van Houtven et al. (2011) investigated choice preferences of medical treatment options by presenting different benefit and risk structures. The authors find that risk tolerances for 2 of the 3 risks presented to the respondents have a highly non-linear structure. Understanding the structural relationship between risk and benefit functions, as the authors point out, could be more relevant for policy and practical implications. More important, such evidence highlights the nonlinear nature of preferences in context of cost–benefit analyses. Lamberton and Diehl (2013) also investigated the value assigned to benefits in contrast to product attributes and associated these preferences with the construal cues. Their study found a significant impact of construal level cues on the valuation of product preferences.

Another way that costs have been associated in the analysis of choices and decisions is by incorporating the cost of transactional choice. While there are several aspects to this issue, Janczyk et al. (2015) assessed the time cost of choices from alternatives when under free choice or forced-choice conditions. The study found performance differences and attributed it to perceptual processing in those two conditions. The choice process could also be seen from the perspective of a business owner. For instance, Ndoro et al. (2015) investigated whether transaction costs impacted the farmers' decisions to choose a particular marketing channel versus another. Some of the interesting findings of this study suggest that marketing channel choice not only depended on market conditions, such as market uncertainty but also on the owners' knowledge of the market and their age. Outsourcing is another business decision where transaction cost and benefits have been evaluated. Schermann et al. (2016) review the extensive literature that has investigated the technology outsourcing decision using the transaction cost approach. The authors highlight a critical issue surrounding TC approach in general: operationalization of transaction cost needs to be enhanced. Furthermore, we would add that such enhancements also need to consider the context of TC given the nuances that are prevalent in transactional attributes.

Having provided a brief overview of the current issues associated with costs and benefits in our proposed analytical model, we now review the thinking around the evaluation of these costs and benefits. In this, we take an inclusive approach, rather than limiting ourselves with strong assumptions around the rationality appearance of individuals. We explain more in the following section.

1.5.4.4   Evaluation of Costs and Benefits

Evaluation and assessment of costs and benefits can be a complex process. The context of evaluation could further increase complexities in this phenomenon. While traditionally we have assumed individuals are capable of making unbiased, and rational decisions, for the most part, there is now agreement that such may not be the case, or at least always. At the least, there is general agreement that it would be naïve to assume that such processes are conducted in a perfectly rational manner, all the time, by all of us. In other words, there are bounds to our rationality. Our bounds to rationality are particularly evoked by the less rational aspects of our decision processes, mostly associated with our beliefs, and heuristics and perceptions to the rational information presented for decision-making.

In fact, even when we make decisions based on our beliefs, research shows that we are often not well aware of our own beliefs and can often become confused (Alcott, 2010). Such subjectivity of beliefs has indeed been linked to food choices and preferences (Grankvist and Biel, 2001; Lusk et al., 2013; Wardle et al., 2014). There is more that can be understood on how certain factors can predict or describe our beliefs about food and, in turn, guide us in understanding how we make food choice decisions (Bell et al., 1981).

Another manner in which individuals evaluate the information for making choices and decisions is through the use of simple heuristics or rules of thumbs. These can be considered as shortcuts to evaluating and decision making. Heuristics have attracted much attention of researchers. There is a fair amount of argument for and against them. Irrespective, heuristics are real, or at least so far as we understand the decision-making phenomenon. Biases can also emerge in choices and decision making, often due to the use of heuristics or simply through other triggers or influences, whether internal or environmental/external.

The literature in the area of heuristics is extensive and ever-expanding. There is evidence to suggest that heuristics could be an automated phenomenon, less in our control, and more implemented as default choices in our decision process (Frederick, 2002). Often times these decision rules can also be triggered by external influences such as those persuading one to make certain type of choices (Whittler, 1994). Whether through internal mechanisms or through external influences, several heuristics and biases have been identified in the literature. Here are a few that particularly concern us in food choice decisions, and those that would be fruitful foci for future research efforts to help us better understand the food choice and decision process: Anchoring, automation through habits, availability, bandwagon, choice supportive, endowment effect, framing effect, hyperbolic discounting, loss aversion, optimism, time saving bias, and overconfidence.[2,3]

Not all choices and decisions require the use of heuristics. Where we can, could we provide the sufficient skills, knowledge, ability, motivation for individuals that would facilitate food choices and decision-making with intent rather than through heuristics? On the other hand, can heuristics take

---

[2]https://en.wikipedia.org/wiki/Heuristic
[3]https://en.wikipedia.org/wiki/List_of_cognitive_biases

a more legitimate and justifiable role in our food choices and decisions? Can individuals be intentional in even choosing the decisions that could require heuristics rather than a structural process of making decisions? If so, what might that process be?

Evaluation of costs and benefits and other information is not the least bit a given process. We have discussed that measures might be imprecise, uncertain, and often may not even exist. The evaluation process itself could be less versus more rational. These several, often confounding dimensions of the evaluation process could impact choices. Better understanding the evaluation process, and how it impacts choices, remains an interesting research pursuit, particularly in the context of food choice decisions.

1.6 INFORMATION PROCESSING

Information asymmetry (IA) in assessing tradeoffs, by using cost–benefit analysis could exist in several forms. The procedural aspects of CBA could involve IA at each stage of the process. Identification of alternatives and stakeholders in the process of making food choices is not always

1.6.1 Information Asymmetry

Tradeoffs would result in acquiring and understanding the information needed to make certain choices. This decision process could essentially reduce the information gap that might exist to make such choices. Or in other words, trade-off analysis could reduce information asymmetry in such transactions. Information asymmetry in a transaction occurs when one party has more or better information than another. This could negatively impact the transaction and lead to inappropriate consequences. The most obstructive consequence of IA would be a market failure of some sorts. However, without even getting as far as market failure (whether partial or complete), at the individual level IA could lead to adverse selection, moral hazard, and information monopoly (De Meza and Webb, 1990; Bawden and Robinson, 2009). Each of these could negatively impact the food choices and associated damaging consequences of such choices. Clearly then reducing information asymmetry could enhance the decision-makers' ability to conduct cost–benefit tradeoffs, and thereby improve the resulting food choices.

IA associated with cost and benefit analysis of decisions have been referred to, but there is an opportunity to better understand what these information gaps are, and how they might be reduced, or removed. Efforts to inform and educate individuals that would reduce IA, and enhance the cost–benefit tradeoff process have been received with mixed success. Several challenges exist when attempting to reduce IA at the individual level. Information asymmetry of costs and benefits or the lack of knowledge of this information is closely associated with the type of information that is consumed. What is not available and/or consumed eventually becomes the source of IA. While information availability is of concern, that area of inquiry falls into the policy environment. At the individual level then, we are left primarily with the challenge of cost–benefit information that could be accessible, but often gets ignored or unattended due to individual preferences.

The context of this information, food choices along the supply and demand continuum in the foodservice environments, may also play a role in this process. Undoubtedly, food is an intricate part of our existence. From a consumer perspective, some of our food preferences are a product of influences of our social and cultural environment, while others have become habits over years of acting in a certain manner, due to individual choices. The supply chain aspects of the foodservice system continue to be in flux, driven by the tradition of historical perspectives, and contemporary trends. Therefore, the educational or informational interventions to reduce cost–benefit IA often have to counter these influences to engage individuals in enhancing food choice decisions. Stemming from these issues is the fact that mass attempts to reduce IA alone may not always work for everyone. Certain level of customization would be required, given the particular contextual and other factors impacting ones' choices. This is no different than the customized approaches being adopted in other spheres of life, such as education and medicine. Whether the mass-produced or customized, individuals would need to be receptive to reducing cost–benefit IA. This brings us to the two key elements of the cost–benefit process as discussed in this paper in context of food choices: The ability to predict consequences, and the willingness to evaluate them based on the costs and benefits assessed.

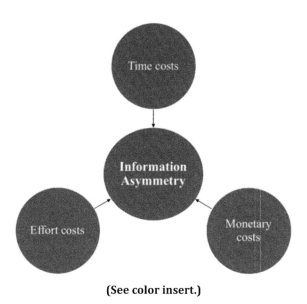

(See color insert.)

The information would be assessed only after it is accessible. How information might get ignored or is inaccessible in the choice and decision process? One proposition for the reason that this information gets ignored could be viewed from a resource allocation perspective. How might the allocation or thereof resource allocation could impact information asymmetry. We propose that transactional costs, such as time, effort, and money, could influence informational asymmetry, particularly at the individual level.

Understanding this process of how individuals would engage in tradeoffs in a food choice transaction, we believe, could significantly enhance our approaches to ensure better food choice decisions along all aspects of the food choice system. Furthermore, understanding how individual-level processes such as working memory, executive processes (executive functioning), and experience might enhance such individual-level tradeoffs in context of information, could also provide valuable insights into the food choice and decision-making phenomenon.

1.6.2   Information Asymmetry in the Information Age

Tabarrok and Cowen (2015) recently argued that in this age of information, the idea of asymmetric information may not exist. This, however, assumes that individuals are able to access that information at relatively minimal or no transaction costs. Furthermore, it assumes this information would be processed at relatively minimal or no costs, and furthermore would lead to enhanced choices through a better decision process (Shiffrin and Schneider, 1977). In fact, there has been a relatively scattered investigation of this phenomenon: How transaction costs could influence the access of relevant information, the ability of individuals to process information in the presence of transaction costs, and impact on their choices through an informed decision process. There are other concerns/ issues associated with the apparent abundance of information. Researchers have argued that more information could also lead to information overload (Bawden and Robinson, 2009). Information overload could disrupt any stage of information processing, thereby reducing or nullifying the benefit of information availability. If the availability of more vegetables and fruits could help us eat healthier than salad bars would be an answer to all our unhealthy eating worries. Another challenge associated with an abundance of information is verifying information credibility (Metzger et al., 2010). All information may not be trustworthy. Abundance of information along with the implications of unreliable information sources could further overburden the decision-maker. Therefore, while the availability of information could be perceived as reducing the risks of information asymmetry, several other aspects of information access and processing need to be incorporated before leading to this conclusion.

1.7 CONCLUDING REMARKS

In this paper, we present the ACE food choice model that focuses on foodservice decisions from a transactional perspective. There are several aspects to the transaction. Foremost is the availability of potential alternatives. These alternatives can be derived from several sources. Once available, the alternatives would need to be evaluated using a multitude of criteria. Despite the terminology used, such criteria are not always precise and even absolute. The evaluation of criteria itself presents challenges for individuals, even within the often unassuming food contexts. Together the alignment or lack thereof of these constructs could define and impact food choice decisions.

The transactional approach in developing the ACE model has been that of leveraging the cost–benefit viewpoint. The balance of those two ideas, costs and benefits, we believe could encapsulate the critical perspectives to enhance an effective approach to optimizing food choice decisions. Why do we care? Theoretically, food choices represent a critical and interesting day-to-day decisions that individuals make, repeatedly. Therefore, understanding the processes that govern our repeated decisions would be critical from a social behavioral point of view. Short term choices lead to long term decisions. Therefore, this understanding of repeated choices in the short term could also give us a view of the mechanisms that eventually begin to influence long term decisions.

Much has been written and explored on the topic of decision making, and this by no means will be the last of those perspectives. The reason choice and decision making attract so much of our attention is because of their importance in our lives, and also in the complexity of the phenomenon. Food choices in away from home environments are untrivial. Individual food choices have potential impact on health and well-being. Coupled with other decisions, such as those related to financial well-being, could have broader impacts on individuals and households. The broader societal aspects of food away from home, associated with food security, access, consumption, waste, and the issues related to our global food supply chain are enormous. It behooves us to not trivialize food choices and decisions. As we propose the ACE model, we do so with the hope that these guiding principles will provide us an overarching evaluative framework in this pursuit.

KEYWORDS

- **food decisions**
- **transaction cost economics**
- **cost–benefit analysis**
- **information asymmetry**
- **foodservice system**

REFERENCES

Alfnes, F.; Sharma, A. Locally Produced Food in Restaurants: Are the Customers Willing to Pay a Premium and Why? *Int. J. Revenue Manag.* **2010,** *4* (3–4), 238–258.

Allcott , H. Beliefs and Consumer Choice. Manuscript: New York University, 2010.

Bawden, D.; Robinson, L. The Dark Side of Information: Overload, Anxiety and Other Paradoxes and Pathologies. *J. Inform. Sci.* **2009,** *35* (2), 180–191.

Becher, S. I. Behavioral Science and Consumer Standard Form Contracts. *La. L. Rev.* **2007,** *68*, 117.

Bell, A. C.; Stewart, A. M.; Radford, A. J.; Cairney, P. T. A Method for Describing Food Beliefs which may Predict Personal Food Choice. *J. Nutr. Edu.* **1981,** *13* (1), 22–26.

Birch, S.; Donaldson, C. Applications of Cost-benefit Analysis to Health Care: Departures from Welfare Economic Theory. *J. Health Econ.* **1987,** *6* (3), 211–225.

Birch, S.; Donaldson, C. Cost-benefit Analysis: Dealing with the Problems of Indivisible Projects and Fixed Budgets. *Health Policy* **1987,** *7* (1), 61–72.

Birch, S.; Gafni, A. Cost Effectiveness/Utility Analyses: Do current Decision Rules Lead us to Where we Want to be? *J. Health Econ.* **1992,** *11* (3), 279–296.

Birkenhead, K. L.; Slater, G. A review of factors influencing athletes' food choices. Sports medicine, *45* (11), 1511–1522.

Boadway, R. W. The Welfare Foundations of Cost-Benefit Analysis. *Econ. J. 84* (336), 926–939.

Boger, S. Quality and Contractual Choice: A Transaction Cost Approach to the Polish Hog Market. *Eur. Rev. Agri. Econ.* **2001,** *28* (3), 241–262.Boudreau, M. C.; Watson, R. T.; Chen, A. J.; Greiner, M. E.; Sclavos, P. The Benefits of Transaction Cost Economics: The Beginning of a New Direction. In *ECIS;* 2007; (pp 1124–1135).

Brouthers, K. D. Institutional, Cultural and Transaction Cost Influences on Entry Mode Choice and Performance. *J, Int. Bus. Stud.* **2002,** *33* (2), 203–221.

Bublitz, M. G.; Peracchio, L. A.; Andreasen, A. R.; Kees, J.; Kidwell, B.; Miller, E. G.; Vallen, B. Promoting positive change: Advancing the food well-being paradigm. Journal of Business Research, **2013,** *66* (8), 1211–1218.

Burns, C.; Cook, K.; Mavoa, H. Role of Expendable Income and Price in Food Choice by Low Income Families. *Appetite, 271,* 209–217.

Cardello, A. V.; Schutz, H. G.; Lesher, L. L. Consumer Perceptions of Foods Processed by Innovative and Emerging Technologies: A Conjoint Analytic Study. *Inn. Food Sci. Emer. Technol.* **2007,** *8* (1), 73–83.

Cellini , S. R.; Kee, J. E. Cost-effectiveness and Cost-benefit Analysis. *Handbook of Practical Program Evaluation;* 2010; Vol. 3.

Coates IV, J. C. Cost-Benefit Analysis of Financial Regulation: Case Studies and Implications. *Yale LJ* **2014,** *124*, 882.

Cowburn, G.; Stockley, L. Consumer Understanding and Use of Nutrition Labelling: A Systematic Review. *Public Health Nutr.* **2005,** *8* (1), 21–28.

Cox Jr, L. A.; Popken, D. A.; Sun, R. X. Improving Individual, Group, and Organizational Decisions: Overcoming Learning Aversion in Evaluating and Managing Uncertain Risks. In *Causal Analytics for Applied Risk Analysis;* Springer, Cham, 2018; pp. 457–492.

Cruwys, T.; Bevelander, K. E.; Hermans, R. C. Social Modeling of Eating: A Review of When and Why Social Influence Affects Food Intake and Choice. *Appetite* **2015,** *86,* 3–18.

Cuéllar , M. F.; Mashaw, J. L. *The Oxford Handbook of Law and Economics;* Public Law and Legal Institutions, 2017; Vol. 3p 59.

Damart, S.; Roy, B. The Uses of Cost-benefit Analysis in Public Transportation Decision-making in France. *Transport Policy* **2009,** *16* (4), 200–212.

Dansereau, D. F.; Knight, D. K.; Flynn, P. M. Improving Adolescent Judgment and Decision Making. *Prof. Psychol. Res. Pr.* **2013,** *44* (4), 274.

Davis, B.; Payne, C. R.; Bui, M. Making Small Food Units Seem Regular: How Larger Table Size Reduces Calories to be Consumed. *J. Assoc. Consum. Res.* **2016,** *1* (1), 115–124.

De Meza, D.; Webb, D. Risk, Adverse Selection and Capital Market Failure. *Econ. J.* **1990,** *100* (399), 206–214.

Devine, C. M. A Life Course Perspective: Understanding Food Choices in Time, Social Location, and History. *J. Nutr. Edu. Behav.* **2005,** *37* (3), 121–128.

DiLeone, R. J.; Taylor, J. R.; Picciotto, M. R. The Drive to Eat: Comparisons and Distinctions Between Mechanisms of Food Reward and Drug Addiction. *Nat. Neurosci.* **2012,** *15* (10), 1330.

DiLeone, R. J.; Taylor, J. R.; Picciotto, M. R. The Drive to Eat: Comparisons and Distinctions Between Mechanisms of Food Reward and Drug Addiction. *Nat. Neurosci.* **2012,** *15* (10), 1330.

Dimitri, C.; Rogus, S. Food choices, Food Security, and Food Policy. *J. Int. Aff.*, **2014,** 67(2), 19.

Doucerain, M.; Fellows, L. K. Eating Right: Linking Food-related Decision-making Concepts from Neuroscience, Psychology, and Education. *Mind Brain Edu.* **2012,** *6* (4), 206–219.

Drewnowski, A.; Darmon, N. Food Choices and Diet Costs: An Economic Analysis. *J. Nutr.* **2005,** *135* (4), 900–904.

Drewnowski, A.; Kawachi, I. Diets and Health: How Food Decisions are Shaped by Biology, Economics, Geography, and Social Interactions. *Big Data* **2015,** *3* (3), 193–197.

Dubé, L.; LeBel, J. L.; Lu, J. Affect Asymmetry and Comfort Food Consumption. *Physiol. Behav.* **2005,** *86* (4), 559–567.

Ekehammar, B. Psychological Cost-benefit as an Intervening Construct in career Choice Models. *J. Vocat. Behav.* **1978,** *12* (3), 279–289.

Epstein, L. H.; Robinson, J. L.; Roemmich, J. N.; Marusewski, A. L.; Roba, L. G. What Constitutes Food Variety? Stimulus Specificity of Food. *Appetite* **2010,** *54* (1), 23–29.

Erramilli , M. K.; Rao, C. P. Service Firms' International Entry-mode Choice: A Modified Transaction-cost Analysis Approach. *J. Marketing* **1993,** 19–38.

Evans, J. S. B. Two Minds: Dual-Process Accounts of Reasoning. *Trends in Cognitive Sciences* **2003,** *7* (10), 454–459.

Feuillette, S.; Levrel, H.; Boeuf, B.; Blanquart, S.; Gorin, O.; Monaco, G.; ..., Robichon, S. The Use of Cost–benefit Analysis in Environmental Policies: Some Issues Raised by the Water Framework Directive Implementation in France. *Environ. Sci. Policy* **2016,** *57,* 79–85.

Firoozzare, A.; Kohansal, M. R. Applying Multinomial Logit Model for Determining Socio-Economic Factors Affecting Major Choice of Consumer s in Food Purchasing: The Case of Mashhad, 2018.

Frederick, S. Automated Choice Heuristics. In *Heuristics and Biases: The psychology of Intuitive Judgment;* Gilovich, T., Griffin, D., Kahneman, D., Eds.; Cambridge University Press: New York, NY, 2002; pp 548–558.

Frederick, S. Cognitive Reflection and Decision Making. *J. Econ. Perspect.* **2005**, *19* (4), 25–42.

Frederiks, E. R.; Stenner, K.; Hobman, E. V. Household Energy Use: Applying Behavioural Economics to Understand Consumer Decision-making and Behaviour. *Renew. Sustain. Energy Rev.* **2015**, *41*, 1385–1394.

French, S. A. Pricing Effects on Food Choices. *J. Nutr.* **2003**, *133* (3), 841S–843S.

Furst, T.; Connors, M.; Bisogni, C. A.; Sobal, J.; Falk, L. W. Food Choice: a Conceptual Model of the Process. *Appetite* **1996**, *26* (3), 247–266.

Giboreau , A. Sensory and Consumer Research in Culinary Approaches to Food. *Curr. Opin. Food Sci.* **2017**.

Gibson, E. L. Emotional Influences on Food Choice: Sensory, Physiological and Psychological Pathways. *Physiol. Behav.* **2006**, *89* (1), 53–61.

Gustafson, A.; Christian, J. W.; Lewis, S.; Moore, K.; Jilcott, S. Food Venue Choice, Consumer Food Environment, but not Food Venue Availability Within Daily Travel Patterns are Associated with Dietary Intake Among Adults, Lexington Kentucky 2011. *Nutr. J.* **2013**, *12* (1), 17.

Guthrie, J. F. Integrating Behavioral Economics into Nutrition Education Research and Practice. *J. Nutr. Edu. Behav.* **2017**, *49* (8), 700–705.

http://dx.doi.org/10.1017/CBO9780511808098.032.

Janczyk, M.; Dambacher, M.; Bieleke, M.; Gollwitzer, P. M. The Benefit of no Choice: Goal-directed Plans Enhance Perceptual Processing. *Psychol. Res.* 2015; *79* (2), 206–220.

Jensen, K. K.; Sandøe, P. Food Safety and Ethics: The Interplay Between Science and Values. *J. Agri. Environ. Ethics* **2002**, *15* (3), 245–253.

Jung, J. M.; Sydnor, S.; Lee, S. K.; Almanza, B. A Conflict of Choice: How Consumers Choose Where to go for Dinner. *Inter. J. Hosp. Manag.* **2015**, *45*, 88–98.

King, J. L.; Schrems, E. L. Cost-benefit Analysis in Information Systems Development and Operation. *ACM Computing Surveys (CSUR)* **1978**, *10* (1), 19–34.

King, S. C.; Weber, A. J.; Meiselman, H. L.; Lv, N. The Effect of Meal Situation, Social Interaction, Physical Environment and Choice on Food Acceptability. *Food Qual. Prefer.* **2004**, *15* (7–8), 645–653.

Kornhauser, L. A. On Justifying Cost-benefit Analysis. *J. Legal Stud.* **2000**, *29* (S2), 1037–1057.

Köster, E. P. The Psychology of Food Choice: Some Often Encountered Fallacies. *Food Qual. Prefer.* **2003**, *14* (5–6), 359–373.

Köster, E. P. Diversity in the Determinants of Food Choice: A Psychological Perspective. *Food Qual. Prefer.* **2009**, *20* (2), 70–82.

Lamberton, C. P.; Diehl, K. Retail Choice Architecture: The Effects of Benefit-and Attribute-based Assortment Organization on Consumer Perceptions and Choice. *J. Consum. Res.* **2013**, *40* (3), 393–411.

Larrick, R. P.; Nisbett, R. E.; Morgan, J. N. Who Uses the Cost-benefit Rules of Choice? Implications for the Normative Status of Microeconomic Theory. *Organiz. Behav. Human Decis. Process.* **1993,** *56* (3), 331–347.

Lazaridis, P.; Drichoutis, A. C. Food Consumption Issues in the 21st Century. The Food Industry in Europe, 2005, 21–33.

Leiblein, M. J. The Choice of Organizational Governance Form and Performance: Predictions from Transaction Cost, Resource-based, and Real Options Theories. *J. Manag.* **2003,** *29* (6), 937–961.

Lepping, R. J.; Papa, V. B.; Martin, L. E. Cognitive Neuroscience Perspectives on Food Decision-Making: A Brief Introduction. *J. Agricul. Food Indus. Organiz.* **2015,** *13* (1), 5–14.

Loh, J. The Possibilities of Reducing Food Choice to Improve the Economical (profits), Nutritional/Psychological (people) and Environmental (planet) Performance of University Residential College Foodservices. Doctoral Dissertation, University of Otago, 2015.

López-Ospina, H. A.; Martínez, F. J.; Cortés, C. E. Microeconomic Model of Residential Location Incorporating Life Cycle and Social Expectations. *Comput. Environ. Urban Syst.* **2016,** *55*, 33–43.

Lusk, J. L.; Schroeder, T. C.; Tonsor, G. T. Distinguishing Beliefs from Preferences in Food Choice. *Eur. Rev. Agricul. Econ.* **2013,** *41* (4), 627–655.

Lytle, L. A. Measuring the Food Environment: State of the Science. *Am. J. Prevent. Med.* **2009,** *36* (4), S134–S144.

Macher, J. T.; Richman, B. D. Transaction Cost Economics: An Assessment of Empirical Research in the Social Sciences. *Bus. Politics* 2008, *10* (1), 1–63.

Mai, R.; Hoffmann, S. Taste Lovers Versus Nutrition Fact Seekers: How Health Consciousness and Self-efficacy Determine the Way Consumers Choose Food Products. *J. Consum. Behav.* **2012,** *11* (4), 316–328.

Marcum, C. S.; Goldring, M. R.; McBride, C. M.; Persky, S. Modeling Dynamic Food Choice Processes to Understand Dietary Intervention Effects. *Annals Behav. Med.* **2018,** *52* (3), 252–261.

Marette, S.; Roosen, J.; Blanchemanche, S.; Verger, P. The Choice of Fish Species: An Experiment Measuring the Impact of Risk and Benefit Information. *J. Agricul. Res. Econ.* **2008,** 1–18.

Marshall, D. Appropriate meal Occasions: Understanding Conventions and Exploring Situational Influences on Food Choice. *Int. Rev. Retail Distribut. Consum. Res.* **1993,** *3* (3), 279–301.

Marty, L.; Nicklaus, S.; Miguet, M.; Chambaron, S.; Monnery-Patris, S. When do Healthiness and Liking Drive Children's Food Choices? The Influence of Social Context and Weight Status. *Appetite* **2018,** *125*, 466–473.

McIntosh, E. Using Discrete Choice Experiments within a Cost-benefit Analysis Framework. *Pharmacoeconomics* **2006,** *24* (9), 855–868.

Metzger, M. J.; Flanagin, A. J.; Medders, R. B. Social and Heuristic Approaches to Credibility Evaluation Online. *J. Commun.* **2010,** *60* (3), 413–439.

Ndoro, J. T.; Mudhara, M.; Chimonyo, M. Farmers' Choice of Cattle Marketing Channels Under Transaction Cost in Rural South Africa: A Multinomial Logit Model. *Afr. J. Range For. Sci.* **2015,** *32* (4), 243–252.

Nickel, J.; Ross, A. M.; Rhodes, D. H. In Comparison of Project Evaluation Using Cost-benefit Analysis and Multi-attribute Tradespace Exploration in the Transportation Domain. In 2nd International Symposium on Engineering Systems, 2009, June.

Nicklaus, S. Development of Food Variety in Children. *Appetite* **2009,** *52* (1), 253–255.

Perez-Burgos, A.; Mao, Y. K.; Bienenstock, J.; Kunze, W. A. The Gut-Brain Axis Rewired: Adding a Functional Vagal Nicotinic "Sensory Synapse." *The FASEB J.* **2014,** *28* (7), 3064–3074.

Prasad, S. Crisis, Identity, and Social Distinction: Cultural Politics of Food, Taste, and Consumption in Late Colonial Bengal. *J. Historical Sociol.* **2006,** *19* (3), 245–265.

Prescott, S. L.; Logan, A. C. Each Meal Matters in the Exposome: Biological and Community Considerations in Fast-Food-Socioeconomic Associations. *Econ. Human Biol.* **2017,** *27*, 328–335.

Ratchford, B. T. Cost-benefit Models for Explaining Consumer Choice and Information Seeking Behavior. *Manag. Sci.* **1982,** *28* (2), 197–212.

Reily, N. M.; Vartanian, L. R. The Portion Size Effect on Food Intake is Robust to Contextual Size Information. *Appetite* **2016,** *105*, 439–448.

Reimann, M.; Bechara, A.; MacInnis, D. Leveraging the Happy Meal Effect: Substituting Food with Modest Nonfood Incentives Decreases Portion Size Choice. *J. Exp. Psychol.: Appl.* **2015,** *21* (3), 276.

Rizk, M. T.; Treat, T. A. Sensitivity to Portion Size of Unhealthy Foods. *Food Qual. Prefer.* **2015,** *45*, 121–131.

Roberto, C. A.; Larsen, P. D.; Agnew, H.; Baik, J.; Brownell, K. D. Evaluating the Impact of Menu Labeling on Food Choices and Intake. *Am. J. Public Health* **2010,** *100* (2), 312–318.

Roitman, M. F.; Stuber, G. D.; Phillips, P. E.; Wightman, R. M.; Carelli, R. M. Dopamine Operates as a Subsecond Modulator of Food Seeking. *J. Neurosci.* **2004,** *24* (6), 1265–1271.

Sadler-Smith, E.; Shefy, E. Developing Intuitive Awareness in Management Education. *Acad. Manag. Learn. Edu.* **2007,** *6* (2), 186–205.

Samson, A.; Voyer, B. G. Two Minds, Three Ways: Dual System and dual Process Models in Consumer Psychology. *Ams Rev.* **2012,** *2* (2–4), 48–71.

Schermann, M.; Dongus, K.; Yetton, P.; Krcmar, H. The Role of Transaction Cost Economics in Information Technology Outsourcing Research: A Meta-analysis of the Choice of Contract Type. *J. Strategic Inform. Syst.* **2016,** *25* (1), 32–48.

Sharma, A. Self-Rationing Efficiency of Repeated Eating-Out Expenses: Does Experience Matter? *J. Hosp. Tour. Res.* **2017,** *41* (3), 259–277.

Shepherd , R., Raats, M., (Eds.; *The Psychology of Food Choice;* 2006; Vol. 3. Cabi. http://ssu.ac.ir/cms/fileadmin/user_upload/Mtahghighat/taghzie_imani/book/The-Psychology-of-Food-Choice.pdf#page=30

Shiffrin, R. M.; Schneider, W. Controlled and Automatic Human Information Processing: II. Perceptual Learning, Automatic Attending and a general Theory. *Psychol. Rev.* **1977,** *84* (2), 127.

Siegrist, M. Factors Influencing Public Acceptance of Innovative Food Technologies and Products. *Trends Food Sci. Technol.* **2008,** *19* (11), 603–608.

Sinayev, A.; Peters, E. Cognitive Reflection vs. Calculation in Decision Making. *Frontiers Psychol.* **2015,** *6*, 532.

Steenhuis, I.; Poelman, M. Portion Size: Latest Developments and Interventions. *Curr. Obes. Reports* **2017**, *6* (1), 10–17.

Steyn, N. P.; Nel, J. H.; Nantel, G.; Kennedy, G.; Labadarios, D. Food Variety and Dietary Diversity Scores in Children: Are They Good Indicators of Dietary Adequacy? *Public Health Nutr.* **2006**, *9* (5), 644–650.

Tabarrok , A.; Cowen, T. The End of Asymmetric Information. *Cato Unbound*.

Taylor, J. E.; Adelman, I. (Agricultural Household Models: Genesis, Evolution, and Extensions. *Rev. Econ. Household* **2003**, *1* (1–2), 33–58.

Terzimehić, N.; Schneegass, C.; Hussmann, H. In *Towards Finding Windows of Opportunity for Ubiquitous Healthy Eating Interventions*. In International Conference on Persuasive Technology, April, 2018, Springer: Cham, pp 99–112.

Tiu Wright, L.; Nancarrow, C.; Kwok, P. M. Food Taste Preferences and Cultural Influences on Consumption. *Br. Food J.* **2001**, *103* (5), 348–357.

Vadiveloo, M.; Morwitz, V.; Chandon, P. The Interplay of Health Claims and Taste Importance on Food Consumption and Self-reported Satiety. *Appetite* **2013**, *71*, 349–356.

Van Houtven, G.; Johnson, F. R.; Kilambi, V.; Hauber, A. B. Eliciting Benefit–risk Preferences and Probability-weighted Utility Using Choice-format Conjoint Analysis. *Med. Decis. Mak* **2011**, *31* (3), 469–480.

Verbeke, W.; Vackier, I. Individual Determinants of Fish Consumption: Application of the Theory of Planned Behaviour. *Appetite* **2005**, *44* (1), 67–82.

Viswanathan, V.; Jain, V. A Dual-system Approach to Understanding "generation Y" Decision Making. *J. Consum. Market.* **2013**, *30* (6), 484–492.

Volkow, N. D.; Wang, G. J.; Maynard, L.; Jayne, M.; Fowler, J. S.; Zhu, W.; Pappas, N. Brain Dopamine is Associated with Eating Behaviors in Humans. *Int. J. Eating Disorders* **2003**, *33* (2), 136–142.

Wardle, J.; Haase, A. M.; Steptoe, A.; Nillapun, M.; Jonwutiwes, K.; Bellisie, F. Gender Differences in Food Choice: The Contribution of Health Beliefs and Dieting. *Annals Behav. Med.* **2004**, *27* (2), 107–116.

Weiss , C. R. Consumer Demand for Food Variety. In *The Oxford Handbook of the Economics of Food Consumption and Policy;* 2011.

Whittler, T. E. Eliciting Consumer Choice Heuristics: Sales Representives' Persuasion Strategies. *J. Personal Selling Sales Manag.* **1994**, *14* (4), 41–53.

Wilcock, A.; Pun, M.; Khanona, J.; Aung, M. Consumer Attitudes, Knowledge and Behaviour: A Review of Food Safety Issues. *Trends in Food Sci. Technol.* **2004**, *15* (2), 56–66.

Worsley, A. Nutrition Knowledge and Food Consumption: Can Nutrition Knowledge Change Food Behaviour? *Asia Pacific J. Clin. Nutr.* **2002**, *11*, S579–S585.

CHAPTER 2

U.S. Trends in Food Away from Home

JUNGTAE SOH

Pennsylvania State University

E-mail: jks5501@psu.edu

ABSTRACT

Eating out among Americans has become important part of life lives due to the tremendous growth of foodservice industry and various social and economic changes. The purpose of this study is to investigate the factors affecting eating out trends and to explore the structural reasoning of eating out behavior. There have been various reasons (trends) to eat out or away from home. Leisure, pleasure, and necessity can be common reasons to eat out but they can be classified into more detailed causes. People are likely to eat out to experience something new and different from the everyday diet, and consumers are motivated from hedonic or utilitarian reason in terms of individual and environmental influences. Markets and demographic characteristics could also be factors impacting eating out so socio-cultural elements play a critical role. The choice of eating out can also be interpreted as a preference to avoid home meal preparation for convenience. One of the motivating reasons for such choices could be the lack of time for cooking and preparing food, given the pressures of day to day life. On the other hand, the looming caution for such choices could be the potential unhealthiness of eating out. Individuals also enjoy eating out when they want to socialize for special occasions with their family and friends. Besides, there are effects of family on eating out decisions, such as the size and composition of the family. Lastly, the socio-economic status of households could affect out-of-home eating decisions, thereby increasing the importance of understanding the economics of this phenomenon.

2.1   INTRODUCTION

There have been significant changes in eating habits of Americans over the past few decades. Eating out in North America has become an important part of life due to ongoing social, cultural, demographic, and economic changes. While America is going through a massive generational change, peoples' perceptions and views on eating out and food away from home have changed significantly. A recent report on global eating out trends (Nielsen, 2016) finds peoples' perceptions and attitudes toward factors such as health, wellness, diversity, and culture are reshaping the way people dine out. For example, due to increased health and wellness awareness, more and more consumers choose food options that can fit their specific dietary needs. The globalization and cultural integration have provided people with an opportunity to experience food from all over the world. A recent consumer report (Nielsen, 2016) shows that consumers between the age of 18 and 34 consider diversity and uniqueness to be important factors when choosing a restaurant. In addition, the rapid growth of foodservice industry has also allowed more dining options available for people to choose from when eating away from home.

Consequently, studies have found that people are likely to eat out more often and spend more on commercially prepared food, resulting in dramatic increase in expenditure on food away from home. According to a report by United States Department of Agriculture (USDA) (2016), total food away from home expenditures reached $731 billion in 2014, $265 billion increased from $466 billion in 2004. Another consumer report (Marks, 2016) shows that an average person in the U.S. would spend approximately $2200 per year on food away from home while food away from home expenditures surpassed 50% of the total food dollars in 2014. Overall, the findings of these studies show that food away from home expenditures have steadily increased over the past years, suggesting that there is a need to better understand the factors that contribute to the increase in food away from home expenditures. Therefore, this paper aims to identify important factors affecting peoples' eating out decisions in relation to recent social, cultural, demographic, and economic changes and discuss recent eating out trends in North America. The findings will provide useful framework and guidelines for researchers to investigate consumers' eating out decision-making processes.

2.2   DETERMINANTS OF CONSUMER DEMAND

A number of studies have shown the significant factors affecting eating away from home. According to French et al. (2001), there are various factors influencing fast food restaurant use such as demographic, behavioral, and nutritional factors. In this previous study, the authors investigated the relationship between frequency of fast food restaurant use and those factors by using a sample of 4746 adolescent students. As expected, frequency of fast food restaurant use was positively associated with intake of total energy, percent energy from fat, daily servings of soft drinks, cheeseburgers, French fries, and pizza. Fast food restaurant visits were negatively related to daily servings of fruit, vegetables, and milk. Interestingly, individuals of non-white ethnicity were significantly more likely to use fast-food restaurants. The study also found that frequent use of fast food restaurant would lead to poor nutritional intake of food. A number of studies have also investigated the structure of factors affecting eating out. For instance, Rashid (2003) developed nine dimensions for the relational marketing and these reflect the factors influencing customers' choice in eating out. The author described the role of relationship marketing (RM) in terms of the benefits of its application by evaluating nine dimensions for successful RM such as trust, commitment, social bonding, empathy, experiences, fulfillment of promise, customer satisfaction, internal RM, and communication. According to Edwards (2013), besides just eating a meal there are a number of elements affecting the eating away from home behavior such as time, social surroundings, physical surroundings, and atmosphere or ambience. Those factors overlapped with other study findings, and demonstrated similar effects on eating out behavior. However, the author emphasized that all those factors are required to be considered together not individually and thus eating away from home behavior can be evaluated.

Ryu et al. (2010) found that hedonic and utilitarian values affect customer satisfaction, which in turn has significant influence on behavioral intentions. In this study, utilitarian value displayed a greater influence than hedonic value. Several studies investigated the relationships between household characteristics and eating away from home demand (Stewart et al., 2004). It was found that household's income, time constraints faced by the household manager, household manager's age, number of people in the household, education level of the household manager, household's region of residence, and the household's race and ethnicity were the important factors impacting food away from home decisions. For instance, if the income of household is high then the members of household are likely to spend more time and money eating food away from home for leisure purposes.

Finally, environmental elements on eating behaviors were significant influences in another study by Story et al. (2008). They developed conceptual framework with factors affecting adolescent eating behaviors and food choices. For instance, there are four levels of influence: individual or intrapersonal influences (e.g., psychosocial, biological); social environmental or interpersonal (e.g., family and peers); physical environmental or community settings (e.g., schools, fast food outlets, and convenience stores); and macrosystem or societal (e.g., mass media, marketing and advertising, and social and cultural norms). According to the study, it is not easy to facilitate multilevel ecological research with variety of possible factors due to lack of valid measurements. Eating behavior and diet habit are multifaceted action and related to various contexts. Therefore, the following section of this paper presents broader causes of demand for food away from home, and at different types of food outlets. The paper also reports on eating away from home trends during the period of 1929–2014.

2.3   HEDONIC VERSUS UTILITARIAN VALUE

There are two types of consumer behavior values usually of interest to social scientists: first, a "utilitarian value" is incurred from the conscious pursuit of an intended consequence; secondly, when an outcome is associated more with voluntary hedonic responses it is called "hedonic value" (Babin et al., 1994). According to Park (2004), Hedonic factors are related to mood, quick service, cleanliness, food taste, employee kindness, and facilities, while utilitarian value is associated with price, quick service, and promotional incentives. Interestingly, in Park's study when Korean consumers make decision on eating out at fast food restaurant they consider the trendy and exotic aspects of the place (the hedonic perspective), and it affects their frequency of eating out significantly. Studies have also shown the consumers purchase meals according to hedonic and utilitarian reasons. However, the criteria for hedonic and utilitarian reasons are quite different from culture to culture. For instance, fast food restaurants appear to be more exotic and refreshing to Koreans than Korean restaurants, given that Koreans would usually eat their own food at home. In the study of different setting (Seo et al., 2012), researchers examined the differences in foreign residents' attitudes toward Korean foods and behavior intentions toward Korean restaurants by using acculturation and uncertainty avoidance level. They found that foreigners in Korea are most affected by income, nationality, and education level through the acculturation and uncertainty avoidance. These two studies suggest that the values customers consider when they eat out depend on their background, and can be quite different from culture to culture.

In case of special occasions for eating out, utilitarian and hedonic influence played different role in choosing healthy food (Boo et al., 2008). It seemed that hedonic motivation leads to selecting unhealthy food items and also the number of healthy items affected the eventual food choices. It was found that utilitarian and hedonic values have dynamic relationship with the construal level (Jeong and Jang, 2015). Either abstract or concrete level of construal was activated according to the long-term or immediate benefits during healthy menu promotion. When consumers focus more on hedonic value, they are likely to have more positive attitudes and purchasing intentions of healthy menu items with long-term benefits advertised than with immediate benefits advertised. Conversely, when consumers focus more on utilitarian values, they are likely to have more positive attitudes and purchasing intentions for healthy menu items with immediate benefits advertised than with long-term benefits advertised. According to Story et al. (2008), there are four levels of influence affecting adolescent eating behaviors and food choices: individual or intrapersonal influences (e.g., psychosocial and biological); social environmental or interpersonal (e.g., family and peers); physical environmental or community settings (e.g., schools, fast food outlets, and convenience stores); and macrosystem or societal (e.g., mass media, marketing and advertising, and social and cultural norms). At each level of influences, individual or intrapersonal level is basic component and the construct of level is hierarchical with level increasing. Thus, to change individual behavior, first it is necessary to address the context in which people make decisions, because an individual belongs to the lowest level and their behaviors are affected by upper levels such as social environmental, physical environmental, and macrosystem level. Also, the hedonic or utilitarian value possibly could interact with these four levels of eating behavior factors and might affect trend of eating out increasingly. Hedonic or utilitarian value is not working alone by itself and has close relationship to four levels of influence.

2.4 MARKETS AND DEMOGRAPHICS

Market segments and demographic factors play a critical role in eating out decision. Socio-cultural aspects are probably the most basic determinants for choosing a menu for eating out. People are willing to buy food away from home when it is more familiar with their background and experience. According to Olsen et al. (2000), there exist socio-demographic variations in the use of restaurants. There were significant impacts of household income, earnings, and age but complicated interaction of occupation, education, age, income, ethnicity, and gender was found. In a similar manner, Adams et al. (2015) investigated relationship between frequency and socio-demographic factors and eating out and take-away meals at home using U.K. data. They found differences in ratio of eating out between age groups of children and adults, but did not find any gender variations in eating out. Adults in higher income families tend to eat out at least once per week, but children in lower-income households tend to eat take-away meals at home at least once per week. There was no correlation between socio-economic status and consumption of take-away meals at home in case of adults. Thus, impact of socio-demographic factors varied depending on specific population or context of data. In another study of eating away from home (Oyewole, 2013), there were detailed and distinguished socio-economic and demographic factors that determined African–American customers' frequency of patronage in all-you-can-eat buffet restaurant. Therefore, socio-demographic factors might also have varied impact on eating out decisions under specific settings.

In another study when demographic factors were combined with other factors, their influence was still significant (Binkley, 2006). Binkley added nutritional factors on demographic and economic factors and analyzed their effects on food-away-from-home (FAFH). The research found that demographic influences were similar to those in the past studies and nutritional factors had some effect on fast food consumption due to their negative image. Also, trends in eating out seem to be in favor of full-service sector as the population is aging and the incomes of these older individuals continue to grow. Thus, the interaction and combination between each demographic factor components could be key to the change of trend in eating out.

2.5 AVAILABILITY AND CONVENIENCE

Food availability plays an important role in eating out decision because it provides convenience and also easy access to food for the consumers. There are links between community and consumer food environments, and dietary outcomes (Ni Mhurchu et al., 2013). In their study, Ni Mhurchu et al. (2013) tried to devise an empirical framework to observe the availability of healthy and unhealthy foods and non-alcoholic beverages in local food environments. The study results show that there is a correlation between community and consumer food environments and dietary outcomes but it is hard to conclude the firm relationship due to variation in the study. Availability of foodservice establishments may encourage consumption and may lead to poor diet quality. According to Murakami et al. (2011), eating out frequency was not related to availability of foodservice facilities but to quality of diet. This study aimed to examine for young Japanese women whether the neighborhood restaurant availability and eating out frequency correlate with dietary intake and with body mass index and waist circumference. It was expected that neighborhood restaurants would influence frequency of eating away from home but interestingly the study found that there was no relationship between those two.

In terms of convenience, it is also important to save time and effort for food preparation at home. According to Scholderer and Gruner (2005), "convenience" in the access to food usually means that some kind of effort is saved or reduced. The researchers in this study focused on household production approach and the convenience orientation approach. This expenditure of time and effort in cooking at home might impact the decision of eating away from home and eating taking-away food at home. According to Warde and Martens (2000), interviewees in their study repeatedly mentioned a break from everyday cooking and serving meal was an important aspect for eating away from home. However, there was conflicting outcome of this relationship in the past studies. The consumption of restaurant and pub meals was less effected by convenience and more by the importance of social events in the Irish market (De Boer et al., 2004). In this study, ready meals and take-away meals displayed close relationship to convenience. Smith et al. (2014) investigated whether state-level unemployment during the recession impacted patterns of home food preparation and away-from-home (AFH) eating among the low-income and minorities. State-level unemployment had little effect on patterns of cooking and eating AFH consumption and also there was no variation for low-income or minority groups. It was obvious that although a major economic crisis existed, adults in the US tried to keep their pre-crisis eating behavior despite rising costs and decreased employment. In case of frequent cooking at home, there was significant influence of being married, unemployed, larger households, presence of children aged less than 12 years, and lower frequency of eating out (Tiwari et al., 2017). To summarize, convenience of eating out and availability of food could play major role in decision of eating away from home but influence of other factors may attenuate their extent of influence.

2.6   FAMILY AND EATING AWAY FROM HOME

Family dynamics also has an influence on eating away from and at home. Looney et al. (2015) found that time and convenience were major factors affecting eating away from home for parents. Eating away from home was more relaxing and satisfying than cooking dinner and provided better quality time for a family with less conflict of choice. Also, early school lunches resulted in purchase of food on the way home or not being hungry at dinner. In another study by Robson et al. (2016), the results showed that parents with middle-to high-income had similar reasons such as quality family time, less conflicts and low costs to eat away from home for their families. Parents tended to eat out more because children were affected by school activity and school lunchtime. In terms of parent and child perspectives on eating out, if parents were satisfied with their expectations in foodservice, then they would be more likely to be loyal to these foodservice establishments (McGuffin et al., 2015). When families considered eating away from home a treat, they did not prioritize health and related health to quality of food. Besides, children could be more responsible for their own food choice. However, according to the income level of the family, home cooking is preferred to eating away from home in some cases.

2.7   ECONOMICS OF EATING OUT

In terms of household consumption of eating out, household income, time value, size and composition, and the environment of production and consumption affected total household expenditures on FAFH (McCracken and Brandt, 1987). These factors contributed to decision of eating out as criteria. Interestingly, there were differences in the importance of these factors by type of food facility: conventional restaurants, fast-food facilities, and other commercial food places. This could suggest that foodservice establishments need to focus on those factors differently according to their types of facility. In another study by Lee and Brown (1986), the study investigated factors affecting eating out decision and expenditure of eating out. The results showed that income positively affected the decision to eat out but affected the amount spent away from home positively only at upper levels of income. In addition, food expenditures at home were similarly affected by income only at higher levels of household income if the household also ate AFH. When the household did not eat out, food expenditures at home were positively affected by income at all levels, the effect decreasing in magnitude with the level of income. Thus, there is a major role of household income in case of decisions associated with eating out.

It is also crucial to see the changing trend of demand for FAFH and its effect on volume of full-service and fast-food restaurant segments (Stewart et al., 2004). The study simulated model with modest growth in household income and economic and demographic developments. The results showed that consumers kept expending increasingly at full-service and fast-food restaurants but they are expected to spend more at full-service restaurants. Expenditure per person would rise in two segments of full-service and fast-food restaurants respectively when the proportion of households of a single or multiple adults without live-at-home children increases. Nevertheless, the aging population is expected to reduce expenditure on fast food by little amount (Stewart et al., 2004). This study suggested that restaurant industry needs to adapt itself to changing atmosphere by preparing different strategies such as providing new, expanded menus, and services. It was also found that household's income, time constraints faced by the household manager, the household manager's age, number of people in the household, education level of the household manager, the household's region of residence, and the household's race and ethnicity were important factors influencing food away from home.

In terms of price and cost of eating out, there are several studies from the perspective of economics. Richards and Mancino (2013) examined how prices influence the demand for FAFH by looking at price-elasticity of demand for different FAFH. The researchers used a new dataset from NPD Group, Inc. and employed physiological measures of obesity, physical activity and health status in a theoretical framework. They found that there exists price elasticity in all the types of FAFH but little cross-price elasticity of demand, so consumers are reluctant to substitute between food-at-home and any type of FAFH or among types of FAFH. Thus, this could affect the demand of FAFH consumption in the period of economic changes due to traits of cross-price elasticities. Prochaska and Schrimper (1973) investigated whether the opportunity cost of the homemaker's time affected food consumption by considering the household a producing and consuming unit, and by analyzing factors such as income, family composition and size, and race as influences on AFH food consumption. They found that opportunity cost of time positively affected AFH consumption for employed homemakers and unemployed homemakers. This could play a critical role as the society becomes more modernized and women work more hours outside home. Equal opportunity between genders has been one of the most dramatic changes in the western countries and it has reached a status of stabilization where women are now moving forward and settling down their roles in the society by competing with their opposite gender partners (Olsen and Sharma, 1998). With the changing role of women, preparing meals at home takes up efforts and time and eating out could be the best alternatives for saving them. According to Lee and Brown (1986), income positively affected the decision to eat out but affected the amount spent away from home positively only at upper levels of income. In addition, food expenditures at home were similarly affected by income only at higher levels of household income if the household also ate away from home. When the household did not eat out, food expenditures at home were positively affected by income at all levels, the effect decreasing in magnitude with the level of income. Therefore, this relationship between cost/price and eating out suggests household production model and consumer behavior would interact and affect decision of eating away from home.

2.8 TREND OF EATING OUT

Dining out continues to grow in popularity, with consumer expenditure increasing from $4 billion in 1929 to over $731 billion in 2014. Therefore, it would be necessary and meaningful to see the trend of eating out so far with regard to influencing factors. This study used the United States Department of Agriculture (USDA) data of total expenditure on food away from home for the periods of 1929–2014 and 1987–2014. These data were calculated by the Economic Research Service, USDA, from various data sets from the U.S. Census Bureau and the Bureau of Labor Statistics. The data were analyzed using a series of descriptive statistics. According to the USDA data, there has been a significant increase of total expenditures on food away from home between 1929 and 2014. Table 2.1 shows the descriptive information of the USDA data during the period with the retail stores, direct selling, and recreational places which have data only from 1954 to 2014. Total expenditure on food away from home gradually increased at the beginning of the data period until the beginning of the 1970s and then expenditure at eating and drinking places surged incredibly after that time, pulling up the total expenditure at the same time (Fig. 2.1). The average expenditure on food away from home is $173 billion over the period of 1929–2014 and eating and drinking places take up average 71% of total expenditure in the same period. The rest of the places accounts only for 29%. Among them, schools and colleges ranked third in

TABLE 2.1 Total Expenditures on Food Away From Home (1929–2014). Dollar (in billions).

	N	Mean	Std. dev.	Proportion (%)
Eating and drinking places	82	$122	$155	71
Hotels and motels	82	$8	$9	5
Retail stores, direct selling[1]	61	$10	$8	6
Recreation places[1]	61	$8	$9	5
Schools and colleges	82	$12	$14	7
All other	82	$16	$15	9
Total	82	$173	$209	–

Note: [1]Data exist only from 1954 to 2014.
Source: Calculated by the Economic Research Service, USDA, from various data sets from the U.S. Census Bureau and the Bureau of Labor Statistics.

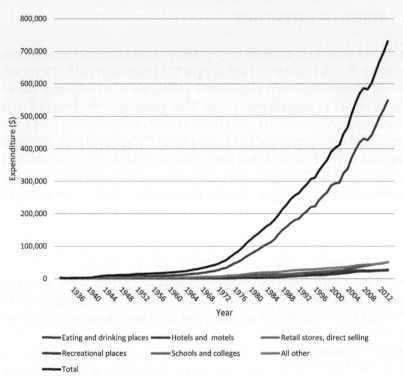

FIGURE 2.1   (See color insert.) Total expenditures on food away from home (1929–2014): Dollar (in billions).

Source: Calculated by the Economic Research Service, USDA, from various data sets from the U.S. Census Bureau and the Bureau of Labor Statistics.

proportion with 7% after all other places (9%), which means quite decent number of meals are served at schools and colleges for students. Most of eating out expenditures have been spent at eating and drinking places and lead the amount spent among the types of outlets. Especially, there are tips included in expenditure at eating and drinking places, and hotels and motels so tips given affected the amount of expenditure.

Total expenditures on food away from home based on a share indicate that the portion of each food-related expenditures also increased almost linearly from 1929 to 2014 (Fig. 2.2). Food away from home as a share of total food dollars reached over the half of total food dollars with 50.1% in 2014. It can be expected that total expenditures on food away from home will go well beyond half of total food dollars after 2014 and continue to grow by year. Interestingly, food away from

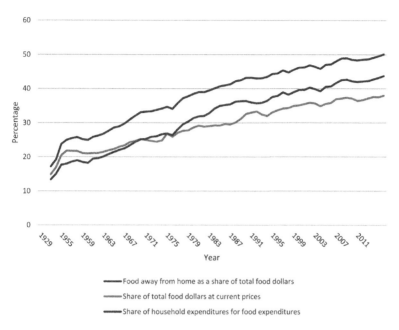

FIGURE 2.2 **(See color insert.)** Food away from home as a share of food expenditures (1929–2014). Share (Percentage).
Source: Calculated by the Economic Research Service, USDA, from various data sets from the U.S. Census Bureau and the Bureau of Labor Statistics.

home as a share of total food dollars stayed over a share of household expenditures for food expenditures by average 6%, which means eating away from home takes up more significant portion within food expenditures than food expenditures does within household expenditures (Table 2.2). Food away from home expenditure as a share of total food dollars accounts for 38% and share of household expenditures for food expenditures is 32% on average. In addition, when total food dollars are calculated at current price its average share decreases to 29% and its share is surpassed by a share of household expenditures for food expenditures in 1969.

Total expenditures on food away from home according to type of outlets shows quite detailed information of expenditure distribution by foodservice facility. For instance, in average, all eating places account for 78% and among them, full-service restaurants account for 42% and limited-service eating places account for 36% over the period of 1987–2014 (Table 2.3). It is noticeable that a share of full-service restaurants

TABLE 2.2   Total Expenditures on Food Away From Home (1929–2014). Share (Percentage).

	N	**Mean (%)**	**Std. dev. (%)**
Food away from home as a share of total food dollars	64	38	9
Share of total food dollars at current prices	64	29	6
Share of household expenditures for food expenditures	64	32	9

Source: Calculated by the Economic Research Service, USDA, from various data sets from the U.S. Census Bureau and the Bureau of Labor Statistics.

TABLE 2.3   Total Expenditures on Food Away From Home According to Type of Outlets (1987–2014). Dollar (in billions).

	N	**Mean**	**Std. dev.**	**Proportion (%)**
Full-service restaurants	28	$163	$66	42
Limited-service eating places	28	$144	$56	36
All eating places	28	$307	$122	78
Hotels and motels	28	$19	$6	4
Schools and colleges	28	$28	$11	7
Stores, bars, and vending machines	28	$19	$7	4
Recreational places	28	$16	$8	5
Others, including military outlets	28	$9	$2	1

Source: Calculated by the Economic Research Service, USDA, from various data sets from the U.S. Census Bureau and the Bureau of Labor Statistics.

has been larger than limited-service eating places except 1995 (Fig. 2.3). Since then the gap between two categories becomes greater year by year and consumers spend more money at full-service restaurants than at limited-service eating places. Also, schools and colleges have been the second largest portion after all eating places which consist of full-service restaurants and limited-service eating places. This was similar trends from 1929 to 2014 in Table 2.1.

There were some prominent percentage changes at the beginning of period for three food outlet types: eating and drinking places, hotels and motels, and schools and colleges. The patterns of changes were relatively similar among them displaying rise and then drop repeatedly. However, percentage change of schools and colleges was larger than the other two outlets in extent and displayed sudden increase around 1947 alone without following the pattern. Also, there was opposite change of schools and colleges in 1987, which was decrease of expenditure by 6%. Thus, food expenditure for schools and colleges had a few exceptional trends compared to eating and drinking places and hotels and motels. Overall, expenditure at the eating out places increased gradually over the years maintaining each proportion between types of eating outlets. Specifically, eating and drinking places had the largest portion among the food places and within them, full-service restaurants became more popular than limited-service restaurants enlarging the gap between two. Thus, observation of these trends by food outlets could help understand the future direction of consumers and manage their reactions   and behavior (Fig. 2.4).

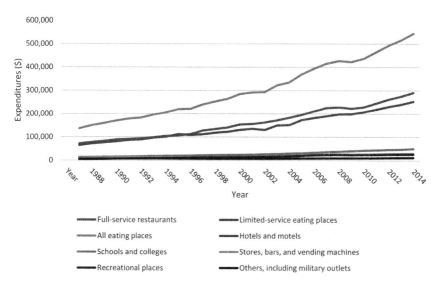

FIGURE 2.3   (See color insert.) Sales of meals and snacks away from home by type of outlet (1987–2014). Dollar (in billions).
Source: Calculated by the Economic Research Service, USDA, from various data sets from the U.S. Census Bureau and the Bureau of Labor Statistics

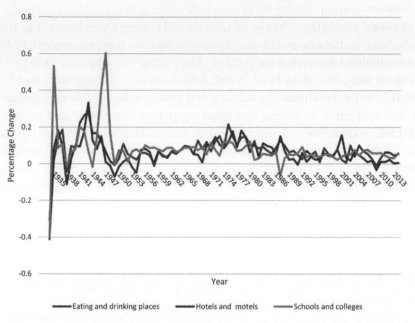

FIGURE 2.4   (See color insert.) Percentage changes in expenditures on food away from home by type of outlet (1929–2014). Dollar (in billions).
Source: Calculated by the Economic Research Service, USDA, from various data sets from the U.S. Census Bureau and the Bureau of Labor Statistics.

2.9   DISCUSSIONS AND IMPLICATIONS

There have been various studies on factors affecting eating out and researchers discussed a number of factors on eating out. This study aims to describe important factors affecting peoples' eating out decisions in relation to recent social, cultural, demographic, and economic changes and to discuss recent eating out trends in North America. After reviewing eating out trends in the United States, explanation for this trends is required over the development of expenditure on eating out according to food outlet types. The factors affecting eating out behavior seem to display relatively dynamic impact in terms of trend. For instance, there might be positive influence of aging baby boom generation at the beginning of trend because they were the first-generation customers of emerging eating out industry while those factors could affect the trend of eating out negatively as they get older (Olsen and Sharma, 1998). Thus, factors affecting eating out decision could play their critical determinant role in every direction in the context of specific time frame. According to Olsen and Sharma (1998), impact of working women changed the whole scene of eating industry as suppliers because they were familiar with hospitality industry traits, which increased the need for their workforce in the industry. This also could bring the change of household income and lack of time to prepare meals at home as consumers. Therefore, the role of women at workplace might create synergy effect for both industries and consumers.

Finally, this paper suggests the potential relationship between afore-mentioned factors and food away from home decisions. Firstly, there could be dynamic relationship between hedonic and utilitarian values on eating out decision. For example, consumers tend to make a decision of eating out when their perceived hedonic and utilitarian values meet their needs.

Proposition 1: consumers purchase food away from home according to their hedonic and utilitarian values.

According to Park (2004), there was a cultural difference in perception of hedonic and utilitarian values which resulted in purchasing food away from home. It might be interesting further study opportunity to compare those perceived values in cross-cultural way. Thus, second propositional statement is as follows:

Proposition 2: consumers' decision of eating out varies according to their culturally perceived hedonic and utilitarian values.

Next, market variety could play significant role in food away from home decision since there exist a number of market segments and compe-tition within them are likely to increase and broaden across each segment.

Proposition 3: eating out decision depends on types of variety of market segments.

In addition, demographic traits could be related to food away from home. Consumers' demographic background would influence the eating out decision and trend overall.

Proposition 4: eating out decision depends on types of demographic traits of consumers.

The availability of food and eating out behavior show conflicting results from the previous studies. There was correlation between commu-nity and consumer food environments and dietary outcomes (Ni Mhurchu et al., 2013). The availability of food would influence quality of eating out consumption. However, there was conflicting output that availability of food did not affect eating out frequency (Murakami et al., 2011). Therefore, further study would be required to examine the effect of availability of food on eating out decision.

Proposition 5: consumers consider the availability of food types when they decide to purchase food away from home.

As women work more and families have double income sources, convenience becomes a critical factor to save time for preparation and consumption of food. Thus, consumers would look for the efficient way in which they could compensate time with eating out. This would be opportunity for further study because change of workforce is likely to emphasize convenience in consumer activities and this trend would be more prevalent in the future due to increasing working population.

Proposition 6: consumers consider the convenience to save time and effort when they decide to purchase food away from home.

Family is also major factor affecting consumption of food away from home. For instance, if family has children, the eating out decision would be greatly affected by children's preference or choice. However, there might be less conflict on selecting the menu due to more inclusive and various capacity of restaurant menus to choose from. Besides, family could save time and enjoy convenience at the same time.

Proposition 7: family affects the eating out decision in terms of preferences and choices of family members.

More importantly, there is a factor of economics such as household income, time value, size and composition, and the environment of production and consumption which would influence total household expenditures on FAFH. Thus, income of household would definitely influence eating out decision and even choice of food places because income is directly related to ability of purchasing menu items at food places. However, there might be different extent of effects along the levels of income.

Proposition 8: consumers choose types of food places according to their income.

In terms of costs, people consider opportunity cost of time before they decide to eat out and it is likely that opportunity cost positively affects AFH consumption for employed homemakers and unemployed homemakers

(Prochaska and Schrimper, 1973). In addition, consumers choose types of food facilities according to the opportunity cost of time which is measured by wage rate.

Proposition 9: opportunity cost of time which consumers perceived could play important role in eating out decision.

This paper has summarized the important factors affecting eating away from home decisions from extant literature and examined the trends of eating out for decades. Also, it provided suggestions for future research in hospitality literature. Our analysis demonstrates that issues on FAFH have been studied broadly but they are not integrated and reviewed thoroughly. Although the trend shows that FAFH expenditure is increasing and its share takes up more than 50% of food expenditure, there have been few studies relating this trend and influencing factor intensively. Also, research on FAFH expenditure by type of food facilities is scarce compared to overall FAFH studies and thus observing food consumption by type of food facilities would provide useful implication to the industry of relevant food facilities. Researchers and practitioners can leverage findings from this paper to better design and implement their research plans on the roles of factors affecting FAFH decision and its trend.

KEYWORDS

- food-away-from-home
- food decision
- eating out trend
- hedonic
- utilitarian
- family

REFERENCES

Adams, J.; Goffe, L.; Brown, T.; Lake, A. A.; Summerbell, C.; White, M.; Adamson, A. J. Frequency and Socio-demographic Correlates of Eating Meals Out and Take-away

Meals at Home: Cross-sectional Analysis of the UK National Diet and Nutrition Survey, Waves 1–4 (2008–12). *Int. J. Behav. Nutr. Phys. Activity* **2015**, *12* (1), 51.

Babin, B. J.; Darden, W. R.; Griffin, M. Work and/or Fun: Measuring Hedonic and Utilitarian Shopping Value. *J. Cons. Res.* **1994**, *20* (4), 644–656.

Binkley, J. K. The Effect of Demographic, Economic, and Nutrition Factors on the Frequency of Food Away From Home. *J. Cons. Affairs* **2006**, *40* (2), 372–391.

Boo, H. C.; Chan, L. T.; Abidin, U. Z.; Fatimah, U. Healthy Eating Away-from-home: Effects of Dining Occasion and the Number of Menu Items. *Int. Food Res. J.* **2008**, *15* (2), 201–208.

De Boer, M.; Mccarthy, M.; Cowan, C.; Ryan, I. The Influence of Lifestyle Characteristics and Beliefs About Convenience Food on the Demand for Convenience Foods in the Irish Market. *Food Qual. Pref.* **2004**, *15* (2), 155–165.

Edwards, J. S. The Foodservice Industry: Eating Out is More Than Just a Meal. *Food Qual. Pref.* **2013**, *27* (2), 223–229.

Jeong, E.; Jang, S. S. Healthy Menu Promotions: A Match Between Dining Value and Temporal Distance. *Int. J. Hosp. Manag.* **2015**, *45*, 1–13.

Lee, J. Y.; Brown, M. G. Food Expenditures at Home and Away From Home in the United States—A Switching Regression Analysis. *Rev. Econ. Stat.* **1986**, *68*, 142–147.

Looney, S.; Crosby, L.; Stark, L. Eating Away From Home: A Parent's Perspective. *FASEB J.* **2015**, *29* (1 Supplement), 132–138.

Marks, T. *Dining Out: Where America Eats*; *Consumer Reports,* 2016; *11*. Retrieved From: https://www.consumerreports.org/restaurants/dining-out-where-america-eats/.

Mccracken, V. A.; Brandt, J. A. Household Consumption of Food-Away-From-Home: Total Expenditure and by Type of Food Facility. *Amer. J. Agric. Econ.* **1987**, *69*, 274–284.

Mcguffin, L. E.; Price, R. K.; Mccaffrey, T. A.; Hall, G.; Lobo, A.; Wallace, J. M.; Livingstone, M. B. E. Parent and Child Perspectives on Family Out-Of-Home Eating: A Qualitative Analysis. *Public Health Nutr.* **2015**, *18* (01), 100–111.

Murakami, K.; Sasaki, S.; Takahashi, Y.; Uenishi, K. Neighborhood Restaurant Availability and Frequency of Eating Out in Relation to Dietary Intake in Young Japanese Women. *J. Nutr. Sci. Vitaminol.* **2011**, *57* (1), 87–94.

Neilson What's in our Food and on our Mind, 2016. Retrieved From: http://www.nielsen.com/us/en/insights/reports/2016/whats-in-our-food-and-on-our-minds.html.

Ni Mhurchu, C.; Vandevijvere, S.; Waterlander, W.; Thornton, L. E.; Kelly, B.; Cameron, A. J.; Swinburn, B. Monitoring the Availability of Healthy and Unhealthy Foods and Non-alcoholic Beverages in Community and Consumer Retail Food Environments Globally. *Obes. Rev.* **2013**, *14* (S1), 108–119.

Olsen, M. D.; Sharma, A. *Forces Driving Change in the Casual Theme Restaurant Industry*; International Hotel and Restaurant Association: Paris, France, 1998.

Olsen, W. K.; Warde, A.; Martens, L. Social Differentiation and the Market for Eating Out in the UK. *Int. J. Hosp. Manag.* **2000**, *19* (2), 173–190.

Oyewole, P. The Role of Frequency of Patronage and Service Quality of All-You-Can-Eat Buffet Restaurant: A Perspective of Socio-economic and Demographic Characteristics of African American Consumers. *Int. J. Hosp. Manag.* **2013**, *34*, 202–213.

Park, C. Efficient or Enjoyable? Consumer Values of Eating-Out and Fast Food Restaurant Consumption in Korea. *Int. J. Hosp. Manag.* **2004**, *23* (1), 87–94.

Prochaska, F. J.; Schrimper, R. A. Opportunity Cost of Time and Other Socioeconomic Effects on Away-From-Home Food Consumption. *Amer. J. Agric. Econ.* **1973,** *55* (4 Part 1), 595–603.

Rashid, T. Relationship Marketing: Case Studies of Personal Experiences of Eating Out. *Br. Food J.* **2003,** *105* (10), 742–750.

Richards, T. J.; Mancino, L. Demand for Food -Away-From-Home: A Multiple-Discrete–Continuous Extreme Value Model. *Eur. Rev. Agric. Econ.* **2013,** 679–707.

Robson, S. M.; Crosby, L. E.; Stark, L. J. Eating Dinner Away From Home: Perspectives of Middle-To High-Income Parents. *Appetite* **2016,** *96,* 147–153.

Scholderer, J.; Grunert, K. G. Consumers, Food and Convenience: The Long Way From Resource Constraints to Actual Consumption Patterns. *J. Econ. Psychol.* **2005,** *26* (1), 105–128.

Seo, S.; Phillips, W. J.; Jang, J.; Kim, K. The Effects of Acculturation and Uncertainty Avoidance on Foreign Resident Choice for Korean Foods. *Int. J. Hosp. Manag.* **2012,** *31* (3), 916–927.

Stewart, H.; Blisard, N.; Bhuyan, S.; Nayga Jr., R. M. *The Demand for Food Away From Home*; US Department Of Agriculture-Economic Research Service Agricultural Economic Report, 2004; 829.

Story, M.; Kaphingst, K. M.; Robinson-O'Brien, R.; Glanz, K. Creating Healthy Food and Eating Environments: Policy and Environmental Approaches. *Annu. Rev. Public Health* **2008,** *29,* 253–272.

Tiwari, A.; Aggarwal, A.; Tang, W.; Drewnowski, A. Cooking at Home: A Strategy to Comply With US Dietary Guidelines at No Extra Cost. *Amer. J. Preven. Med.* **2017,** *52,* 616–624.

Warde, A.; Martens, L. *Eating Out: Social Differentiation, Consumption, and Pleasure*; Cambridge University Press: Cambridge, England, 2000.

CHAPTER 3

Out-of-Home Eating Trends: How Knowledgable Is the South African Foodservice Industry on Healthy Meal Alternatives?

H. KESA* and A. N. MELANI

School of Tourism and Hospitality, College of Business and Economics University of Johannesburg, Johannesburg, South Africa

Corresponding author. E-mail: hemak@uj.ac.za

ABSTRACT

Out-of-home (OH) eating amongst South Africans and globally is on a significant increase. Individuals are increasingly becoming more reliant on meals consumed in restaurants. However, the foodservice industry faces challenges due the perceived nature of poor diet quality of meals they serve, said to be contributing to the prevalence of non-communicable diseases that are related to diet, particularly overweight and obesity. The purpose of this paper was to understand the challenges faced by the food-service industry regarding the nature of meals offered and the perceived poor diet quality thereof. Therefore, the objectives of the study were to examine how knowledgeable foodservice employees are on healthy meals, as well as to evaluate managers' rationale regarding the inclusion of healthier meals on their menus. A mixed method approach was adopted to collect data for this study. Wherein self-administered questionnaires were distributed to waiter while structured interviews were conducted with their managers. The quantitative findings showed that only 29.03% of waiters were knowledgeable about healthier meals as an alternative, and were able to efficiently assist guests with such meal requests. Qualitative findings revealed that managers indeed considered the incorporation of healthier meal alternatives and all managers were influenced by similar factors. From this study, it could be recommended that a considerable amount of training is needed in the foodservice sector, particularly regarding waiters' knowledge on healthier alternative meals. This would be crucial as consumers/guests are increasingly preferring such type of meals, even when dining out.

3.1 INTRODUCTION

The trend toward out-of-home (OH) eating is on a constant increase, as it is evident that individuals and families are now more inclined to eat out than to enjoy a home-cooked meal. This occurrence can be attributed to the fact that consumers are increasingly experiencing scarcity of time to prepare meals at home (Moolman, 2011:131). As a general global trend over the past decades toward fewer meals prepared from home has been observed, resulting from dynamics of busier lifestyles, unconventional working hours, and an increase in the number of working women in households Bevis (2012:online). To this effect, consumers prefer to enjoy a meal prepared OH instead of spending their scarce time preparing a home-cooked meal (Moolman, 2011:131). It is clear that the contemporary way of life coupled with the nature of individuals being extremely busy has led to an increase of meals that are consumed out-of-home (Choi and Rajagopal, 2013:474) and South Africa has not been spared from this occurrence. To this effect, a need for healthier alternatives on menus has been observed. Previous studies reveal that over the past few years, regardless of household income or economic class; individuals have increased the number of meals that they consume OH and with that the average food budget which they spend on eating out has also increased (Glanz et al., 2007:383). Food and eating environments possibly contribute to the increasing prevalence of the obesity epidemic and other Non-Communicable Diseases (NCD's) that are related to diet (NEMS, 2015: Online) and (Story et al., 2008:253). Food that is consumed OH has been made known to have higher calorie/ fat content, added sugars, refined carbohydrates as well as higher salt content than food prepared at home (Fitzgerald et al., 2004:429). Therefore, the foodservice industry has been condemned for the increase in overweight and obesity and other diet-related diseases (Edwards et al.,

2005:85). The increased trend toward OH eating is closely associated with increased ingestion of calories, saturated fats, added sugars, and salt and on contrary the intake of fewer fruits and vegetables, less milk, fiber and vitamins (Glanz et al., 2007:383). Meals prepared OH are known to be of larger portion sizes, which may lead to overconsumption which is closely connected to enlarge body weight and insulin struggle (Glanz et al., 2007:383). The steady increase toward OH eating has also been closely associated with several NCD's that are related to diet, particularly; overweight and obesity and respiratory diseases (Boo et al., 2008:201).

Robson et al. (2016:147) agree with the notion that meals that are prepared OH have higher caloric content and are of poorer nutritional quality. Therefore, McCool and McCool (2010:13) state that it would seem rational that managers within the foodservice industry acknowledge that the industry has a social responsibility regarding the obesity epidemic. Therefore, it is suggested that the prevalence of overweight and obesity has increased considerably concurrently with the increase of OH. Previous studies suggest that over the past few years an increased prevalence of NCD's related to diet such as; overweight and obesity, cardiovascular diseases and diabetes, had been observed as a result of an equal growing focal point on customer nourishment education has been observed (Sharma et al., 2011:146).

3.2   PURPOSE AND OBJECTIVES

The purpose of the study was to acquire literature on new trends regarding OH. The study explores and documents the trends toward OH eating within a global context and provides a focus into the South African context. The research will establish the nature of meals consumed OH, the effects increased OH eating and the prevalence of obesity and other NCDs.

The study was guided by the following research objectives:

(1) The objective of the study was to evaluate the knowledge and awareness of foodservice employees on low-calorie and healthy balanced meal alternatives.

(2) The study also investigated factors which informed restaurant managers' decision regarding the inclusion of healthy balanced meals as well as low-calorie meals.

3.3 OUT-OF-HOME EATING

Tourism is one of the largest and fastest-growing industries globally. The World Travel and Tourism Council (WTTC, 2014:4) reports that the tourism industry contributed 9.5% to the global economy in 2013. According to Statistics South Africa (SSA, 2013:7) despite the challenging global economic conditions, the South African tourism industry reached a record of 9.6 million international tourist arrivals in 2013. Subsequently, the sectors contribution to the gross domestic product (GDP) in South Africa has risen progressively from 8.1% in 2007 to 10.3% in 2013 and is expected to reach 12% in 2014 (WTTC, 2014:4). Restaurants are classified as one of the Standard Industrial Classification (SIC) codes within the hospitality industry that make up the South African Tourism Industry (CATHSSETA, 2014:4). Statistics South Africa (SSA, 2013:11) estimates that restaurants provided for 93,000 jobs in 2013, while the total income generated by restaurants was R1728 million in September 2013. During the past decades, OH eating has been documented to have gained significance in diets worldwide (Lachat et al., 2012:329). Trichopoulou et al. (2009:66) state that OH eating is no longer just for special occasions, however, it has become a common way of life. It is important to note that the defining and describing OH eating is more slippery than what meets the eye. D'Addezio et al. (2014:9) acknowledged that a limitation in their study titled "Out-of-home eating frequency, causal attribution of obesity, and support to healthy eating policies from a cross-European survey" was a lack of a strict definition for OH eating. Warde and Martens (2000:526) suggests that OH eating can be referred to as enjoying a meal at a public dining room, where individuals who afford to go eat, can go eat whilst in the presence of others.

Families are now spending more money eating OH, more than they are preparing food at home (Robson et al., 2016:147). These researchers continued to state that there is no standard definition, however meals that are prepared OH typically refer to meals purchased at a restaurant, fast food outlet, and any other take-out or take away establishment. Lachat et al. (2012:332) state that environmental transitions and personal life-styles are dominant factors of the global increase regarding overweight and obesity. It was publicized that one of the dominant transitions in lifestyles of individuals that took place during the past decades is the increasing prevalence of consumption of foods and beverages OH.

Lachat et al. (2009:332) publicized that a number of researchers have explicitly articulated their apprehensions with the foodservice Industry with regards to; larger portion sizes, high-density energy, lack of conveying nutritional value of meals to consumers, and lack of healthy balanced meal options among other concerns related to OH eating. It is true that worldwide, individuals are eating away from home more often than they used to. Edwards et al. (2005:85) state that the foodservice industry has invigorated this with business tactics to attract consumers by making their meals affordable, accessible, and acceptable through; super-sizing, product bundling and "eat as much as you like buffets." Researchers continued to state that the prevalence of overweight and obesity has increased throughout the world and thus the foodservice industry has been condemned for this occurrence.

3.4   THE GROWTH OF OH EATING

Statistics and recent studies have documented the growing significance of establishments providing foods and beverages (D'Addezio et al., 2014:9). Expenditures regarding the consumption of OH eating have risen not only in developed countries but also in developing countries (Bezerra et al., 2012:65). Bezerra and Sichieri (2009:2037) publicized that the level of spending on OH eating gained prevalence in the USA and rose from 26% of total food expenditure during the 1970s, to 39% in 1996 and it reached 42% in 2002. Therefore, according to Hwang and Cranage (2006:66) the ratio of OH eating to total food dollars was 48.5% in 2004 and 48.9% in 2016. Hwang and Cranage (2010:69) state that as household disposable incomes increase, time for preparing a home-cooked meal becomes scarce and thus OH eating becomes affordable and easily accessible.

Figure 3.1 illustrates the expenditure for food consumed OH in the United States. It shows the incline of the expenditure for food consumed OH from the year 2000–2010. The expenditure increased from nearly $400 billion in 2000 to nearly $580 billion in 2010. The figure depicts the rigorous growth of the foodservice industry, this refers to the private, profit, and commercial segment of the Industry.

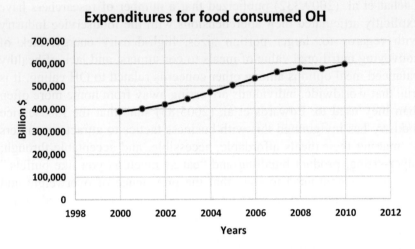

FIGURE 3.1   Expenditures for food consumed OH from 2000 to 2012.
Source: United States Department of Agriculture (2015:Online).

The foodservice industry is a major contributor to the economy in the USA. In 2010, American consumers spent nearly $580 billion on purchasing food OH (National Restaurant Association, 2010: online). According to the National Restaurant Association's 2014 Restaurant Industry Forecast report, restaurant and foodservice sales are projected to total $683.4 billion in 2014, up 3.6% from 2013's sales volume of $659.3 billion.

3.5   THE SOUTH AFRICAN PERSPECTIVE ON OH EATING

Food consumed OH is also on the rife in developing countries, this occurrence may stem from a matter of convenience or simply a pleasurable activity, whatever the reason may be, it has been documented that urbanites spend a substantial amount of their food budget on meals consumed OH (Delisle, 1990:online). OH eating represents an increasing share of food consumption around the world, caused by various factors including increasing urbanization, increased number of females in the workplace, participation and evolving food systems that have made food availability easier (Vakis et al., 2015:online). It is needless to argue that South Africa has not been spared from this occurrence. In an article titled *"More South Africans Are Eating Out,"* it was recorded that in October 2014 consumers had spent R3.95 billion on food and beverages consumed OH (IOL, Independent Online, 2014:online).

Subsequently, the South African consumer foodservice industry experienced growth over the 2003/2004, the number of establishments increased by 8% while value sales increased by 17% and reached R23.3 billion in 2004 (Consumer Foodservice in South Africa 2005: online). The modernization of the South African economy which has led to the changes in OH eating habits and food trends, boosted the restaurant industry, which increased by 47% (Consumer Foodservice in South Africa 2005:online). Researchers suggest that with the increasing number of women in the workplace and busier lifestyles, the convenience that restaurants offer is significant factor in modern-day living.

According to Statistics South Africa (2013:3), the year-on-year percentage on total income generated by the food and beverages industry yielded a growth percentage of 5.2% in October 2013 when compared with October 2012, despite the tough global economic conditions, the South African tourism sector reached a record of 9.6 million international tourists in 2013.

3.6 MANAGEMENT RESPONSIBILITY

The foodservice industry in the commercial sector has experienced a great deal of development in recent years, with an increased focus on healthy eating (Lee et al., 2011). McCool and McCool (2010:13) suggest that it would seem rational that managers within the foodservice industry acknowledge that the industry has a social responsibility regarding the obesity epidemic. The researchers also publicized that managers and menu planners should take the initiative in assuming a foremost role in the nation's exertions to combat obesity, which appears to be a critical public health concern than any other (McCool and McCool 2010:13). However, it may be argued that the foodservice industry is not the prime source of obesity, but the industry and the food that is at the public's disposal, OH, are definitely related to this issue. In this light, it has been debated that the foodservice industry should assume a foremost role to alleviate the epidemic and initiate actions to assist neutralize the obesity prevalence. Lee et al. (2011) state that it is incredibly vital that managers consider what their consumers want and one of the biggest and growing trends currently is to provide healthier food choices on menu offerings.

TABLE 3.1 Factors that Influence Restaurant Managers' Decisions to Incorporate Healthier or Low Kilojoule/Low Fat in the Menu.

Issue	Most influential	Less influential
Most relevant considerations for adding and retaining healthier menu items.	Consumer demands Sales and profit of the item	Ease of cooking Food safety
What healthy foods to add?	Food that is lower in calorie Fruits and veg Fibre	No hydrated fats low carbohydrates low sodium
Perceptions of healthier foods	Need sufficient consumer demand Healthy options avoid	Customers want to indulge when eating out
Obstacles to adding healthier menu offerings	Lower sales margin Note enough appeal Spoils quickly short shelf life ingredient availability	Fruit and veggies Reluctance to identify as food healthy storage requirements Training Employee skill issues
Future trends, opportunities, strategies	Healthier foods may increase slightly Fruits and vegetables add creativity to the menu	Use of ethical products Fresh produce is limited
What trade groups and industry associations can do to support healthier meals	Clearly demonstrate profitability of healthier eating options Partner with various restaurants to market healthy eating	Educate/train new chefs on healthier food use and preparation Improve distribution to increase fresher, riper produce
What public health groups and scientists can do	Conduct consumer research and share with the restaurant industry Publicize good examples of healthy eating	Rate healthfulness of restaurants to drive more people to those restaurants

Source: (Glanz et al., 2007:383).

According to the (Glanz et al., 2007:383), Table 3.1 reflects factors influencing managers' decisions during menu planning. These factors are influenced by decisions informed that are informed by how influential the issue/factor is.

3.7   CONSUMER AND FOODSERVICE EMPLOYEES' NUTRITIONAL KNOWLEDGE AND EDUCATION

Harneck and French (2008:3) publicized that there is no published literature that discusses the need for nutritional knowledge among foodservice employees. However, literature outlines the need to educate and inform consumers on nutritional knowledge through; healthful programs and calorie labeling on meal items Harneck and French (2008:3). Published literature on calorie labeling on restaurant menus state that it is one policy concerning health issues linked to the public that has been selected to assist consumers in making healthy informed food choices when dining out. Furthermore, Harnack and French (2008:4) state that it had been debated that consumers require to be well-informed with regards to calorie and fat content in meals on the menu in restaurants as this may create awareness on the amount of fat content in the food that they order. Over the past decade, there has been an increase in the dominance of diet-related diseases; overweight and obesity, diabetes, heart diseases, and cardiovascular diseases as well as other chronic diseases, subsequently there has been an equal incline focusing on consumer nutritional education (Sharma et al., 2011:146). The importance of consumer nutrition education and awareness cannot be over emphasized as several diseases, obesity and heart disease, which are on rife are closely related to diet and food consumption.

Igumbor et al. (2012:6) concluded that there is a dire need to mitigate the adverse health implications of the transitioned food environment in South Africa. The authors suggested that the deeds should combine accelerated efforts to educate and inform the public about the consequences of consuming increased fatty foods and generally unwholesome foods. In this light, it was also suggested that the South African government develops a strategic outline to make healthier foods; fruits, vegetables, whole grains, and a variety of wholesome foods more affordable, accessible, and acceptable.

3.8   SUCCESSFUL HEALTHY PROMOTIONAL RESTAURANT PROGRAMS

The Healthy Dining Program was established after a caption in The Nation's Restaurant News in the United States asked whether restaurants should be held accountable for tracking people's diets (Gregory et al., 2006:43) and after other researchers suggested that to address health concerns (NCD's); hospitals, community care centers, tertiary institutions, and health departments need to work cohesively with point-of-purchase outlets like; restaurants, hotels, and supermarkets. These should act as mediums of prospect to connect patrons with community nutritional education workshops that will serve as local support groups for a positive lifestyle development (Catherine et al., 2004:429)

The Healthy Dining Program (HDP) was a joint venture between community restaurants and the health departments. The core aim of the joint venture was to promote and identify healthy balanced menu options to assist consumers in making healthier food choices when dining out (Hwang and Crange, 2010: 69). In South Africa, healthy dining initiatives are very new. Eat Out is an online program that partners with restaurants owners in all provinces in South Africa. It advertises the restaurants that offer healthy eating choices (Buxton et al., 2016). Business Tech (2015) publishes on the healthiest fast food meals in South Africa and offers the nutritional analysis of some of the food items on menus. The healthy eating trend is new but it is growing in South Africa.

Regardless of the amount of published literature and media reporting around issues of the unhealthy nature of eating out, previous studies reveal that people have adopted a taste for that kind of lifestyle. However, there was an equal increase surrounding the interest in dietary value of eating out because people have become more conscious about their health (Hwang and Crange, 2010:69). The researchers continued to state that the trend was that customers demanded meals that were lower in calories and healthier balanced meals. Therefore, in these circumstances, restaurant marketers need to understand how customers think of their menu options and how to take heed and incline their focus on keeping up with the trend in preferences of meals that are lower in calories and healthier balanced meals (Hwang and Crange, 2010: 69).

In the effort to assist restaurants to facilitate and encourage the emerging interest on nutrition by customers, the Colorado State University developed the *Dine to Your Hearts' Delight Restaurant Program* (Wenzel et al., 2008:63). These researchers publicized that the program was developed to aid restaurant managers to design and encourage healthy menu options through selected menu items that were lower in calories, cholesterol, saturated fats, and salts. Therefore, post the establishment of the program; these restaurants' marketing departments and newspaper publishers revealed that restaurant menus now offer healthier food choices. This revealed that the trend incorporated meals that were lower in calories such as; grilled chicken, and the preferences of lean low-fat meats, low sodium and in contrary, an increased utilization of fruits and steamed vegetables (Wenzel et al., 2008:63). The researchers also added that as restaurant patrons became more health-conscious there has been some sort of response from the restaurant industry.

It is evident that the restaurant industry and various Health Policy boards in the United States have responded to the trend and the need for healthier food consumption for consumers eating out. However, no published research discusses the need for nutrition knowledge among foodservice employees; in contrary published research outlines the need to inform and educate consumers through means of healthful programs and calorie labeling on menu items.

3.9   THE PREVALENCE OF OBESITY IN SOUTH AFRICA

Obesity has been documented as one of the chronic diseases affecting society by the World Health Organization (WHO); this is since the disease has reached its epidemic proportions, and it is evident that South Africa is not spared (Van de Merwe and Pepper, 2006:315). The researchers continued to state that obesity is identified by the modification in metabolic utility that results from an increase in total body weight as well as a gathering of visceral adipose tissue; these metabolic modifications are associated with the development of important other diseases such as; type 2 diabetes, hypertension and dyslipidemia (Van de Merwe et al., 2006:315).

South Africans are getting fatter. We are placed third in the world obesity ranking according to Compass Group Southern Africa's 2011 report, and the first developing country on the list. We are a game-changer in the global obesity epidemic, proof that fatness does not have to be an exclusively first world problem (The South African food taboo, confronting the obesity crisis 2013: online). Previous studies state that the widespread prevalence of obesity is poorly explained by individual-level psychological and social correlates of diet and physical activity behaviors. In addition, advice like "eat less and move more" pays no attention to the complex influences of the social and built environments on individuals' access to affordable, healthful food and activity environments (Glanz et al., 2005:330). For several years, there has been an increase in the prevalence of obesity in South Africa, particularly among women, and a recent increasing prevalence has been observed in children, predominantly among girls (Van de Merwe et al., 2006:315).

Previous studies reveal that obesity is a risk factor among the NCDs and is a global public health concern. It is however estimated that over one billion adults are overweight, of which at least 300 million are obese (Kruger et al., 2005:491). These researchers believe that countries in economic transition from undeveloped to developed are particularly affected and have seen an increased rate of obesity across all economic levels and age groups. Health consequences of obesity are increased morbidity and mortality with significantly increased healthcare costs. In addition, obese individuals are at a social disadvantage and may be discriminated against in employment opportunities (Kruger et al., 2005).

3.9.1   Urbanization and Globalization

A study conducted by Kruger et al. (2005) reveals that the obesity epidemic among South Africans reflects globalization which of late is the reason behind the transformation of nutritional consideration of food. The researches added previously people would consume traditional food that was low in fat and rich in fiber which has now transitioned into consuming meat and dairy products which are high in saturated fats and more highly refined foods. Therefore, globalization increased the risk amongst the urban population by creating an environment that promotes consumption of food rich in fat and sugar (Kruger et al., 2005:493).

3.9.2   Dietary Practices

Weak correlations between dietary energy, fat intakes, and body mass index (BMI) of South Africans have been reported; however, food that is consumed by urban suburban individuals indicate a high fat intake and are said to contribute to increasing obesity among South Africans (Kruger et al., 2005:493). Previous studies reveal that a U.S. Surgeon General announced that obesity was leading cause of preventable deaths in the world. This condition has come about, in large part, as a result of diets that are high in fat content (Gregory et al., 2006:44). The researchers continued to state that for many years, the restaurant industry, as well as fast -food restaurants, has faced criticism from consumer groups that their products place emphasis on taste and minimal emphasis on health. As previously stated, the great consumption of eating away from home has been associated with increased intake of; calories, total fat, saturated fat, added sugars and sodium and in contrary the intake of fewer fruits and vegetables, less milk, fiber, and vitamins (Glanz et al., 2007:383). However, in the vast majority of people, the condition of being overweight and obesity is characterized by excess calorie intake and/or inadequate physical activity (Gregory et al., 2006:45).

3.10 METHODOLOGY

The study made use of mixed methods; both qualitative and quantitative research methods in order to address the research objectives and answering the research questions. The investigator employed a survey technique to collect the quantitative data from waiters, data was collected by means of a pilot-tested, self-developed (by investigator) instrument. The instrument was a closed-ended, self-administered questionnaire. For the collection of the qualitative data, a structured open-ended interview was conducted with managers.

The following questions were selected to be categorized into relevant themes to facilitated data analysis:

(1) During the menu planning process, do you consider adding low fat/calorie items? What criteria do you use?
(2) In your opinion, is the hospitality industry adapting to the trend of food that is lower in fat/calories? Please elaborate.
(3) How often does the menu change, and what factors contribute to "altering" the menu?

(4) Would you say that the menu in your establishment is flexible enough to accommodate various food preferences?

The sampling method used in the study was nonprobability sampling method; purposive sampling which was utilized for the collection of qualitative data, and convenience sampling which was adopted for the quantitative data. The sample consisted of restaurant managers and waiters from three hotels, north of Johannesburg. The research sample for the quantitative approach consisted of relevant data that were collected from $n = 60$ waiters ($n = 20$ waiters from each hotel), while $n=3$ managers were interviewed ($n = 1$ manager from each hotel).

3.11   RESULTS

The qualitative and quantitative approach findings were compared against the core objectives of the study and the literature review that was related to findings. This assisted in determining whether the researcher achieved the objectives of the study. The findings were also compared to the literature review; this also assisted the researcher in analyzing the research against the relevant literature.

3.12   QUESTIONNAIRES

This approach was aimed at the foodservice employees (waiters), and this was conducted through self-administered questionnaires. These employees were randomly selected according to their availability as they work shifts varying from early shift to late shift.

3.13   DEMOGRAPHIC VARIABLES OF RESPONDENTS

Participants represented a diversity of ethnic groups, in which 33% of the population was Black, 25% of them were White and 17% were Colored and the remaining 25% were both Indian and Asian (Fig. 3.2).

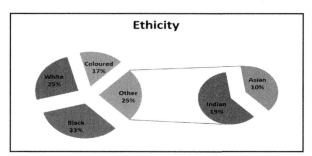

FIGURE 3.2   (See color insert.) Ethnicity.

The highest level of education of the quantitative population that participated, 33% have a post matric qualification while 32% completed their Grade 12 and only 10% have a postgraduate degree (Fig. 3.3).

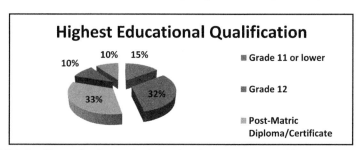

FIGURE 3.3   (See color insert.) Highest level of education qualification.

Employees were asked whether they had noticed a change in consumer eating out habits, regarding a shift to healthier balanced or low-calorie preferences.

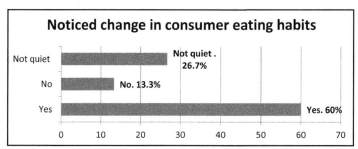

FIGURE 3.4   (See color insert.) Level of awareness with regards to changes in consumer eating out habits.

According to Figure 3.4, it is evident that majority of the waiters who participated (60%) in the study were aware of the changes in consumer preferences, particularly toward meals that were healthier and lower in calories and total fat. While 26.7% were uncertain about the changes and the remaining 13.3% were not aware of the changes at all.

Employees were asked whether menus at their establishments were, according to their knowledge, catering for health-conscious guests.

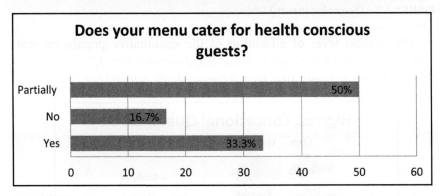

FIGURE 3.5   (See color insert.) Restaurant menus cater for health-conscious guests.

According to Figure 3.5, it is evident that 33.3% of the waiters who participated were of the view that the menu at the establishment where they work does cater for guests who prefer meals that were healthier and were lower in calories or total fat. While 50% of participants were of the view that the menus at their establishment moderately or partially accommodated guests who prefer meals that were lower in calories or total fats and the remaining 16.7% of the participants felt that the menu at their establishments do not cater for guests who prefer meals that are lower in calories or total fats.

Participants were then asked whether they had experienced serving a guest who had requested a meal that was either healthier or lower in calories

Looking at the participants' responses, Figure 3.6 reveals that there was somewhat a demand for meals that are healthier and lower in calories or total fats. As 51.7% of waiters who participated in the study have experienced guests who have requested meals that are lower in calories or total fat.

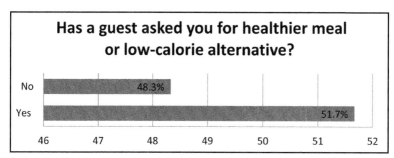

FIGURE 3.6 (See color insert.) Waiters requested by guests to assist with healthy alternative meals.

Subsequent to this, participants were then asked whether they were able to assist these guests adequately, or if they had to request assistance from a more experienced

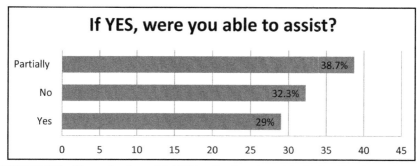

FIGURE 3.7 (See color insert.) Ability of waiters to assist with healthy alternatives.

Figure 3.6 shows that 51.7% waiters who said that they have had to serve a guest who requested a meal that was lower in Calories or an alternative meal. Therefore, according to Figure 3.7, only 29.03% of those waiters could assist these guests efficiently. This shows that there is a knowledge gap in the area of low-calorie or healthier meals as an alternative.

Participants were requested to identify a meal that was the healthiest alternative between the following meals:

(1) grilled beef fillet with sautéed mixed veggies,
(2) batter-fried hake with fries,
(3) deep-fried chicken schnitzel with steamed veggies, and
(4) grilled hake with steamed veggies.

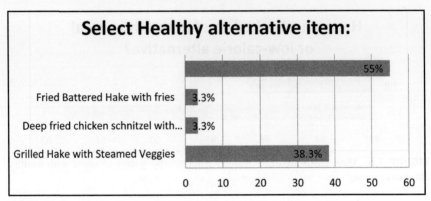

FIGURE 3.8   (See color insert.) Meal selected as the healthiest alternative.

From Figure 3.8, responses reveal that only 38.33% of the respondents could correctly select the meal that was lowest in calories, even though 55% of the respondents were of the impression that a meal which consisted of "pan-fried" vegetables was lower in fat. The remaining 6.66% had no idea which item was lowest in calories. This depicts that there is a need for nutritional knowledge/training to be implemented for restaurants.

3.14   INTERVIEWS

This section will provide feedback and findings from the qualitative approach; this section will illustrate the responses of each of the three managers that were interviewed.

3.14.1   Comparisons on Related Subjects Regarding Three Interviews Transcripts

To facilitate qualitative data analysis, the researcher first transcribed the responses of each of the three food and beverage managers and categorized the recurring content into themes.

The following are the questions selected to be categorized into relevant themes to facilitated data analysis:

(1) During the menu planning process, do you consider adding low fat/calorie items? What criteria do you use?

(2) In your opinion, is the hospitality industry adapting to the trend of food that is lower in fat/calories? Please elaborate.

(3) How often does the menu change, and what factors contribute to "altering" the menu?

(4) Would you say that the menu in your establishment is flexible enough to accommodate various food preferences?

Responses lead to the following themes derived from similarity or recurring content in the responses.

(1) During the menu planning process, do you consider incorporating healthier or low-calorie items? What criteria do you use?

Themes that emerged were:

(1) Consumer demand   55%
(2) Costs of "healthier" ingredients   25%
(3) Seasonal availability of ingredients   20%

The three factors that the food and beverage managers considered as important when or before adding healthier meals or meals lower in calories. Managers agreed that the most important factor is consumer demand; it will not make any senses to amend a menu when there is no demand for it.

(1) In your opinion, is the hospitality industry adapting to the trend of food that is lower in fat/calories? Please elaborate.

The most common responses where categorized into the following themes.
Themes:

(1) It is a relatively new and emerging trend in South Africa.
(2) It depends on the market and location of the establishment.
(3) Observation: it is a growing phenomenon, slowly but surely.

Responses from the three interviews were quite similar, from the above the researcher deduced that it is clear that the trend of consumer preferences moving toward healthier meals or low-calorie or low-fat meals is still relatively a new emerging trend in South Africa.

(1) How often does the menu change, and what factors contribute to "altering" the menu?

Themes (important factors):

(1) Changes seasonally (winter, summer, spring, autumn)   35%
(2) Stock availability   30%
(3) New creative recipes   20%
(4) Consumer demand   15%

The three factors that influence food and beverage managers' decisions on changing the menus. The most common and highly ranked response viewed to be important is seasonal changes.

(1) Would you say that the menu in your establishment is flexible enough to accommodate various food preferences? Please elaborate

Themes:

(1) Yes, with the exception of low-calorie /fat meals.
(2) Wide variety to select from.
(3) Variation between fine dining and standard gourmet meals.
(4) Chefs specials: custom made selections.

The final themes that guided the study are as follows:

(1) consumer demand,
(2) availability of ingredients, and
(3) costs of ingredients.

The above-mentioned themes guided the study throughout as food and beverage managers agreed that they would never amend a menu by incorporating healthy or low-calorie meals if there was no demand for it. They also stated an issue of seasonal availability of ingredients was a major issue as it also affects the costs of the ingredients.

3.15 CONCLUSIONS

As stated in the background of the study, the trend of eating out in restaurants is continuously increasing, whether for social reasons or due to traveling for leisure or traveling for work-related reasons. South Africans, now more than ever are more inclined to eat out than to enjoy a home cooked meal. It is significantly important that the Foodservice Industry prepares, accommodates and caters for the needs of these individuals who are constantly on the move. However, it became evident that the great consumption of eating away from home had been associated with increased intake of; Calories, total fat, saturated fat, added sugars and sodium and in contrary the intake of fewer fruits and vegetables, less milk, fiber, and vitamins (Glanz et al., 2007:383). A study conducted by (Gregory et al., 2006:43) showed the drastic change in consumer eating out habits, showing that consumers are making the move from fast food consumption to healthy, low-calorie preferences.

Therefore, the objectives of the study were guided by whether there was knowledge and awareness of the food and beverage employees and their ability to understand and serve guests who had requested meals that were either; healthier or lower in calories or total fat.

In conclusion of the results there is a knowledge gap with regards to low-calorie meals in the hospitality/restaurant industry. Regardless of the fact that it is still an emerging phenomenon in South Africa, the industry should be able to adapt to the trends of both local and international consumers, therefore, these deficiencies in knowledge should be addressed and the willingness of managers to amend menus should also be addressed. Incorporating more healthful menu items will make a significant difference in the society, in terms of alleviating the health risks associated with increased away from home eating.

3.16   RECOMMENDATIONS

The following recommendations are to be considered in terms of the topic in question:

(1) It is recommending that the hospitality industry sets standards for menu planners that enforce them to offer more healthful, low-calorie meals in their menus.
(2) It is recommended that food and beverage managers train and equip foodservice employees.

3.17 AN AGENDA FOR FUTURE RESEARCH

To conclude, the purpose of the study was to show the need for the hospitality industry as a dynamic industry that contributes significantly to health issues in society; obesity, cardiovascular diseases, and diabetes, to adapt to the various needs of consumers concerning healthy eating. As the research has pointed out that away from home eating had led to the increases of the diseases, the researcher deems it necessary for the industry to yield to the knowledge and training gaps to enable a more positive contribution from the industry.

(1) Research should be published that is related to knowledge and training of food and beverage employees on healthful menu items or alternatives in South Africa.
(2) Further studies in a broader spectrum, in a different Province in South Africa, can be done with the topic in question.
(3) A similar study could be conducted on restaurant managers in order to identify training needs.

KEYWORDS

- out-of-home eating
- healthy meal alternatives
- diet quality
- obesity
- knowledge
- foodservice

REFERENCES

Bevis, E. Home Cooking and Eating Habits: Global Survey Strategic Analysis [Online] 2012. Retrieved from: http://blog.euromonitor.com/2012/04/home-cooking-and-eating-habits-global-survey-strategic-analysis.html (accessed June 22, 2016).

Bezerra, I. N.; Sichieri, R. Eating Out of Home and Obesity: A Brazilian Nationwide Survey. *Public Health Nutr.* 2009, *12* (11), 2037–2043.

Bezerra, I. N.; Curioni, C.; Sichieri, R. Association Between Eating Out of Home and Body Weight. *Nutr. Rev.* **2012,** *70* (2), 65–79.

Boo, H. C.; Chan, L. T.; Fatimah, U. Healthy Eating Away-From-Home: Effects of Dining Occasion And the Number of Menu Items. *Int. Food Res. J.* **2008,** *15* (2), 201–208.

Buxton, N.; Emond, M. L.; Fisher, H. Eat Out [Online]. Retrieved from: http://www.eatout.co.za (accessed Nov 29, 2016).

Catherine, M.; Fitzgerald, M. A.; Kannan, S.; Sheldon, S.; Eagle, K. A. Effect of a Promotional Campaign on Heart-Healthy Menu Choices in Community Restaurants. *Amer. Diet. Assoc.* **2004,** *104,* 429–432.

CATHSETTA. Role of Hospitality Industry in the Tourism Sector [Online] 2013. Available From: http://www.cathsetta.gov.za (accessed July 21, 2016).

Choi, J. H.; Rajagopal, L. Food Allergy Knowledge, Attitudes, Practices, and Training of Foodservice Workers at a University Foodservice Operation in the Midwestern United States. *Food Control* **2013,** *31* (2), 474–481.

Consumer Foodservice in South Africa [Online] 2005. Available From: http://www.restaurant.org.za/pdf/consumer_foodservice_in_south_africa.pdf (accessed May 6, 2016).

D'Addezio, L.; Turrini, A.; Capacci, S.; Saba, A. Out-of-Home Eating Frequency, Causal Attribution of Obesity and Support to Healthy Eating Policies from a Cross-European Survey. Epidemiol. Biostat. *Public Health* **2014,** *11* (4), 1–13.

Delisle, H. Patterns of Urban Food Consumption in Developing Countries: Perspective From the 1980s; Food Policy and Nutrition Division, FAO: Rome, 1990.

Edwards, J. S.; Engström, K.; Hartwell, H. J. Overweight, Obesity and the Foodservice Industry. *Food Serv. Technol.* **2005,** *5* (2–4), 85–94.

Fitzgerald, C. M.; Kannan, S.; Sheldon, S.; Eagle, K. A. Effect of a Promotional Campaign on Heart-Healthy Menu Choices in Community Restaurants. *J. Amer. Diet. Assoc.* **2004,** *104* (3), 429–432.

Glanz, K.; Resnicow, K.; Seymour, J.; Hoy, K.; Stewart, H.; Lyons, M.; Goldberg, J.. How Major Restaurant Chains Plan Their Menus: The Role of Profit, Demand and Health. *Amer. J. Prev. Med.* **2007,** *32* (5), 383–388.

Glanz, K.; Sallis, J. F.; Saelens, B. E.; Frank, L. D. Healthy Nutrition Environments: Concepts And Measures. *Sci. Health Prom.* **2005,** *19* (5), 330–333.

Gregory, S.; Mctyre, C.; Dipietro, R. B. Fast Food to Healthy Food. *Int. J. Hosp. Tour. Admin.* **2006,** *7* (4), 43–64.

Harnack, L. J.; French, S. A. Effect of Point-of-Purchase Calorie Labeling on Restaurant and Cafeteria Food Choices: A Review of Literature. *Int. J. Behav. Nutr. Phys. Activity* **2008,** *5* (51), 1–6.

Hwang, J.; Crange, D. Consumer Health Perceptions of Selected Fast-Food Restaurants According to Their Knowledge and Health Consciousness. *J. Foodserv. Bus. Res.* **2012,** *13* (2), 68–84.

Igumbor, E. U.; Sanders, D.; Puoane, T. R.; Tsolekile, L.; Schwarz, C.; Purdy, C. et al. "Big Food," The Consumer Food Environment, Health, and the Policy Response in South Africa. *PLoS Med.* **2012,** *9* (7), E1001253.

IOL (Independent Online). Business News. More South Africans Are Eating Out [Online] 2014. Available From: http://www.iol.co.za/business/news/more-south-africans-are-eating-out-1792438 (accessed June 8, 2016).

Kruger, S. H.; Pauoane, T.; Senekal, M.; Van De Merwe, M. T. Obesity in South Africa: Challenges for Government and Health Professionals. *Public Health Nutr.* **2005,** *8* (5), 491–500.

Lachat, C.; Nago, E.; Verstraeten, R.; Roberfroid, D.; Van Camp, J.; Kolsteren, P. Eating out of Home and its Association With Dietary Intake: A Systematic Review of the Evidence. *Obes. Rev.* **2012,** *13* (4), 329–346.

Lee, S. M.; Jin, N. H.; Jeon, Y.; Huffman, L. Definition and Classification of Healthy Foodservice for Business and Industry, 2011.

Mccool, A. C.; Mccool, B. N. The Foodservice Industry's Social Responsibility Regarding the Obesity Epidemic, Part I: Parallels to Other Public Health Issues and Potential Legal Implications. *Hosp. Rev.* **2010,** *28* (1), 1.

Mccool, A. C.; Mccool, B. N. The Foodservice Industry's Social Responsibility Regarding the Obesity Epidemic, Part II: Incorporating Strategic Corporate Social Responsibility into Foodservice Operations. *Hosp. Rev.* **2010,** *28* (2), 2.

Moolman, H. J. Restaurant Customer Satisfaction and Return Patronage in a Bloemfontein Shopping Mall. *Acta Commercii* **2011,** *11* (1), 111–128.

NEMS. Nutrition Environment Measurement Survey [Online] 2015. Available From: http://www.med.upenn.edu/nems/ (accessed May 26, 2016).

Robson, S. M.; Crosby, L. E.; Stark, L. J. Eating Dinner Away from Home: Perspective of Middle-to-High Income Parents. *Appetite* **2016,** *96*,147–153.

Sharma, S.; Wagle, A.; Sucher, K.; Bugwadia, N. Impact of Point of Selection Nutrition on Meal Choices at a Table-Service Restaurant. *J. Foodserv. Bus. Res.* **2011,** *14* (2), 146–161.

SSA (Statistics South Africa). *Food and Beverages, September2013*; Statistics South Africa: Pretoria, 2013.

Story, M.; Kaphingst, K. M.; Robinson-O'Brien, R.; Glanz, K. Creating Healthy Food and Eating Environments: Policy and Environmental Approaches. *Annu. Rev. Public Health* **2008,** *29*, 253–272.

The Healthiest Fast Food Meals in South Africa [Online]. Business Tech, 2015 (accessed Nov 29, 2016).

The South African Taboo: Confronting the Obesity Crisis (Online) 2013. http://www. news24.com/mynews24/the-south-african-food-taboo-confronting-the-obesity-crisis-20130207 (accessed July 2013).

Trichopoulou, A.; Naska, A.; Orfanos, P. In *Eating Out: Habits, Determinants, and Recommendations for Consumers and the European Catering Sector-The Hector Project*. Annals of Nutrition and Metabolism; Karger:. Allschwilerstrasse 10, Ch-4009 Basel, Switzerland, 2009; Vol. 55, 66.

United States Department of Agriculture (USDA) Economic Research Services. Foodservice Industry, 2015. Retrieved From: http://www.ers.usda.gov/topics/food-markets-prices/food-service-industry/market-segments.aspx (accessed June 22, 2016).

Vakis, R.; Genoni, M. E.; Farfan, G. Let's Talk Development. More People in the Developing World are Eating Out. Measuring this Well Could Change our Understanding of Poverty and Inequality [Online] 2015. Available From: http://blogs.worldbank.org/developmenttalk/more-people-developing-world-are-eating-out-measuring-well-could-change-our-understanding-poverty (accessed June 23, 2016).

Van De Merwe, M. T.; Pepper, M. S. Obesity in South Africa. *Natl. Prev. Obes.* **2006,** *7,* 315–322.

Warde, A.; Martens, L. Eating Out: Social Differentiation, Consumption and Pleasure; Cambridge University Press, 2000.

Wenzel, L.; Anderson, J.; Gregory, S.; Pineda, C. Identifying Healthy Menu Items. *J. Rest. Foodserv. Market.* **2008,** *3* (2), 63–76.

WTTC (World Travel and Tourism Council). *Travel and Tourism Economic Impact Summary* [Online] 2014. Available From: http://www.wttc.org/bin/pdf/temp/2014_ exec_summary_final.htm (accessed July 15, 2016).

CHAPTER 4

Nutritional Status of Children Participating in the Supplementary Nutritional Programme (SNP) and Mothers' Perceptions of Services Provided

ANGELINE JEYAKUMAR* and MRUDULA HOLKAR

*Interdisciplinary School of Health Sciences,
Savitribai Phule Pune University, Maharashtra, India*

Corresponding author. E-mail: angelinejaykumar@gmail.com

ABSTRACT

Government of India invests substantial resources in the Supplementary Nutrition Programme (SNP) to prevent undernutrition among preschool children. A cross-sectional survey was performed to asses and compare the nutritional status of children (2-6 years) who participated in the SNP, with non-participants. Mothers' perception of undernutrition and perceived barriers to participation were assessed using health belief model. A sample of mother–children pairs N=144 were randomly recruited from Budruk Taluka, Kondhwa, in Pune, Maharashtra. As per WHO standards underweight was observed among 36% and 22% of children attending government and private preschools, in addition 28% and 19% were stunted, respectively. Results indicated that a significantly higher proportion children in government centers were underweight (p=0.001) and stunted (p=0.011). Despite agreeing upon the benefits of SNP, mothers of children who were non-participants, perceived the services provided to be of lesser standards. Improving the quality of services and creating awareness among mothers about the importance of government services would enable better participation and ensure better utilization of resources.

4.1 BACKGROUND

The Sustainable Development Goals (SDG, 2015)[1] reports that among the 836 million people who live in poverty, a significant proportion is from the Southeast Asian region. A majority of the population who are affected by hunger are those from the developing countries. Among these, two-thirds of the Asian population remains hungry.[1] In India, despite the economic growth and improvement in nutritional status among children under 5 years, a significant number is yet undernourished.[2] Socioeconomic status is a major determinant of undernutrition, as poverty manifests as hunger and results in undernutrition. According to the global hunger index (GHI), India scores 28.5 which indicate a "serious" state of hunger.[3] The Government of India, through the Integrated Child Development Scheme (ICDS) is addressing undernutrition and its consequences among children 0–6 years of age since 1975.[4] The intervention includes immunization, health checkup, and referral services, treatment of minor illness, nutrition and health education to women, preschool education for children (2.5–6 years), and also addresses adolescent and maternal health. Thus, it aims to use a life course approach to address the multiple risk factors of undernutrition. Among the multi-component integrated intervention-free, hot, cooked supplementary meal is provided to children. The aim of this Supplementary Nutrition Program (SNP) is to address food insecurity and provide one-third of the nutrient requirement per day for preschool children. In addition to the government-run preschool centers, there exist private pre-schools that charge low fees but do not provide a meal for the children. However, many children attend these centers. Although participation in ICDS and nutritional status of children has been well studied, the barriers to participation and perception of the program by the beneficiaries are less studied. Understanding the perception of mothers that influence participation would contribute to strengthening of the existing public health program and prevention and control of undernutrition nationwide. This work primarily aims to assess the nutritional status of children who participate in the SNP. It also aims to ascertain the reasons for non-utilization of services in a random sample drawn from anganwadi centers (AWC, government-run preschool centers) in urban slums of Pune city, Maharashtra, India.

4.2 METHODS

The study design was a cross-sectional survey. The locale for the study was Ghorpadi–Kodhawa Budruk block (BibawewadiVibhag) in Pune city (Maharashtra, India), where a block is an administrative subdivision of Pune City. The selected block consisted of 25 anganwadis. Of these, five AWCs were randomly selected from the slums. The list of all children less than 6 years in the slums is maintained by the anganwadi workers (AWW). Among these children, some are enrolled in the AWC and others in a private preschool. All children (2.5–6 years of age) enlisted by the AWW, both registered and not registered in the AWC were included in the study. In all, 144 children from five slums formed the study sample.

4.2.1 Study Variables

(1) *Nutritional indicators*: Height for age (HAZ), weight for height (WHZ) and weight for age (WAZ) Z scores were used to detect malnutrition. HAZ scores measures cumulative effects of growth deficiency and WHZ scores measures short term nutritional status and WAZ scores reflects both short term as well as long term nutritional status. Classification of nutritional status was as per the WHO reference standard applying Z scores. Height was measured using a stadiometer (Seca Model no: 213) and weight was recorded using a digital portable weighing scale (Omron). Measurements were recorded in duplicates and average was considered. Measurements were taken to nearest 0.1 mm for height and 0.1 kg for weight.

(2) *Economic status* of the participants was studied through a structured interview. Kuppuswamy scale[5]was used for assessing socioeconomic status. Data was collected on education of head of the household, occupation, and monthly family income of each household and was used to categorize the socio-economic class.

(3) *Maternal perceptions through health belief model (HBM)*: A pretested interview schedule was used to elicit information on maternal characteristics such as mother's education and mother's awareness of her child's health and the supplementary nutrition program. Mother's perception about undernutrition was assessed using HBM. The HBM was developed by Irwin M. Rosenstock in

1966. It is a model for studying and promoting the uptake of health services through behavior change and psychology.[6]

The original model included the following constructs:

(1) Perceived susceptibility (an individual's assessment of their risk of getting the condition).
(2) Perceived severity (an individual's assessment of the seriousness of the condition, and its potential consequences).
(3) Perceived barriers (an individual's assessment of the influences that facilitate or discourage adoption of the promoted behavior).
(4) Perceived benefits (an individual's assessment of the positive consequences of adopting the behavior).

The tool used in this study comprised of 13 questions representing the four constructs. The scores for the questions were given based on Likert scale where a score of 1 represented strongly agree, score 2: agree, score 3 partly disagree, score 4 disagree, and score 5 strongly disagree.

4.3 RESULTS

4.3.1 Population Characteristics

The mean age of the children was 3.4 ± 1.3 years. Of the total children selected from five slums, the average number of children enrolled in each AWC was 25 ± 6.8 children. In the study sample, about 74% (106/144) children were enrolled in government AWC and participated in supplementary nutrition program of ICDS, while 26% (38/144) children attended private preschool and did not participate in SNP.

Of the studied sample, 55% (79/144) were girls and 45% (65/144) were boys. About 40% (57/144) of the children belonged to families with size ≤ 4 family members, 43% (62/144) of size 5–6 family members, and 17% (25/144) of size more than eight family members. Results show a substantial number of children belonged to larger families. About 54% (78/144) of children were from upper lower socioeconomic status, 33% (48/144) were from lower middle class, and 13% (18) were from upper middle class. Although 98% of the mothers were literate, three-fourth of them received up to primary school education.

4.3.2 Nutritional Status of Children

Table 4.1 shows the distribution of undernutrition among children who participated and did not participate in the SNP. As per the WHO, classification of undernutrition using Z scores, 36% and 22% of the children were underweight (WAZ <–2SD) from the government anganwadi and private preschools respectively. Nearly 28% and 19% of the children were stunted respectively from government and private anganwadis (HAZ <–2SD). Results indicate that significantly higher percentage of children from government anganwadis who participate in supplementary nutrition program were underweight ($P=0.001$) and stunted ($p=0.011$). About 4% of children were wasted in both government and private anganwadis.

TABLE 4.1 Distribution of Undernutrition Among Children Who Participated and Did Not Participated in the SNP

WHO classification of undernutrition	Nutritional status of children participating in SNP ($n = 106$)	Nutritional status of children not participating in SNP ($n = 38$)	p value
Underweight < –2 SD WAZ	36% (38)	22% (8)	0.001
Stunted < –2SD HAZ	28% (30)	19 % (7)	0.011
Wasted < –2 SD WHZ	4% (5)	4% (2)	NS

NS, not significant.

4.3.3 Mothers Perceptions of Undernutrition and SNP

Table 4.2 compares the mean scores of mothers' perception in various constructs of HBM between participants and non-participants of SNP. HBM is widely used to assess health-related behavior. Among the domains studied, almost all mothers (from both groups) strongly agreed (Score 1) that maternal undernutrition, poor dietary intake and poor monitoring of growth increases the risk of undernutrition. Similar results of agreement were obtained in domains that assessed perceived severity of undernutrition and benefits of participation in SNP. Despite agreeing upon the benefits of participation, the scores of mothers whose children who did not participate

TABLE 4.2   Mean Scores of Mothers' Perception in Various Constructs of HBM Among Participants and Nonparticipants of SNP.

Constructs of health belief model	Mean scores		*p*-value
	Participants of SNP	Nonparticipants	
Perceived risk of undernutrition			
An undernourished mother is likely to have an undernourished baby	1.44	1.90	0.15
If the child does not consume a balanced diet the risk of undernutrition is high	1.08	1.45	
Lack of constant monitoring would prevent the mother from knowing the nutritional status of the child	1.36	1.28	
Perceived severity of undernutrition			
Having an undernourished child is a serious condition	1.52	1.63	0.22
Management of an undernourished child is expensive	1.38	1.35	
Having an undernourished child would affect the quality of life	2.30	1.49	
Perceived benefits of participation in SNP			
SNP prevents undernutrition in children	1.67	1.42	0.38
Participation in SNP saves time and cost	1.55	1.65	
SNP makes the children independent	1.32	1.34	
Perceived barriers to participation in SNP			
Supplementary food provided by the anganwadi is nutritious	2.72	4.35	**0.03***
The environment in the anganwadi is good	3.57	4.08	
The preschool education provided good foundation for further education	1.28	4.22	
The teachers and care providers are well trained	1.20	2.37	

*Significant at 95% CI.

in SNP, were significantly lower (scores 2–4) in the construct of perceived barriers. As per the HBM, significantly higher percent (*p*=0.03) of mothers from private preschools less appreciated the nutrition provided through SNP.

4.4   DISCUSSION

Of the 144 children studied, 74% (106/144) children participated in government preschool and benefitted through the SNP. This reflects that nearly three-fourth of the children are dependent on the SNP for food security. The ICDS has significantly increased the number of anganwadi centers to avail preschool education along with nutritious meal for children.[7] The criticism from World Bank that children under three would miss out on the nutrition services of ICDS has to be considered. Expansion of the program for younger children would address their nutritional needs as well.[8] Compared to the results of the present study, other studies and evaluations have reported high non-participation.[9,10] This study identifies the need to improve the services provided and encourage participants to utilize the service provided.

The fact that 26% (38/144) of the children attend a private school by paying fees and carry their snack reflects the slightly better economic status within the same locale. Also, a lesser proportion of children attending private preschool were undernourished compared to those in government preschool centers. This underscores the decreased risk of undernutrition with a marginal variation in the economic status. It highlights the need for addressing poverty and improving economic status of the vulnerable. However, 19% (7/38) stunting even among those who are economically better reflects a chronic state of undernutrition. This is suggestive of food insecurity among those attending private centers too. A larger proportion of those in government preschool were stunted despite participating in the SNP. It is therefore of prime importance to address chronic undernutrition as it is widespread among slum-dwelling children. Wasting was seen among a very small proportion of children who are participants of both private and government centers. As the children come from similar environment, they share similar exposure to infections and morbidities that manifest as wasting. Work done in Chandigarh in India showed higher prevalence of undernutrition among ICDS beneficiaries similar to the present study.[11] The results of the present study vary from other literature evidence that suggest better nutritional status of ICDS beneficiaries.[12] However, the sample size of the present study is limited compared to others. Further studies with larger samples are needed to gain further understanding of the nutritional status of children participating in ICDS.

In this study, perception of mothers on risk of undernutrition, its severity and the benefits and barriers of participation in SNP were studied. The results indicate that even with high prevalence of undernutrition and good perception of the SNP, some parents chose private centers. The qualitative descriptions of barriers to participation identified the following. They felt that the medium of instruction in English would result in enrollment in better schools. Also, the mothers who chose the private centers perceived that the personnel at the private centers are better trained than the government centers. However, the consequences of alternate choices for preschool facility did reflect in the qualitative findings. The mothers whose children attended a private school were not aware of the nutritional status of the children as growth monitoring was not carried out routinely. On the contrary, mothers of ICDS beneficiaries were aware of the nutritional status of children.

Quality of food provided at the anganwadi centers has been a priority for the Government of India. Despite providing a well-balanced meal, with variety in weekly menu, it has been a challenge to ensure maximum participation. The perception that the food served in the anganwadi is for the poor needs to be changed.[13] There is a need to reduce the stigma associated with free meals. If an intervention by the government that addresses food insecurity and ensures diet diversity is not perceived well, the strategies to achieve SDG would be complex. Ensuring better infrastructure and improving the quality of services provided would encourage mothers to participate in the Government programs.

4.5 CONCLUSIONS

India has a robust "nutrition-specific" program (Integrated Child Development Scheme—ICDS) to address undernutrition among preschool children. The Supplementary Nutrition Program (SNP) under ICDS has been successful in addressing severe forms of undernutrition and food insecurity among millions of children. Although the program extends to the poor, ensuring maximum participation remains a public health challenge. This work identifies the need to bridge the program to the people.

At the program level, convergence of sectors and coordination of services would ensure effective delivery of services. Careful planning to incorporate micronutrient-rich foods would add variety to the menu. The budget allotted for infrastructure needs to be revised as most of the facilities need to be improved. At the implementation level, more emphasis is needed for maintenance of hygiene and cleanliness in storage, preparation, and service of foods. Monitoring and evaluation have been an integral part of ICDS program. Gaps identified during evaluation needs to be worked upon to achieve maximum benefit from inputs. At the participant level, feedback from children and parents needs to be considered to make feasible changes for betterment of quality of the service provided. Improving awareness among mothers on the significance of SNP and involving parents in the delivery of services would increase the enrollment ICDS centers. Along with "nutrition-specific" intervention there is great need to improve "nutrition-sensitive" interventions such as poverty alleviation to ensure household food security.

4.6   AREAS OF FUTURE RESEARCH

Further research in this area of institutional foodservice should focus on addressing questions such as, who needs these interventions and who does not? This would identify the true vulnerable for whom the services should reach. With socio-demographic variation in rural–urban settings it would be worth exploring the variation in perceptions and participation. Action research following monitoring and evaluation would help to address region-specific issues encountered in the delivery of services.

KEYWORDS

- SNP participation
- preschool children
- nutritional status
- perceived barriers

REFERENCES

Bhasin, S. K.; Bhatia, V.; Kumar, P.; Aggarwal, O. P. Long Term Nutritional Effects of ICDS. *Ind. J. Pediatrics* **2001**, *68* (3), 211–216.

Bhatia, R.; Jones, P.; Reicker, Z. Competitive Foods, Discrimination, and Participation in the National School Lunch Program. *Amer. J. Public Health* **2011**, *101* (8), 1380–1386.

Global Hunger Index, 2016. Available in ghi.ifpri.org/countries/IND/. (accessed Sept 2016).

Integrated Child Development Scheme, (ICDS), Maharashtra, 2016. Available in www. icds.gov.in (accessed Sep 2016).

National Family health Survey, India, 2016. Available in rchiips.org/nfhs/factsheet_nfhs-4. shtml. (accessed Sep 2016).

Raghunandan, T. R. Rural Infrastructure, Panchayati Raj, and Governance. *India Infrastructure Report 2007*, 2007.

Rosenstock, I. M. Historical Origins of the Health Belief Model. *Health Educ. Monogr.* **1974**, *2* (4), 328–335.

Saxena, N. C.; Srivastava, N. ICDS in India: Policy, Design and Delivery Issues. *IDS Bulletin* **2009**, *40* (4), 45–52.

Sharma, R.; Saini, N. K. A Modification Regarding the Kuppuswamy Socioeconomic Scale. *Chron. Young Sci.* **2014**, *5* (1), 84.

Sustainable Development Goals. 17 Goals to Transform our World, 2015. Available in http://www.un.org/sustainabledevelopment/sustainable-development-goals/ (accessed Sept, 2016).

Swami, H. M.; Thakur, J. S.; Bhatia, S. P.; Bhatia, V. Nutritional Status of Pre-School Children in an Integrated Child Development Service (ICDS) Block of Chandigarh. *J. Ind. Med. Assoc.* **2001**, *99* (10), 554–556.

Vaid, S.; Vaid, N. Nutritional Status of ICDS and Non ICDS Children. *J. Human Ecol.* **2005**, *18* (3), 207–212.

World Bank. South Asia Regional Office. *Reaching Out to the Child: An Integrated Approach to Child Development*; Oxford University Press, 2004.

PART II

Foodservice Systems

CHAPTER 5

To Be Green or Not to Be Green: Costs and Benefits Related to Sustainability Decision-Making in the Restaurant Industry

ROBIN B. DIPIETRO

School of Hotel, Restaurant and Tourism Management,
College of Hospitality, Retail and Sport Management,
University of South Carolina, Columbia, SC 29208, USA

*Corresponding author. E-mail: rdipietr@mailbox.sc.edu

ABSTRACT

This chapter addresses the costs and challenges of using sustainable practices in the restaurant/foodservice industry while also highlighting the benefits of implementing such practices. Foodservice organizations have had pressures put on them by customers, but also they have an ethical obligation to assess the sustainable practices that make sense for them to implement. Not implementing any sustainable practices seems to be not an option anymore. The costs/challenges include price, lack of access or information, resources, management attitudes and actual financial costs. The benefits can range from environmental, financial, societal, health, and social for varying sustainable practices. Implications for decision making are discussed in detail.

5.1 INTRODUCTION

The questions that many organizations face of late are not about whether they should be implementing sustainable practices, but how they should be doing this and what is the most cost-effective way to implement these practices. It is not a question anymore about participating in sustainable efforts, but rather what those activities should be. The decision making related to these questions regarding sustainability can be very daunting for organizations.

The foodservice industry has felt increasing demand by customers for sustainable practices due to the environmental, economic, and social impact of the industry. As a result of this increased pressure, they have incorporated more sustainability initiatives into their operations (Choi and Parsa, 2006; Peregrin, 2011). Using sustainable practices can become a competitive advantage for organizations, but determining the comprehensive costs and benefits of a variety of sustainable practices can be hard. For example, the costs of using local foods will vary greatly in different parts of the world, the ability to recycle and reuse components in foodservice operations vary, the interest of consumers regarding these practices vary depending on the part of the world or cultural pressure, and all of these factors contribute to effectively making decisions regarding sustainability initiatives.

The following section presents a review of the literature related to sustainability practices in foodservice operations, a discussion of the types of practices, and the costs and benefits related to these decisions for foodservice operators to make. The intent of the paper is to discover the best ways for foodservice operators to analyze the decisions of whether to use these sustainable practices or not as they determine how to create a competitive advantage for themselves in an ever more competitive marketplace.

5.2 LITERATURE REVIEW

5.2.1 Restaurant Sustainability Practices and Local Food Purchasing

Sustainability is a complex, multifaceted concept for which there are varying interpretations and components. It is broadly defined as the use of natural resources in a manner that prevents overuse or depletion (Hunter and Rinner, 2004). Generally, researchers assert that it is comprised of three key elements: An economic element, a social element, and an environmental element (Maloni and Brown, 2006; Sloan et al., 2012). Effective sustainable practices are those that balance the needs and wants of these three elements among all stakeholders (Figge et al., 2002; Honey, 2008; Taiwo, 2011). This balancing of economic, social, and environmental needs is also referred to as the "three pillar" approach to sustainability (Gibson, 2006).

The foodservice industry represents an area where the concept of sustainability is both applicable and important. The foodservice industry represents a large part of the economic make-up of many countries and for example, represents 4% of the GDP of the USA with sales expected to reach $783 billion in 2016. It also represents the second-largest private-sector employer in the USA (National Restaurant Association, 2016), thus showing its relative importance economically. Because of the relevance and size of the industry, it represents an area that can have a big impact on the sustainability initiatives of a country and can greatly reduce environmental harm by making some slight changes to the industry.

Sustainable restaurants are those that are built and operated in an energy-efficient and environmental-friendly manner (Lorenzini, 1994). This means that for their operations, there is a greater emphasis on reducing waste and energy usage, reusing items, recycling, and being more efficient (Gilg et al., 2005). Sustainable restaurants also strive to maintain food systems over the long term. This is to say that they attempt to meet the present needs of their customers without compromising the ability to meet the needs of customers in the future. To do this, sustainable restaurants conserve raw materials during the food production process (Harmon and Gerald, 2007).

One of the most evident forms of sustainability utilized by restaurants is the purchasing and preparation of local foods (Darby et al., 2008). In fact, 87% of fine dining restaurants and 75% of family dining restaurants source local food for their menus (Blay-Palmer and Donald, 2007; Boniface, 2003; Martinez et al., 2010). This ability to source more local foods for their menus is because of the flexibility of their menus as well as the ability to absorb slightly higher costs for the ingredients. Sourcing local foods means that these restaurants are purchasing and preparing produce, meat products, cured items, and cheeses that are manufactured or processed in a given region (Enteleca Research and Consultancy, 2000;

Nummedal and Hall, 2006). They are also typically purchasing from independent farmers and companies who have a more environmental approach to agriculture and manufacturing (Morgan et al., 2006).

Overall, many restaurants are implementing certain sustainable practices, including recycling, minimizing waste products, implementing energy-saving practices and purchasing energy-saving equipment, as well as purchasing local foods. The following section will detail the decision-making process for foodservice operations as well as the costs and benefits for restaurant stakeholders implementing these practices.

5.2.2   The Decision-making Process: Costs and Benefits

Research on restaurant sustainability practices generally approaches the subject from one of two perspectives: from a stakeholder, owner or operator perspective, or from a customer perspective. As the purpose of this research is to explore the decision making that takes place to determine specifically why restaurant stakeholders would implement sustainable practices, the relevant literature pertaining to stakeholders will be reviewed in detail. A review of the extant literature suggests that restaurant stakeholders implement sustainable practices due to perceived environmental, economic/financial, social, and health benefits (Choi and Parsa, 2007; Gibson, 2006; Pearson et al., 2011). There are also many perceived barriers (costs) that have been assessed related to why restaurant operators and managers do not implement sustainability practices (Chou et al., 2012) and these will also be discussed. These perceived factors will be reviewed to highlight their influence, whether positive or negative, on the restaurant stakeholder decision-making process.

5.2.3   Barriers or Costs of Implementing Sustainable Practices into Restaurant Operations

There are many challenges with implementing sustainability practices for restaurant operators, especially independent operators that run in effect small to medium enterprises (SMEs) as these operations are typically limited on management strength, knowledge and a lack of funding. Some of the challenges or barriers brought out in a study of SMEs stated that lack of information and time, ineffective dissemination of information regarding regulations and legislation, high costs of implementing sustainable practices, personal attitudes of owners and employees, and lack of customer demand were reasons for the hesitancy in implementing sustainable practices (Revell and Blackburn, 2007; Revell et al., 2010; Taylor et al., 2003).

Because of the financial pressure on restaurants of all kinds, whether chain or independent, to work hard to even make very small margins for profitability in the industry, the limitations of resources, such as money and time, are very critical barriers that impact all restaurants. This lack of resources related to implementing sustainable practices impacts the industry tremendously (Revell and Blackburn, 2007; Revell et al., 2009; Wang, 2012). In a study by Chou et al. (2012), the theory of innovation adoption and the theory of planned behavior were used as a framework to assess managers' attitudes about implementing green practices. The study found that by increasing managers' knowledge of green practices and reinforcing their positive beliefs about these practices, they would increase their use of the practices. By eliminating barriers and obstacles, the managers felt more able to implement the practices. The study also found that if the managers perceived that their innovation could lead to the adoption of green behaviors, they were more apt to adopt them (Chou et al., 2012).

In a study of restaurant managers from upscale restaurants in Penang, Kisam and Ismail (2012) found that the greatest barriers to implementing sustainable practices are top management's attitude about the green practices and the costs of implementing practice especially the start-up costs of implementation. The study found that if top management's attitudes about sustainable practices were not positive, there were limited resources allocated for the efforts in sustainability, and the employees and other managers did not feel the support needed to implement the practices. The restaurant managers were unsure as to whether implementing sustainability practices could really make a lasting impression on their guests, which is their ultimate goal. Other factors that are considered barriers to restaurant managers are the poor enforcement of the regulations related to sustainability initiatives and also the higher prices that have to be paid for purchasing local or organic foods and the lack of internal and external pressures to be green and participate in environmental-friendly practices (Kasim and Ismail, 2012).

Through this discussion, it is clear that there are barriers and costs that are related to implementing sustainable practices in restaurants. In general, the barriers or costs to implementing sustainable practices are lack of regulations and enforcement mandating changes be made, poor management attitudes about making the changes, limited resources, higher costs for implementing sustainable practices, and therefore higher prices for the end customers for the sustainability efforts. In making decisions about whether to implement these practices regarding sustainability initiatives, restaurants have benefits to consider as well. The benefits related to sustainability are discussed below.

5.2.4 Benefits of Implementing Sustainable Practices

5.2.4.1 Environmental Benefits

Since the 1960s, environmentalists and researchers have been increasingly concerned about the interconnected issues of pollution management, land preservation, population management, climate change, resource and biodiversity depletion, and food safety (Dryzek, 2013). In recent years, environmentally sustainable practices have gained greater attention on a global level. This can be seen by the fact that while only 83 countries committed to the 1997 United Nations' Kyoto Protocol to reduce greenhouse gasses, 195 have agreed to commit to its 2015 successor (Breidenich et al., 1998; Goldenberg, 2016). Similarly, there has been a growing focus on the environmental impact of the restaurant industry with studies focusing on preservation, the management of natural resources, and conservation (Cui et al., 2004; Sloan et al., 2013).

The foodservice industry itself relies upon the large-scale production of consumable material. This production process can have major negative impacts on the environment. Food production generates 70% of river pollution in the United States and 30% of global greenhouse gasses (Bellarby et al., 2008). The combination of hotels and restaurants also comprises 14% of commercial building energy usage in the United States (Pérez-Lombard et al., 2008). According to Pacific Gas and Electric Foodservice Technology Center, restaurants are the retail world's largest energy user as they use almost five times more than other types of commercial buildings (Horovitz, 2008). The negative effects of the traditional production process related to food production also influence weather patterns and subsequently lead to instability in the food supply (Baldwin et al., 2011).

Because of these concerns related to the potential environmental damage and impact of the restaurant industry, many restaurant stakeholders believe that they can mitigate these effects via the introduction of sustainable practices into restaurant and foodservice operations (Choi and Parsa, 2007; Harmon and Gerald, 2007; Maloni and Brown, 2006; Peregrin, 2012). For example, Choi and Parsa (2007) observed via likelihood ratio tests of their regression model that individuals who had a strong preference for operating an environmental-friendly restaurant were willing to accept higher prices to support the implementation of sustainable practices. This shows that the restaurant owners that want to implement environmental-friendly practices also will be willing to take on one of the barriers and pay slightly higher prices for implementing these practices.

Evidence suggests that reductions in resource usage in restaurants and foodservice operations do have benefits for the environment. In the United States, approximately 40 "green" restaurants have been developed in recent years (Rotelli, 2013). These are restaurants which are "new or renovated structures designed, constructed, operated, and demolished in an environmentally friendly and energy-efficient manner" and that have reduced their environmental footprints when compared with conventional restaurants (Gilg et al., 2005; Lorenzini, 1994, p. 119). They have reduced energy use, water use, carbon dioxide emissions, and use of natural resources (United States Green Building Council, 2016). While it is harder for conventional restaurants to reduce their energy usage, there are nonetheless sustainable practices that they can implement which will benefit the environment. For example, The United States Environmental Protection Agency (2009) and Turenne (2011) assert that all restaurants, which reduce the idling times of their equipment, have marked declines in their energy consumption. Some energy savings fixes are very easy to implement at the foodservice operations level, thus helping the environment overall.

Regarding the use of local food, studies suggest that it can be both beneficial and costly to the environment. Pearson et al. (2011) argue that purchasing local food leads to the creation of less waste. It is beneficial primarily due to the fact that products are not being shipped long distances and do not require the packaging material traditionally required for shipping. On the other hand, Edwards-Jones et al. (2008) argue that one's carbon footprint can increase via the purchasing of some local foods due to reductions in economies of scale and mass transportation. Growth in local food industries may also necessitate the development of local food processing plants (Jones et al., 2004). These processing plants have a history of environmental problems including issues with smell, pollution, and waste disposal, and visual intrusion. Thus, in areas where there are local processing plants, support for the local food industry is often diminished. This is notably the case in coastal towns with fish processing plants (Jones et al., 2004).

Overall, research suggests environmental benefits serve as a key influence on restaurant stakeholder intentions to implement sustainable practices. Further research suggests that reductions in resource usage are beneficial for the environment while the use of local foods can also be a benefit to the environment if done effectively. The following will discuss the perceived financial benefits of implementing sustainable practices.

5.2.4.2   Financial Benefits to a Restaurant

Research suggests that restaurant stakeholders are willing to implement certain sustainable practices if there are possible financial incentives to do so (Ayuso, 2007; Bohdanowicz, 2005). This is particularly the case for restaurant stakeholders who have independently-owned operations (Curtis and Cowee, 2009). Choi and Parsa's (2007) study of restaurant managers' perceptions of sustainability observed a positive relationship between willingness to adopt sustainable practices and desire to charge higher menu prices. This is to say that these managers believed that they can obtain greater financial returns by adopting sustainable practices. Conversely, restaurant stakeholders will also adopt sustainable practices to avoid paying penalties. For example, Chan and Wong (2006) argue that legal compliance is the strongest influence on whether businesses adopt sustainable practices. Ibrahim and Parsa's (2005) assessment of French and American restaurant manager's perceptions of corporate social responsibility also determined that legal compliance was a key variable influencing the implementation of sustainable practices. Having legal regulations related to sustainability practices was found as a motivator to implement sustainable practices.

Many restaurant stakeholders perceive there are financial incentives to purchase local foods. For example, many chefs perceive local food to cost less than nonlocal foods (Inwood et al., 2009). They also perceive it to be fresher and higher quality than nonlocal foods (Inwood et al., 2009;

Sharma et al., 2014). This is a key financial incentive for restaurants to use local foods as food quality has been found to positively influence restaurant customer return intentions (Namkung and Jang, 2007).

Recent research supports restaurant stakeholders' perception that implementing sustainable practices will financially benefit their restaurant. These benefits occur primarily through (1) reductions in cost and (2) changes in customer behavior. These benefits will now be discussed.

In recent years, researchers have utilized lifecycle assessments as a means of determining the financial and environmental impact of different industries. More specifically, a lifecycle assessment highlights these impacts at each stage of production. A limited number of lifecycle assessments have been conducted in the foodservice industry, but of keynote with regard to financial benefits is a study by Baldwin et al. (2011), which argues that restaurants that reduce their food waste production can save as much as $50,000 each year. Further, Baldwin et al. (2011) argued that restaurants that reduce their energy usage can save approximately $5000 each year. This reduction in costs definitely provides financial incentives to restaurants that can take advantage of them by reducing energy usage and waste.

Along with reductions in cost, multiple recent studies have determined that restaurant sustainable practices can positively influence restaurant customers' behavior via increases in (1) willingness to pay and (2) intentions to patronize.

Pertaining to the willingness to pay, results from multiple studies suggest that restaurant customers are willing to pay greater amounts for sustainable practices implemented by restaurants. It should be noted that this amount varies based on respondent nationality, type of restaurant, and type of practices being implemented. Dutta et al.'s (2008) study of customer perceptions of green practices in a commercial restaurant compared levels of willingness to pay by American customers with Indian customers. In the both India and the United States, approximately 75% of respondents were willing to pay an additional 1% for enhanced environmental practices while approximately 25% of respondents were willing to pay more than a 7% increase. Further, approximately 66% of respondents were willing to pay an additional 1% for an increase in socially-conscious practices, while approximately 25% of respondents were willing to pay more than a 7% increase.

Hu et al.'s (2010) study of customers in Taiwan determined that a majority of respondents were willing to pay up to 6% more for green practices. Further, approximately one-third of respondents were willing to pay a premium of between 8% and 12%. DiPietro and Gregory's (2012) study of customer perceptions of green practices at fast-food restaurants determined that customers were willing to pay 1% more at restaurants implementing sustainable practices. Similarly, DiPietro et al. (2013) determined customers were willing to pay 1% more at quick-serve restaurants implementing sustainable practices. Parsa et al.'s (2015) study of customer perceptions of green practices at commercial restaurants determined that all respondents were willing to pay up to 4% more at restaurants implementing green practices. Lastly, a study by Remar et al. (2016) specifically focused on customers' willingness to pay for locally grown food. Data was collected in quick-service restaurant locations and results determined that customers were willing to pay up to 10% more for locally produced food. This finding suggests that local food may have a stronger influence on customer's willingness to pay than other sustainable practices.

Certain demographics and psychographic groups also appear to have enhanced levels of willingness to pay for sustainable practices. DiPietro et al. (2013) determined that individuals who are more educated are more willing to pay a premium for sustainable practices. More specifically, individuals with graduate degrees had the strongest positive opinions regarding sustainable practices in restaurants and were willing to pay up to 5% more than respondents with lesser educational attainment. Campbell et al. (2014) determined that individuals with higher levels of local food involvement are more willing to pay a premium for local foods in a foodservice establishment. Similarly, Parsa et al. (2015) determined that individuals who have positive attitudes toward sustainable practices, as well as strong involvement with local foods and sustainable practices, are more likely to pay a "high premium" greater than 10% for sustainable practices at a restaurant. These factors related to strong involvement include a belief that society is more important than low prices, a desire to dine at sustainable restaurants, a desire to research sustainable practices, the presence of positive feelings when eating at a sustainable restaurant, the avoidance of restaurants who are not socially responsible, and the acceptance of inconvenience in order to help society.

Pertaining to intentions to patronize, multiple studies have demonstrated that there is a positive relationship between one's concern toward sustainable practices and intentions to patronize a sustainable restaurant (DiPietro and Gregory, 2012; DiPietro et al., 2013; Hu et al., 2010). It can be insinuated from these findings that individuals who have higher concerns for green practices have a higher likelihood of patronizing a restaurant that utilizes sustainable practices. Hu et al.'s (2010) study of customer perceptions of green practices in Taiwan observed a positive correlation between knowledge of green restaurants and intentions to patronize as well as one's daily ecological behavior (including recycling, energy saving, and environmental purchasing) and intentions to patronize. DiPietro and Gregory's (2012) study of customer perceptions of green practices at fast food and upscale casual restaurants observed a positive correlation between one's green practices utilized at home and their intention to visit a restaurant using green practices for both restaurant formats. Similarly, DiPietro et al.'s (2013) study of customer perceptions of sustainable practices at quick-service restaurants observed a positive correlation between one's personal level of implementation of green practices and their intended patronization rate of green restaurants.

Certain demographic segments are also more likely to patronize restaurants which implement sustainable practices. Notably, DiPietro et al.'s (2013) study of patronage at upscale green restaurants determined individuals with higher levels of education (and notably those who held doctorate degrees), as well as females, demonstrated elevated levels of preference toward patronizing a green restaurant.

While research suggests that the implementation of certain sustainable practices may financially benefit a restaurant by lowering operating costs and positively influencing customer behavior, further research suggests that the implementation of sustainable products may be financially inconsequential for restaurants. Notably, Ham and Lee's study of green practices at 53 American chain restaurants determined that their sustainable practices had no significant influence on their financial performance (Ham and Lee, 2011).

A study by Sharma et al. (2009) assessed the costs and benefits of using locally grown food at independent restaurants and observed there to be no financial incentive to source local food as it was priced similarly to nonlocal food. Other studies have also argued that sourcing local foods has the potential to be more costly than sourcing nonlocal foods. This is due to the fact that local foods can be produced inefficiently at times. Both Pearson et al. (2011) and Oglethorpe (2008) argue that local growers are at a disadvantage to mass producers with regard to economies of scale. Oglethorpe (2008) notes that local food producers often have their own small processing facilities, which is a much more inefficient system than the centralized processing methods used by large-scale food producers. Similarly, Pearson et al. (2011) note that all slaughterhouses in the United Kingdom require inspectors to be on site. Thus, the local, small scale facilities lose economies of scale as they only butcher small quantities of meat, but still need to hire full-time inspectors.

As can be seen, restaurant stakeholders often perceive the implementation of sustainable practices to be financially beneficial to their businesses. Research suggests that it can positively influence customer behavior as well as operating costs, but further research suggests that sourcing local food may be more expensive than sourcing nonlocal food. The following section will discuss the perceived economic benefits to the local community of implementing sustainable practices in restaurants and foodservice operations.

5.2.4.3   Economic Benefits to the Community

Along with a perception that there are economic incentives for their restaurants to implement sustainable practices, some restaurant stakeholders implement certain sustainable practices with the intention of supporting the local economy (Meade and Sarkis, 1998).

The research appears to support this perception with regard to the purchasing of local food. Pretty's (2001) study of local food consumption in the United Kingdom notes that increases in local food consumption in the city of Devon led to the creation of 113 jobs. Ward and Lewis's (2002) study of local food spending in the city of Cornwall, England determined that £52 million would be added annually to the local economy for every percentage increase in local food sales. Ward and Lewis (2002) also determined that every £1 spent on local food led to a contribution of £2.59 to the local economy. This contrasts with a contribution of only £1.40 to the local economy for every £1 spent on nonlocal food.

Research also suggests that the purchasing of local food can have benefits in other sectors of the local economy. For example, Pearson et al. (2011) argue that the tourism industry can benefit in areas where the restaurants promote their use of local foods as this will pique food tourists' interest to travel to those places.

To sum up, research suggests that some restaurant stakeholders implement sustainable practices due to a perception that it is economically beneficial to their community. Further research supports this perception. The following section will discuss the perceived social benefits of implementing sustainable practices.

5.2.4.4   Social Benefits

Along with perceived environmental and economic benefits, there is some research to suggest that restaurant stakeholders implement sustainable practices due to perceived social benefits. These benefits have traditionally gained limited attention from practitioners and researchers when compared with environmental or economic benefits. This has been attributed to the fact that working and living conditions around farms are often obscured from the consumer (Gotlieb and Joshi, 2010). Yet in recent years, the issue has started to gain the attention of major advocates of local foods and sustainability initiatives. For example, at a recent food advocacy conference, Eric Schlosser, author of *Fast Food Nation* posed the question "Does it matter whether an heirloom tomato is local and organic if it was harvested with slave labor?" (Organic Consumers Association, 2009). Schlosser's question pushes restaurant stakeholders to consider the social consequences of food production and the role that restaurants play in that need for cheap food production.

There is contradicting evidence that restaurant stakeholders implement certain sustainable practices due to their perceived social benefits. Choi and Parsa's (2007) study of sustainable purchasing decisions determined that restaurant stakeholders who were more socially conscious were more likely to implement sustainable practices. On the other hand, Chou et al.'s (2012) assessment of restaurant stakeholders' intentions to implement sustainable practices, which was based on the theory of planned behavior, determined that social concerns did not influence intentions to implement sustainable practices.

Several studies suggest that the implementation of certain sustainable practices and in particular the purchasing of local foods can lead to greater awareness of farmers, their growing practices, and the crops that they grow. First, since local foods are seasonal in nature, it often leads to greater diversity in the types of food added to menus and consumed. This means that restaurant chefs are often forced to create new, unique dishes. This leads to individuals, and particularly children, having a greater awareness and knowledge for different fruits and vegetables throughout the various growing seasons in different parts of the country throughout the year (Strohbehn and Gregoire, 2005). Further, a study by Pretty (2001) observed that the purchasing of local foods positively influenced trust and connectedness between consumers and growers in the United Kingdom. This is an important phenomenon that has the potential to increase social and societal integration between those who live in rural areas and those who live in urban centers (Pearson et al., 2011).

Overall, there is conflicting research to suggest that restaurant stakeholders implement sustainable practices due to their social benefits. Yet, research suggests that those who do implement sustainable practices do perpetuate social benefits. The following section will discuss the perceived health benefits of implementing sustainable practices in foodservice operations.

5.2.4.5 Health Benefits

The local food sector has gained attention with foodservice practitioners and researchers noting the hazards that have befallen the unsustainable, "conventional" foodservice industry. Notably, the conventional food production sector has been in the media on a regular basis with multiple foodborne illnesses scares including mad cow disease, salmonella, E-coli, as well as hoof and mouth disease (Blay-Palmer and Donald, 2007; Boniface, 2003). Similarly, a recent report from the Centers for Disease Control and Prevention determined that industrially grown produce and nuts cause 46% of foodborne illnesses (Painter et al., 2013). These hazards have led to perceptions that the local food industry is safer and more reliable when it comes to contamination and food safety issues (Zepada and Deal, 2009). With regard to the foodservice industry, Strohbehn and Gregoire's (2003) case study of restaurant purchasing behavior in Iowa determined that restaurant stakeholders purchased local foods, in part, due to a perception that it was safer.

Although there is a perception that local foods are safer than nonlocal foods, outbreaks of foodborne illnesses have originated from local distributors as well, albeit on smaller scales than for large, industrial producers (Sharma et al., 2014). It is therefore not surprising that a study by Smith-Spangler et al. (2013) determined that the levels of contaminants were similar between organically and conventionally raised meat and produce.

Pearson et al. (2011) even argue that local foods can have a greater prevalence of pests and bacteria. This is due to the fact that local growers often use intercropping techniques instead of pesticides.

Along with a perception that local foods are safer than nonlocal foods, restaurant stakeholders perceive local food to be more nutritious (Sharma et al., 2014). There is research which both supports and rejects this assertion. Local food requires less transport and storage time than nonlocal food. This means that their nutrient levels can be elevated due to reduced storage and transport durations (Pearson et al., 2011). Yet, Edwards-Jones (2010) argues that the perception that local foods are more nutritious is inherently flawed as a plant's nutritional value is more likely to be influenced by the environment in which it is grown including levels of sunshine, rainfall, and levels of disease or pests.

Overall, research suggests that perceptions that local foods are safer and more nutritious influence restaurant stakeholder purchase intentions. Further research supports and questions these viewpoints. Overall, the perceived benefits of implementing sustainable food practices are environmental, financial/economic for the restaurant organization and the community, social benefits, and health benefits.

The next section discusses one of the challenges regarding sustainable restaurant practices that influence the decision-making process, and that is the potential lack of access to information provided to restaurant stakeholders, which is one of the key reasons that sustainable practices may not be implemented on a regular basis.

5.2.4.6   Information Access

While there are many reasons that restaurant stakeholders opt to implement sustainable practices, there are reasons that dissuade them from doing so as well. Notably, in situations where businesses only have access to limited information, they face challenges in altering their operations (March and Simon, 1993).

Restaurant stakeholders often do not have the tools or materials to assess the benefits of implementing sustainable practices (Kasim, 2007). For example, they may not have access to scientific data regarding the environmental problems which exist in their locale as well as the environmental benefits of implementing sustainable practices (Donaldson and Preston, 1995).

Restaurant stakeholders also may not be aware that local foods are produced in their community. This can be seen from the interviews conducted by Curtis and Cowee (2009) with chefs in Nevada. Almost all of the chefs expressed surprise that any agricultural industry existed near their restaurants.

Overall, research suggests that restaurant stakeholders will not implement sustainable practices if they are confronted with a lack of information. This includes the inability to assess the benefits of sustainable practices, as well as a lack of awareness, that local foods are produced in their region.

The following section discusses the implications of these costs, benefits, and challenges for implementing sustainable practices in the restaurant industry and how they relate to decision making for restaurant owners and operators. The decision of whether to implement sustainable practices is a complex process that involves looking at the costs, benefits and also the results of what may or may not happen when these sustainability efforts are implemented, such as behavioral intentions and willingness to pay of customers to the restaurants.

5.2.5   Discussion and Implications for Decision Making

When restaurateurs make decisions about whether or not to implement sustainable practices into their restaurants, the questions of why do it and how to do it come into their minds. There is almost always a cost to implementing sustainable practices, whether it is based on the increased cost of the food when produced locally or organically, or the cost of the equipment needed to implement recycling programs, decrease utility waste, or other sustainability initiatives. The benefits for implementing sustainable decisions can be many and can be varied depending on the interest of a restaurants' target market and depending on what the restaurant hopes to achieve.

When assessing the costs and benefits of the decisions related to implementing sustainable practices, it is important to understand what your restaurant can do well. It does not make any sense to implement practices, such as sourcing local foods if the location of the country is not conducive to grow the foods all year or the excessive demand of the restaurant company cannot be met. The practices should be practical and supported by top management of the company and should be seen as a benefit to the management of the company as well as to the guests that frequent the restaurant.

There also should be some time spent in assessing whether sustainable practices will bring the desired positive outcomes, such as positive behavioral intentions and willingness to pay. Despite the fact that there are social and socially economic benefits that can occur as a result of implementing sustainable practices, the primary reason that a restaurant is in business is to facilitate profit and increased customer counts. The decisions made by restaurants should be based in logic and using knowledge from previous studies, it can be determined that in general if the benefits of implementing sustainable practices outweigh the costs, the restaurant should implement the practice. See Figure 5.1 for a visual depiction of the analysis of costs and benefits for restaurants.

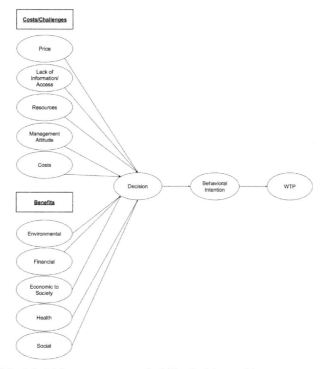

FIGURE 5.1   Model for restaurant sustainability decision making.

Restaurant owners and operators should assess their current customer needs and wants as well as their desire for future customers before making decisions. They also need to assess their tolerance for the potential costs of implementation before going through with any new changes. The benefits can be numerous, but not if you do not look at the costs and challenges first. For example, the owners of a fast food restaurant chain may have the strong desire for implementing local foods, but because of the lack of supply of this food, or the costs of the raw materials, they may not be able to implement this practice. On the other hand, recycling their cooking oil may be cost-effective and feasible.

5.3 CONCLUSIONS

The current paper discusses the literature related to the costs/challenges and the benefits that exist in making decisions related to implementing sustainable restaurant practices. The paper focused on the five costs of the price of raw materials (including local foods) that may be prohibitive, the lack of information or access to information on sustainable practices, the limited resources that restaurants may have, the attitude of management, which must be supportive of the practices, and the costs involved in implementing some of the sustainable practices.

The benefits that have been shown to actually support the implementation of sustainable practices are the positive impact that these practices can have on the environment, the financial benefits related to saving money (for example in lower utility costs), the economic benefits to society, the health benefits of using local foods or organically grown foods, and the social benefits to the use of sustainable restaurant practices. The costs and benefits must be carefully analyzed and the priorities of the restaurant and management must be assessed to determine if there will be enough support to allow for the successful implementation of the sustainable practices and will help determine which sustainable practices should be implemented.

Given the size of the restaurant industry globally, it is critical for restaurants to look at what they are currently doing related to sustainability efforts and assess how and what they can do in the future. Costs and benefits should be used in decision making to determine what will help increase guest behavioral intentions and whether that might influence willingness to pay for those sustainability practices. The current paper looks at the ways that specific costs and benefits can influence decision making and provides a visual way to look at the process of decision making related to sustainability efforts in the restaurant industry.

KEYWORDS

- foodservice
- sustainable practices
- financial decision-making
- behavioral intentions

REFERENCES

Baldwin, C.; Wilberforce, N.; Kapur, A. Restaurant and Foodservice Life Cycle Assessment and Development of a Sustainability Standard. *Int. J. Life Cycle Assess.* **2011**, *16* (1), 40–49.

Bellarby, J.; Foereid, B.; Hastings, A.; Smith, P. *Cool farming: Climate Impacts of Agriculture and Mitigation Potential;* Greenpeace: Amsterdam, 2008.

Blay-Palmer, P. Donald, B. Manufacturing Fear: The Role of Food Processors and Retailers in Constructing Alternative Food Geographies in Toronto, Canada. In *Alternative food geographies;* Maye, D., Holloway, L., Kneafsey M., Eds.; London: Elsevier, 2007.

Bohdanowicz, P. European Hoteliers' Environmental Attitudes Greening the Business. *Cornell Hotel Restaur. Adm. Q* **2005**, *46* (2), 188–204.

Boniface, P. *Tasting Tourism: Travelling for Food and Drink;* Ashgate: Burlington, VT, 2003.

Breidenich, C.; Magraw, D.; Rowley, A.; Rubin, J. W. The Kyoto Protocol to the United Nations Framework Convention on Climate Change. *Am. J. Int. Law* **1998**, *92* (2) 315–331.

Campbell, J.; DiPietro, R. B.; Remar, D. Local Foods in a University Setting: Price Consciousness, Product Involvement, Price/Quality Inference and Consumer's Willingness-to-Pay. *Int. J. Hosp. Manag.* **2014**, *42*, 39–49.

Carson, R. *Silent Spring;* Houghton Mifflin Harcourt: Boston, 2002.

Chan, E. S.; Wong, S. C. Motivations for ISO 14001 in the Hotel Industry. *Tourism Manag.* **2006**, *27* (3), 481–492.

Choi, G.; Parsa, H. G. Green Practices II: Measuring Restaurant Managers' Psychological Attributes and Their Willingness to Charge for the "Green Practices". *J. Foodserv. Bus. Res.* **2007**, *9* (4), 41–63.

Chou, C. J.; Chen, K. S.; Wang, Y. Y. Green Practices in the Restaurant Industry from an Innovation Adoption Perspective: Evidence from Taiwan. *Int. J. Hosp. Manag* **2012**, *31* (3), 703–711.

Cui, Y.; Hens, L.; Zhu, Y.; Zhao, J. Environmental Sustainability Index of Shandong Province, China. *Int. J. Sustainable Development World Ecology*, **2004**, *11* (3), 227–233.

Curtis, K. R.; Cowee, M. W. Direct Marketing Local Food to Chefs: Chef Preferences and Perceived Obstacles. *J. Food Distrib. Res.* **2009**, *40* (2), 26–36.

Darby, K.; Batte, M. T.; Ernst, S.; Roe, B. Decomposing Local: A Conjoint Analysis of Locally Produced Foods. *Am J. Agric. Econ.* **2008**, *90* (2), 476–486.

DeWeerdt, S. Is local food better?. *World Watch Magazine*, **2009**, *22* (3). Retrieved Jan 22, 2016, from http://www.worldwatch.org/node/6064

DiPietro, R.; Cao, Y.; Partlow, C. Green Practices in upscale Foodservice Operations: Customer Perceptions and Purchase Intentions. *Int. J. Contemp. Hosp. Manag.* **2013,** *25* (5), 779–796.

DiPietro, R. B.; Gregory, S. A Comparative Study of Customer Perceptions Regarding Green Restaurant Practices: Fast Food vs. Upscale Casual. *FIU Hosp. Rev.* **2012,** *30* (1).

DiPietro, R. B.; Gregory, S.; Jackson, A. Going Green in Quick-service Restaurants: Customer Perceptions and Intentions. *Int. J. Hosp. Tourism Adm.* **2013,** *14* (2), 139–156.

Donaldson, T.; Preston, L. E. The Stakeholder Theory of the Corporation: Concepts, evidence, and Implications. *Acad. Manag. Rev.* **1995,** *20* (1), 65–91.

Dryzek, J. S. *The Politics of the Earth: Environmental Discourses;* Oxford University Press: Oxford, 2013.

Dutta, K.; Umashankar, V.; Choi, G.; Parsa, H. G. A Comparative Study of Consumers' Green Practice Orientation in India and the United States: A Study from the Restaurant Industry. *J. Foodserv. Bus. Res.* **2008,** *11* (3), 269–285.

Edwards-Jones, G. Does Eating Local Food Reduce the Environmental Impact of Food Production and Enhance Consumer Health?. *Proc. Nutr. Soc.* **2010,** *69* (4), 582–591.

Edwards-Jones, G.; Canals, L. M.; Hounsome, N., Truninger, M.; Koerber, G.; Hounsome, B.; Cross, P.; York, E., Hospido, A.; Plassmann, K.; Harris, I.; Edwards, R.; Day, G.; Tomos, A.; Cowell, S.; Harris, I. M. Testing the Assertion that 'Local Food is Best': The Challenges of an Evidence-based Approach. *Trends Food Sci. Technol.* **2008,** *19* (5), 265–274.

Enteleca Research and Consultancy *Tourist Attitudes Towards Regional and Local Foods;* Enteleca Research and Consultancy: London, 2000.

Environmental Protection Agency. *Energy Star Guide for Restaurants*, 2009 Retrieved from Energystar Website: http://www.energystar.gov/ia/business/small_business/restaurants_guide.pdf

Figge, F.; Hahn, T.; Schaltegger, S.; Wagner, M. The Sustainability Balanced Scorecard–Linking Sustainability Management to Business Strategy. *Bus. Strategy Envir.* **2002,** *11* (5), 269–284.

Gibson, R. B. Beyond the Pillars: Sustainability Assessment as a Framework for Effective Integration of Social, Economic and Ecological Considerations in Significant Decision-Making. *J. Envir. Assess. Policy and Manag.* **2006,** *8* (03), 259–280.

Gilg, A.; Barr, S.; Ford, N. Green Consumption or Sustainable Lifestyles? Identifying the Sustainable Consumer. *Futures* **2005,** *37* (6), 481–504.

Goldenberg, S. Paris Climate Deal Offers Flame of Hope, Says UN Official. *The Guardian.* Retrieved Jan. 25, 2016, from http://www.theguardian.com/environment/2016/jan/17/paris-climate-deal-flame-of-hope-diplomacy-christiana-figueres

Gottlieb, R.; Joshi, A. *Food Justice.* MIT Press: Cambridge, 2010.

Ham, S., Lee, S. US Restaurant Companies' Green Marketing via Company Websites: Impact on Financial Performance. *Tourism Econ.* **2011,** *17* (5), 1055–1069.

Harmon, A. H.; Gerald, B. L. Position of the American Dietetic Association: Food and Nutrition Professionals can Implement Practices to Conserve Natural Resources and Support Ecological Sustainability. *J. Am. Dietetic Assoc.* **2007,** *107* (6), 1033–1043.

Honey, M. *Ecotourism and Sustainable Development;* 2nd ed; Island Press: Washington, DC, 2008.

Horovitz, B. Can Restaurants go Green, Earn Green?, 2008. Retrieved on Mar 12, 2016 from http://usatoday30.usatoday.com/money/industries/environment/2008-05-15-green-restaurants-eco-friendly_n.htm

Hu, H. H.; Parsa, H. G.; Self, J. The Dynamics of Green Restaurant Patronage. *Cornell Hosp. Q* **2010,** *51* (3), 344–362.

Hunter, L. M.; Rinner, L. The Association Between Environmental Perspective and Knowledge and Concern with Species Diversity. *Soc. Nat. Resour.* **2004,** *17* (6), 517–532.

Ibrahim, N. A.; Parsa, F. Corporate Social Responsiveness Orientation: Are There Differences Between US and French Managers? *Rev. Bus.* **2005,** *26* (1), 27.

Ilbery, B.; Morris, C.; Buller, H.; Maye, D.; Kneafsey, M. Product, Process and Place: An Examination of Food Marketing and Labeling Schemes in Europe and North America. *Eur, Urban Reg. Stud.* **2005,** *12*, 116–132.

Inwood, S. M.; Sharp, J. S.; Moore, R. H.; Stinner, D. H. Restaurants, Chefs and Local Foods: Insights Drawn from Application of a Diffusion of Innovation Framework. *Agri. Human Values* **2009,** *26* (3), 177–191.

Jones, P.; Comfort, D.; Hillier, D. A Case Study of Local Food and its Routes to Market in the UK. *Br. Food J.* **2004,** *106* (4), 328–335.

Kasim, A. Towards a wider Adoption of Environmental Responsibility in the Hotel Sector. *Int. J. Hosp. Tourism Adm.* **2007,** *8* (2), 25–49.

Kasim, A., & Ismail, A. Environmentally Friendly Practices Among Restaurants: Drivers and Barriers to Change. *J. Sustainable Tourism* **2012,** *20* (4), 551–570.

Lorenzini, B. The Green Restaurant, Part II: Systems and Service. *Restaur. Instit.* **1994,** *104* (11), 119–36.

Maloni, M. J.; Brown, M. E. Corporate Social Responsibility in the Supply Chain: An Application in the Food Industry. *J. Bus. Ethics* **2006,** *68* (1), 35–52.

March, J. G. Simon, H. A. Organizations Revisited. *Indus. Corp. Change* **1993,** *2* (1), 299–316.

Martinez, S.; Hand, M. S.; Da Pra, M.; Pollack, S.; Ralston, K.; Smith, T. A.; Vogel, S.; Clark, L.; Low, S.; Newman, C. Local Food Systems: Concepts, Impacts, and Issues. *Econ. Res. Rep.* **2010,** *97*, 1–49

Meade, L.; Sarkis, J. Strategic Analysis of Logistics and Supply Chain Management Systems Using the Analytical Network Process. *Logistics and Transportation Review* **1998,** *34* (3), 201–215.

Morgan, K.; Marsden, T.; Murdoch, J. *Worlds of Food;* Oxford University Press: Oxford, 2006.

Namkung, Y.; Jang, S. Does Food Quality Really Matter in Restaurants? Its Impact on Customer Satisfaction and Behavioral Intentions. *J. Hosp. Tourism Res.* **2007,** *31* (3), 387–409.

National Restaurant Association 2016 Restaurant Industry Forecast: News and Research, 2016. Retrieved on Mar 12, 2016 from http://www.restaurant.org/News-Research/Research/Forecast-2016

Nummedal, M.; Hall, C. M. Local Food in Tourism: An Investigation of the New Zealand South Island's bed and Breakfast Sector's Use and Perception of Local Food. *Tourism Rev. Int.* **2006,** *9* (4), 365–378.

Oglethorpe, D. *What's so Good About Local Food?* Paper presented at the Agricultural Economics Society Conference on Our Food Economy, London, England, 2008.

Organic Consumers Association. Sustainable Food Movement Calls out Crist on Slavery [Press release], 2009. Retrieved from https://www.organicconsumers.org/news/sustainable-food-movement-calls-out-crist-slavery

Parsa, H. G.; Lord, K. R.; Putrevu, S.; Kreeger, J. Corporate Social and Environmental Responsibility in Services: Will Consumers Pay for it? *J. Retail. Consum. Serv.* **2015**, *22*, 250–260.

Pearson, D.; Henryks, J., Trott, A.; Jones, P.; Parker, G.; Dumaresq, D.; Dyball, R. Local Food: Understanding Consumer Motivations in Innovative Retail Formats. *Br. Food J.* **2011**, *113* (7), 886–899.

Peregrin, T. Sustainability in Foodservice Operations: An Update. *J. Am. Dietetic Assoc.* **2011**, *111* (9), 1286–1294.

Peregrin, T. Sustainability in Foodservice Operations: An Update. *J Acad. Nutr. Dietetics* **2012**, *112* (5), S12–S15.

Pérez-Lombard, L.; Ortiz, J.; Pout, C. A Review on Buildings Energy Consumption Information. *Ener. Buildings* **2008**, *40* (3), 394–398.

Pretty, J. *Some Benefits and Drawbacks of Local Food Systems* (TVU/Sustain AgriFood Network); Sustain: London, 2001.

Remar, D.; Campbell, J.; DiPietro, R. B. The Impact of Local Food Marketing on Purchase Decision and Willingness to Pay in a Foodservice Setting. *J. Foodserv. Bus. Res.* **2016**, *19* (1), 89–108.

Revell, A.; Blackburn, R. The Business Case for Sustainability? An Examination of Small Firms in the UKs Construction and Restaurant Sectors. *Bus. Strategy Environ.* **2007**, *16*, 404–420.

Revell, A.; Stokes, D.; Chen, H. Small Businesses and the Environment: Turning Over a New Leaf? *Bus. Strategy Environ.* **2010**, *19* (5), 273–288.

Rotelli, W. Breaking Ground on LEED-Certified Restaurants, 2013. Retrieved from Restaurants.com: https://www.restaurants.com/blog/breaking-ground-onleed-certified-restaurants/#.VL_Zoj90yUl

Sharma, A.; Gregoire, M. B.; Strohbehn, C. Assessing Costs of Using Local Foods in Independent Restaurants. *J. Foodserv. Bus. Res.* **2009**, *12* (1), 55–71.

Sharma, A.; Moon, J.; Strohbehn, C. Restaurant's Decision to Purchase Local Foods: Influence of Value Chain Activities. *Int. J. Hosp. Manag.* **2014**, *39*, 130–143.

Sloan, P.; Legrand, W.; Chen, J. C.; Chen, J. S. *Sustainability in the Hospitality Industry: Principles of Sustainable Operations;* Routledge: New York, 2012.

Smith-Spangler, C.; Brandeau, M. L.; Olkin, I.; Bravata, D. M. Are Organic Foods Safer or Healthier? *Annals Intern. Med.* **2013**, *158* (4), 297.

Strohbehn, C. H.; Gregoire, M. B. Case Studies of Local Food Purchasing by Central Iowa Restaurants and Institutions. *J. Foodserv.* **2003**, *14* (1), 53–64.

Strohbehn, C. H.; Gregoire, M. B. Local foods: From Farm to College and University Foodservice. *J. Foodserv. Manag. Edu.* **2005**, *25* (1), 1–20.

Taylor, N.; Barker, K.; Simpson, M. Achieving Sustainable Business, a Study of Perceptions of Environmental Best Practice by SMEs in South Yorkshire. *Environ. Plan. C: Gov. Polic.* **2003**, *21*, 89–105.

Taiwo, A. M. Composting as a Sustainable Waste Management Technique in Developing Countries. *J. Environ. Sci. Technol.* **2011**, *4* (2), 93–102.

Turenne, J. *Sustainability in the Food Industry;* Baldwin, C., Ed.; John Wiley & Sons: Hoboken, NJ, 2011.

United States Green Building Counsel. *What LEED is,* 2016 Retrieved Jan 20, 2016, from http://www.usgbc.org/DisplayPage.aspx?CMSPageID=1988

Ward, B.; Lewis, J. *Plugging the Leaks: Making the most of Every Pound that Enters your Local Economy;* New Economics Foundation: London, 2002.

Wang, R. Investigations of Important and Effective Effects of Green Practices in Restaurants. *Procedia- Soc. Behav. Sci. 40*, 94–98.

Zepeda, L.;Deal, D. Organic and Local Food Consumer Behavior: Alphabet Theory. *Int J. Consum. Stud.* **2009,** *33* (6), 697–705.

CHAPTER 6

Cost–Benefit Assessment of Local Foods in Independent Restaurants

AMIT SHARMA[1*] and FRODE ALFNES[2]

[1]*School of Hospitality Management, College of Health and Human Development, the Pennsylvania State University, 201 Mateer Building, University Park, PA 16802, USA*

[2]*UMB School of Economics and Business, Norwegian University of Life Sciences, P.O. Box 5003, N-1432 Ås, Norway*

Corresponding author. E-mail: aus22@psu.edu

ABSTRACT

We propose a cost–benefit approach for assessing the viability of product improvement decisions in independent restaurants. We investigate the costs and benefits associated with using local foods as a product improvement strategy by three independent restaurants. The results of the study suggest that the discounted cash flows of the selected menu items in each of the three restaurants were negative. Based on this analysis, the three restaurants would reject the strategy to source local ingredients for the sample menu items. We apply Monte Carlo simulations to assess the sensitivity of cost and price changes, and suggest price levels at which sourcing local foods would be acceptable in these sample menu items. We discuss the financial implications of adopting local foods as a product improvement strategy. Furthermore, we highlight the value of using menu level microdata, analyzing broader costs and benefits in product improvement decisions, and simulations and sensitivity analysis.

6.1 INTRODUCTION

The goal of a product improvement strategy is to improve an existing product so that existing customers are willing to spend more money on the product (Gilbert and Riordan, 2005). In the restaurant setting, a product improvement strategy can, for example, be sourcing the food from specific producers or origins. To employ a successful product improvement strategy, it is important for restaurants to identify food trends that can be utilized to improve profits. The Food Channel listed "Local Somewhere" as one of its top ten food trends for 2011 (Food Channel, 2011), and the National Restaurant Association ranked local foods as the number one trend the same year (NRA, 2011). Many restaurants have started advertising and using local foods in their menu items.

Food quality is to a large degree in the eye of the beholder. Grunert (2005) argues that consumers' expectations and experience of food quality are affected by, among others, credence attributes. Credence attributes are product attributes that cannot be verified by consumption. Local production of food is a prime example of such an attribute. However, many consumers relate local food with improved product quality due to superior freshness, healthiness, and taste. There are other reasons why consumers buy local food, including environmental concerns related to food miles, and a desire to support local producers. Visitors often wish to taste the products of a region (Gilg and Battershill, 1998).

Such a product quality decision also has economic and financial implications: restaurants could incur additional costs associated with sourcing local foods (Sharma et al., 2009). From a financial perspective, any product improvement strategy is effective only if restaurant firms receive returns on their investment in using local foods to improve product quality, that is, present values of estimated revenues must exceed estimated costs, including those of investing and financing the project.

In general, there is limited research into assessing the financial implications of product quality improvements in the hospitality industry. In this paper, we propose a decision-making framework for restaurant management to make investments, and/or financial and economic commitments to product improvement through the use of locally sourced ingredients. In doing so, we are responding to a critical gap in hospitality literature, particularly in restaurants, where micro-level data are not normally used in traditional financial and economic analyses. This study builds on two prior studies that independently evaluated costs and benefits of using local foods in independent restaurants. In this paper, we compare these costs and benefits in context of managerial decision-making.

6.2   LITERATURE REVIEW

6.2.1   Cost–Benefit Analysis and Capital Budgeting

Cost–benefit analysis (CBA) is a methodical approach of estimating the costs and benefits of a project for the purpose of decision-making. It has been widely used in both government and non-governmental settings. Conceptually, the CBA is a test of the Kaldor–Hicks efficiency criterion, which states that an outcome is more efficient than another if those that are made better off could, in theory, compensate those that are made worse off (Marowsky and Wagner, 2009; Altman, 2011). In a business setting, this implies that the increase in revenues implementing a strategy must exceed the costs. In a product improvement context, this could mean that customers would be able to compensate the company for the added costs of a product improvement. Therefore, a particular product improvement would only be profitable if consumers' willingness to pay (WTP) for the improvement exceeds the added costs. One of the purposes of using CBA is to determine whether a project will represent a sound investment (Scott, 2009). The difference between CBA and capital budgeting is that CBA allows decision-makers to incorporate intangibles in their analysis—costs or benefits that may not have a clearly defined market traded value (Huang and Ritter, 2009; Rosacker and Olson, 2008). CBA can also be used to compare projects to facilitate decision-making. Some of the basic concepts of CBA include estimation of costs and benefits, along with the use of shadow prices (e.g., opportunity costs such as employee time spent on an activity that could have been spent elsewhere), investment criteria (e.g., discounting rates), risk and uncertainty, and decision rules (e.g., cost–benefit ratio, net present value) (Scott, 2008). CBA involves an incremental estimation of costs and benefits associated with the project under investigation. Given that both costs and benefits need to be reconciled, CBA studies must rely on data from a number of sources (Scott, 2009).

CBA allows the decision-maker to include intangible variables in the analysis. For instance, opportunity cost is a frequently used concept to estimate costs within CBA (Lohmann, 2008). Opportunity cost is of interest in the case of labor cost. Time taken in one activity could impact the time available for other activities. Furthermore, wages and salaries that are traditionally used in assessing financial viability of a project represent lump sum costs. Using CBA to identify incremental opportunity, costs of labor could provide a comprehensive analysis of costs. Estimating benefits using CBA can also be conducted comprehensively by accounting for intangibles. Usually, this is achieved by obtaining WTP estimates for certain attributes of a product or service (Steur et al., 2009; Awad, 2012). Such estimates could then be translated into projected estimates of revenues, and included within the CBA framework. The flexibility within the CBA procedure is such that it can be superimposed on a traditional capital budgeting technique like the discounted cash flow analysis (DCF). Therefore, the investment or decision criteria can be a combination of two approaches; to include both a DCF based measure (e.g., net present value) and a cost–benefit ratio (Lin, 2012; Scott, 2008). A CB ratio is also similar to the profitability ratio, and therefore consistent with the capital budgeting methodology. Risk and uncertainty have extensively been incorporated into CBA (Scott, 2008; Newton et al., 2012). In fact, accounting for uncertainty is also highly recommended given that CB estimates based on shadow prices and WTP estimates may not be accurate (Brien, 2005; Scott, 2008).

In summary, CBA is a well-established procedure used to guide management and policy decision-making. Its use in business settings continues to be extensive, however, its application in the hospitality industry has rarely been documented. The objective is to guide decision-makers in selecting an investment project or comparing several projects. In the restaurant industry, capital budgeting procedures such as net present value and profitability ratio are more widely used for decision analysis than CBA. However, an important advantage of the CBA is that it allows researchers and decision-makers to incorporate the effects of intangibles such as opportunity costs and estimated prices of intangible product and service attributes. Opportunity cost of labor time spent on an activity is an important intangible in the restaurant business. Similarly, WTP for certain product attributes, such as locally sourced foods, is another intangible, represented as a benefit for businesses. Application of CBA in the decision to choose locally grown foods as a product improvement strategy could, therefore, enhance the decision-making ability of owners and managers.

6.2.2 Local Foods

The concept of local foods is pluralistic and can be characterized by cultural subjectivity, and the social and political environment (Holt and Amilien, 2007). In this study, we define local food as food grown or processed locally and purchased by restaurants from the local market or primarily through local producers within a 50-mi radius (Sharma et al., 2009).

6.2.2.1 Benefits of Local Food in Restaurants

Independent and regional restaurants have been cognizant of the trend toward offering local foods on their menus and have developed local food sourcing strategies. This has prompted larger restaurant chains to develop local food sourcing strategies to complement traditional supply channels (Yin and Zajac, 2004).

To signal that a product is unique or novel, the price of the product must be right. A credence attribute like local can signal this by using a higher price (Alfnes and Sharma, 2010; Schjøll and Alfnes, 2011). There are several consumer segments that may be willing to pay more for local foods in restaurants. In context of tourism, Sims (2009) argues that local food has the potential to enhance the visitor's experience by connecting consumers to the region and its perceived culture and heritage. Certain consumers may want something novel. For instance, Hobes et al. (2006) found that there are consumer segments that strongly agree with the statement that they "when buying meat at a restaurant look for unique/novel products." This indicates that some consumers, when visiting restaurants, want to buy products that differ from the standard products found in most grocery stores. Most grocery stores sell standardized products available throughout the entire year, while restaurants are able to source more specialized products available in limited amounts and often during a limited time period.

There is a relatively large body of literature that examines the relationship between consumers' WTP and the country-of-origin of food products (Alfnes and Rickersten, 2003). The general finding is that consumers prefer domestic to imported products. If imported, they prefer products from developed countries over products from less developed countries, and products from countries geographically and culturally close to them, to products from more distant countries (Alfnes, 2004). Most of the results in this literature can be attributed to a few factors: (1) higher trust in the food safety of some countries (Alfnes, 2004), (2) perceived better freshness resulting from shorter transportation distances, (3) ethnocentrism (Orth and Firbasova, 2003), and (4) product-specific origin reputation.

So far studies have found that the possible drivers of WTP a premium for local food include similar, and several of the same features: competition among foods produced at other places in the same country, perceived better freshness, ethnocentrism, and product-specific origin reputation.

6.2.2.2   Cost of Local Food in Restaurants

Local food usage is particularly valuable for small and independently owned restaurants that have the flexibility of purchasing from various vendors. However, restaurants continue to be concerned about higher costs that may be associated with using local suppliers as a differentiation strategy (Strohbehn and Gregoire, 2002). Research suggests that local food sourcing can result in incremental costs to restaurants, particularly as employee time costs (Sharma et al., 2009).

Cost, and profit analyses in restaurants and foodservices has been extensive. The cost analysis literature in restaurants and foodservice examines issues such as: the relationship of food expenditures to energy prices (Arbel, 1983); indirect costs and menu pricing (Pavesic, 1990); general revenue and cost analysis (Malk and Schmidgal, 1995); principles of restaurant management (Smith, 1996); profit measurement of menu items (Chan and Au, 1998; Sullivan, 2003); costs associated with hazard analysis critical control points (HACCP) (Cohen et al., 2000); management of energy costs (Stipanuk, 2001); and, activity-based costing (Raab and Mayer, 2003, 2007). However, there is an important gap in systematic research that analyzes cost and profits at the individual menu item level in context of broader product decisions. Research that focuses on small and independently owned restaurants is also relatively limited (Kwansa, 1994; Knychalska and Shaw, 2002; Thompson, 2002, Sharma, 2006a).

We were unable to find any studies that have used DCF analysis using micro-data at the menu level to evaluate the financial viability of investment decisions in restaurants.

6.2.3   Restaurant Decision Making, Product Improvement, and Micro-data Analysis

There is a scarcity of research that could guide the restaurant industry to make investment decisions (Jang and Park, 2012). It is unclear how restaurants determine the financial viability of broader product improvement decisions that involve micro-level individual menu items. Improved understanding of this process could enhance management's decision-making process, and improve their choices and the associated outcomes, such as financial performance and return on investments. Even though systematic research is lacking, evidence points to the fact that small restaurants can be an important source of entrepreneurial activity, employment generation, and economic linkages (Goebel, 2010; Agrawal, 2012). This paper adds not only to small independently owned restaurant literature, but also fills a critical gap of how such restaurants can prudently extend their economic role in the local economy through the purchase of local grown/produced foods.

6.3   METHODS AND DATA

The research design of this study incorporates data and results of two prior investigations that separately evaluated costs and benefits for independent restaurants to source local foods. This approach is consistent with the design of cost–benefit studies that usually require data from several prior studies (Scott, 2009). In the following section, we describe the two studies—cost study and benefit study—that were the source of the data that authors used to conduct analysis for this study.

6.3.1   Cost Study (SSG)

The first study (Sharma et al., 2009) (from here on SSG) assessed the costs of sourcing local foods in independent restaurants. The results of this study indicated that the following were the incremental costs to independent restaurants associated with sourcing local foods: longer delivery, receiving, and storage times, and larger portion sizes.

Sharma et al., (2009) (SSG), in their study of independent restaurants, found that employee costs were higher when sourcing and using local food ingredients, than to source ingredients from national and regional suppliers. Nonemployee costs included storage costs, or the amount of money held as inventory, particularly due to less frequent delivery schedules for local foods. In the current study, we estimated these costs on an incremental basis to evaluate the total costs of using local foods.

6.3.2   Benefit Study (AS)

The second study (Alfnes and Sharma, 2010) (from here on AS) evaluated the WTP for locally grown foods in restaurants. The study was a menu manipulation experiment where products' origin and price were altered from day to day in a restaurant, and sales data analyzed with a discrete choice logit model. Based on the sales data, the authors found that restaurant patrons as a group were willing to pay around 17% more for locally grown foods. While there was a slight preference for chicken, other menu items that demonstrated similar price effects were made of beef and pork. In the current study, we assume the incremental benefits associated with local foods as the increase in price or the price premium that the restaurant would be able to charge for menu items prepared using local foods (Alfnes and Sharma, 2010).

6.3.3   Cost Benefit—Current Study

6.3.3.1   Analytic Framework

We use CBA as a decision procedure in a business context where businesses (in this case local, independently owned restaurants) prefer projects that maximize benefits to related costs (Prest and Turvey, 1965; Adler and Posner, 1999). The decision framework that we propose also describes which costs and benefits could be evaluated, how they could be valued, and at what rate they would need to be discounted (Prest and Turvey, 1965). Within this cost–benefit framework we also highlight the use of WTP estimates as an essential procedure to value potential benefits (Frank and Sunstein, 2001). Furthermore, the inclusion of human factors—such as employee costs—in a CBA framework is consistent with previous literature (Mantei and Teory, 1988). As our study demonstrates, human factor costs are critical in this particular context, and may, in fact, be so in other hospitality decision-making settings.

6.3.3.2   Sample and Data

Cost data from a sample of three independent restaurants that were comparable from the cost study was used in the CBA. This cost data was combined with WTP estimates derived from an experiment in an independent restaurant comparable to the three restaurants in the cost study. The types of cost and benefit data and the source of the data used in the CBA are presented in Table 6.1.

6.3.3.2.1   Cost Data

The three restaurants in the costs study (SSG) were fine dining, quick service, and a member's only club restaurant. From each of these restaurants one menu item was identified for financial analysis. The three menu items identified used chicken, beef, and pork as their main ingredient. Incremental costs of locally sourcing the main ingredients were estimated for each of these three menu items. These cost elements were identified based on the SSG study findings. The total of these costs represented the incremental costs of sourcing locally produced ingredients for the three menu items.

6.3.3.2.2   Benefits Data

WTP estimates from the benefit study (AS) were used as benefits of sourcing local foods. These WTP estimates were used to forecast price increases (and therefore, incremental revenues) for each of the three menu items. While the AS benefit study experiment was not conducted in the same restaurants as the SSG cost study, the AS study restaurant was comparable to the three restaurants of the cost study in its geographical location, clientele, and ownership (independently owned and managed). However, the experiment restaurant of the AS study was different in its menu offering than the other three restaurants. The experiment restaurant had a relatively limited menu choice compared to the other three restaurants of the cost SSG study. In order to reduce this bias for the present study menu items from the cost study (SSG) were carefully chosen. The three menu items identified from the SSG study (that used chicken, beef, and pork as their main ingredient) were comparable to the three main ingredients in the AS study.

TABLE 6.1 Data Sources.

Data	Estimation process
Changes in time to delivery	From survey responses (SSG)
Changes in delivery cost	Function of time to delivery and labor cost per hour, survey responses (SSG)
Changes in receiving time	From survey responses (SSG)
Changes in receiving time cost	Function of receiving time and hourly labor cost, survey responses (SSG)
Changes in time to storage (after delivery)	From survey responses (SSG)
Changes in storage cost	Function of storage time and labor cost per hour, survey responses (SSG)
Total item portion size	From survey responses (SSG)
Labor cost per hour	From survey responses (SSG)
Demand per year	Monthly demand (June–July) from survey results used to forecast annual demand (SSG)
Changes in sourcing time	From survey responses (SSG)
Changes in sourcing time cost	Function of sourcing time and labor cost per hour, survey responses (SSG)
Primary ingredient weight	From survey responses (SSG)
Change in food cost percentage	From survey responses (SSG)
Changes in total food cost	Function of revenue and changes in food cost %, survey responses (SSG)
Initial menu price	From survey responses (SSG)
Menu price increase %	WTP estimates from choice experiment (AS)
Change in revenues	Function of new price and demand – Current study analysis
Forecast percentage	Consumer Price Index for "Food Away from Home"—Current study analysis
Weighted average cost of capital	Industry estimates of restaurants' cost of debt and equity—current study analysis

6.3.3.2.3   Data Analysis

In this current study, we conducted a DCF of the forecasted incremental costs and benefits associated with local foods. Incremental revenues associated with the three menu items represented the benefits associated with local foods. These incremental revenues were forecasted using the WTP estimate of 17% from the benefit study (Alfnes and Sharma, 2010). Incremental costs associated with the use of local foods were identified as employee time (for sourcing, delivering/receiving, and storing local foods), and the incremental food cost (Sharma et al., 2009). The data presented in Table 6.1 were used to create a *pro forma* statement of revenues, costs, and income for the three menu items representing each of the three restaurants. The projected income and resulting cash flows were then discounted by the weighted average cost of capital. This framework was integrated into a Monte Carlo simulation analysis. The Monte Carlo analysis simulated changes in revenues, costs, income, and cash flows based on expected changes in the randomized variables. That is, the simulation analysis automatically varied the randomized variables within the defined probability distributions, and evaluated the output of interest for each combination of changed values. The output of interest, in this case, was the discounted cash flows.

6.3.3.2.4   CBA and Stochastic DCF Using Monte Carlo Simulation

We adopted an incremental CBA framework to evaluate the effects of local foods in selected menu items representing three different types of independently owned restaurants. Within the CBA, a DCF was conducted to compare costs and benefits of local foods as ingredients. The cost–benefit approach allowed us to incorporate incremental costs that are not always accounted in a traditional discounted cash flow approach, for instance, incremental employee time costs. Incremental costs associated with the sourcing of local foods in restaurants were primarily employee time in sourcing, delivery, and storage of local foods (Sharma et al., 2009). The incremental costs were therefore identified as follows:

$$\Delta Costs = \Delta \text{ Sourcing time cost}$$
$$+\Delta \text{ delivery costs} \left(\text{including inventory holding costs}\right)$$
$$+\Delta \text{ receiving time costs} + \Delta \text{ storing time costs}$$

(6.1)

Based on the results of Sharma et al. (2009), all other costs were assumed to be constant or same. This treatment of other costs that do not change between two alternatives (with and without locally-produced foods) is consistent with accounting principles (Scott, 2008). Incremental increase in price was treated as the direct benefit of using local foods. The incremental revenues from the use of local foods were a function of these incremental price increases. Price range estimates of WTP more for local foods were obtained from previous research (Alfnes and Sharma, 2010) that demonstrated independent restaurants could charge a premium of around 17% on certain menu items featuring local ingredients. Incremental costs and revenues were evaluated to calculate the discounted cash flows as follows:

$$\Delta DCF = \sum_{t=1}^{n} \frac{\Delta Revenues_t - \Delta Costs_t}{(1+WACC)^n}, \qquad (6.2)$$

where $n=3$ years. All revenue and cost data was projected for 3 years using the most recent price indices from the Bureau of Labor Statistics (BLS, 2005).

We also applied a Monte Carlo simulation to the DCF to model the stochastic effects of several variables that may not be deterministic, particularly food cost. Equation 6.2 was translated into a stochastic model by specifying probability distributions on the respective variables. Table 6.2 shows the variables that were assumed to be stochastic, $E(.)$, and the distributions that were specified for each of those variables:

$$E(DCF) = \sum_{t=1}^{n} \frac{E(\Delta Revenues_t) - E(\Delta Costs_t)}{\left[1 + E(WACC)\right]^n} \qquad (6.3)$$

The process of defining these distributions is more of an art than a science (Guericke et al, 2012; Meyn and Tweedie, 1993). Researchers use guidelines to specify distributions within the Monte Carlo procedures, particularly when there are limited data available for the stochastic variables.

TABLE 6.2   Stochastic Variables for Monte Carlo Simulation.

Variable	Distribution specified
Time to storage cost	Uniform
Time to storage (h)	Triangle
Receiving time cost	Uniform
Receiving time (h)	Triangle
Time to delivery (from placing order) (h)	Triangle
Sourcing time cost	Uniform
Total sourcing time (h)	Triangle
Food cost difference	Triangle
Price change percentage	Uniform
Weighted average cost of capital	Triangle

Uniform distribution was used if there were some expectations that events had an equal likelihood of occurrence. For instance, there appeared to be an equal chance that either the manager (higher-paid, maximum limit) or a front-line employee (lower-paid, minimum limit) would be engaged in receiving or storing food. Therefore, employee costs per hour were assumed to be uniformly distributed. Time cost for sourcing food was also specified as a uniform distribution but the minimum limit was higher, representing a manager, owner, or chef's likelihood to source food rather than the front-line employee. In cases where there were limited historical data or cost judgment criteria available regarding the behavior of a variable, a triangular distribution was specified (hours required for employee tasks—sourcing, receiving, storage, and food cost) (IBM, 2012). It is recommended that input variables of time required for tasks with no or limited prior data be specified as triangular distributions.

Price change from the experimental results of the WTP estimates was specified as a uniform distribution (Alfnes and Sharma, 2010). That is, we assumed that incremental price increases were equally likely.

The three menu items selected from three different restaurants had lamb, chicken, and pork as the local ingredients. The Table 6.3 shows two sets of results, the first three columns of data present discounted cash flow results that included food cost as one of the incremental cost elements. These results were based on three years of projected costs and revenues.

The forecasts of cash flows were based on the projected consumer price index (CPI, 2012) table published by the Bureau of Labor Statistics, and treated as a deterministic variable. The discounting factor was treated as a random variable, and its maximum and minimum limits were based on recent estimates of cost of debt and equity for restaurants (NYU, 2012). The Monte Carlo simulation provided us with several outputs, discounted cash flow estimates (maximum, minimum, mean, and standard deviation), regression coefficient of inputs with discounted cash flows, and distribution fit on the discounted cash flows. These are discussed in the results section.

6.3.3.2.5   Sensitivity Analysis in Monte Carlo Simulation

Even though our approach of specifying probability distributions is well supported in the literature, we also conducted a baseline sensitivity analysis. In this sensitivity analysis, we specified all stochastic variables as normally distributed. These results are also discussed in the next section.

6.4   RESULTS

As stated earlier, the purpose of this paper was to investigate the implications for restaurant decision-making when considering menu items prepared with locally sourced foods. In Table 6.3, we present the results of the Monte Carlo simulations of the DCF.

In all three cases, the discounted cash flows were negative, implying that if food cost were treated as an incremental cost of using local foods then these three menu items would lead to a negative cash flow. The probability of these results being negative was a 100%, based on the cumulative distribution function.

We also conducted a sensitivity analysis of these results by removing the food cost, in order to assess the impact of other costs. The second set of columns show these results. While the lamb and chicken dishes yielded positive cash flows, pork was problematic. Still, there was a 95% probability that pork would have positive discounted cash flows.

TABLE 6.3 Monte Carlo Simulation of Discounted Cash Flow (in US Dollars).

Measure	Discounted cash flows			Discounted cash flows (without food cost)		
	Lamb	Chicken	Pork	Lamb	Chicken	Pork
DCF Min	−84,969	−349,142	−14,402	11,743	90,797	−1,605
DCF Max	−15,757	−130,957	−4179	38,348	99,409	4186
DCF Mean	−48,984	−130,861	−8757	24,212	95,003	1925
DCF St. Dev.	12,331	45,682	1828	5651	1805	1070
C–B ratio	0.366	0.166	0.029	1.502	0.269	0.030
Probability of negative DCF	100%	100%	100%	0%	0%	0%

In Table 6.4, we present the regression coefficients of various inputs that impacted the discounted cash flow results. As expected, in all three cases, food cost had the strongest negative influence on DCF results. Price had a strong positive influence in the case of pork, but that effect was not enough to prevent negative discounted cash flows. The time and cost associated with storage of pork was the second strongest negative influence on the discounted cash flows. Similarly, time to delivery (from placing the order) of lamb and pork had a negative influence, just as did sourcing time for lamb, and time to storage (from taking delivery to storage), and cost of storage for lamb.

TABLE 6.4 Input Cost Regression Coefficients With Discounted Cash Flows.

Input variables (weekly)	With food cost			No food cost		
	Lamb	Chicken	Pork	Lamb	Chicken	Pork
Food cost difference	−0.860	−0.991	−0.830	–	–	–
Price change percentage	0.428	0.000	0	0.931	0.000	0.000
Time to delivery (h)	−0.235	0.000	−0.156	−0.342	0.000	−0.188
Total sourcing time (h)	−0.067	0.000	0.000	−0.148	0.000	0.000
Sourcing time cost (h)	−0.035	0.000	0.000	−0.079	0.000	0.000
Time to storage (h)	−0.024	0.000	−0.480	−0.049	0.000	−0.836
Time to storage cost	−0.013	0.000	−0.292	−0.027	0.000	−0.502
Receiving time cost	−0.005	0.000	0.000	−0.013	0.000	0.000

A similar analysis of input cost effects was conducted for the DCF without food cost (see Table 6.4). There was no significant change in effects of other input costs, thereby verifying our results from the previous analysis that included food costs.

Table 6.5 presents the results of the sensitivity analysis conducted to assess the price point at which all menu items would be accepted if local food costs were included. That is, the lamb menu item price would have to increase by over 27% for it to be profitable. Similarly, the chicken menu item price would need to increase by over 23%, and the pork menu item price would need to increase by over 26%. This table also shows the type of restaurant concepts represented by those menu items. There appears to be a small difference in price increase percentages among the three indicating that irrespective of the concept, menu prices would need to increase by a significant margin, otherwise sourcing local ingredients would not yield a positive financial outcome.

TABLE 6.5   Sensitivity Analysis of Price Increase.

	Lamb	Chicken	Pork
Restaurant type	Fine dining	Small, quick service	Member's only club
Price increase	27.40%	23.30%	26.90%

In Table 6.6 (see also Appendix for Fig. 6.A1) we present the probability distributions of discounted cash flows for each of the menu items when food cost was included. We see that lamb discounted cash flow distribution could have been approximated by the normal distribution (Fig. 6.A1, from top left and moving clockwise). However, the triangle distribution would be the best approximate for the discounted cash flows associated with the chicken menu item, and beta general would best approximate the discounted cash flows of the pork menu item. A similar distribution fit was applied to the discounted cash flow results without food cost. Those distributions were as follows: normal for lamb, triangle for chicken, and Weibull for pork (see Fig. 6.A2). Table 6.6 also shows the variance functions of each of the distributions fitted to the discounted cash flows. As can be seen, normal distribution is the only one that has a linear variance function. All other variance functions are highly nonlinear.

TABLE 6.6 Distribution Fit for Discounted Cash Flow (Monte Carlo Simulation).

	For reference	Discounted cash flows		
	Normal distribution	Lamb	Chicken	Pork
Distribution	Normal	Normal	Triangular	Beta Central
Mean function M		μ	$\dfrac{a+b+c}{3}$	$\dfrac{\alpha}{\alpha+\beta}$
Variance function	σ^2	σ^2	$\dfrac{a^2+b^2+c^2-ab-ac--bc}{18}$	$\dfrac{\alpha\beta}{(\alpha+\beta)^2(\alpha+\beta+1)}$
	For reference	Discounted cash flows (without food cost)		
	Normal distribution	Lamb	Chicken	Pork
Distribution	Normal	Beta central	Triangular	Weibull
Mean function μ		$\dfrac{\alpha}{\alpha+\beta}$	$\dfrac{a+b+c}{3}$	$\lambda\Gamma\left(1+\dfrac{1}{k}\right)$
Variance function	σ^2	$\dfrac{\alpha\beta}{(\alpha+\beta)^2(\alpha+\beta+1)}$	$\dfrac{a^2+b^2+c^2-ab-ac--bc}{18}$	$\lambda^2\left[\Gamma\left(1+\dfrac{2}{k}\right)-\left(\Gamma\left(1+\dfrac{1}{k}\right)\right)^2\right]$

We also conducted a sensitivity analysis of Monte Carlo simulations to assess the changes due to probability distribution specifications. All stochastic variables in this sensitivity analysis were specified as normally distributed. There was no change in the accept/reject decision of adopting the product improvement strategies for the sample variables based on DCF estimates. Furthermore, Table 6.7 presents the results of DCF distribution fit. As in the original analysis, we found that two of the three menu items had non-normally distributed DCFs.

TABLE 6.7 Sensitivity Analysis of Distribution Fit for Discounted Cash Flow with All Inputs Normally Distributed (Monte Carlo Simulation).

	For reference	Discounted cash flows		
	Normal distribution	Lamb	Chicken	Pork
Distribution	Normal	Beta central	Normal	Weibull
Mean function	μ	$\dfrac{\alpha}{\alpha+\beta}$	μ	$\dfrac{\alpha}{\alpha+\beta}$
Variance function	σ^2	$\dfrac{\alpha\beta}{(\alpha+\beta)^2(\alpha+\beta+1)}$	σ^2	$\dfrac{\alpha\beta}{(\alpha+\beta)^2(\alpha+\beta+1)}$
	For reference	**Discounted cash flows (without food cost)**		
	Normal distribution	Lamb	Chicken	Pork
Distribution	Normal	Logistic	Lognormal	Weibull
Mean function	μ	μ	$e^{\mu+\frac{\sigma^2}{2}}$	$\lambda\Gamma\left(1+\dfrac{1}{k}\right)$
Variance function	σ^2	$\dfrac{\pi^2}{3}s^2$	$\left(e^{\sigma^2}-1\right)e^{2\mu+\sigma^2}$	$\lambda^2\left[\Gamma\left(1+\dfrac{2}{k}\right)-\left(\Gamma\left(1+\dfrac{1}{k}\right)\right)^2\right]$

6.5 CONCLUSIONS

The purpose of this paper was to assess cost–benefits of using local foods in independent restaurants. Local ingredients in menu items were defined in this paper as a product improvement strategy. Commitments to such product improvement strategies require managers to ensure financial prudence or required returns on investment. Results of this analysis suggest that in the case of all three menu items (representing three different types of restaurants), the restaurant management would decide to reject the product improvement strategy of sourcing local food ingredients. The negative discounted cash flows resulted not only from the high food costs but other incremental employee costs that would be overlooked in a traditional analysis. The CBA results also demonstrated that the price increase of 17% would not be sufficient to justify the financial commitment of local ingredients led product improvement strategy. Furthermore, sensitivity analysis of this study showed that menu item prices would have to increase significantly (ranging from 23% to 27%, see Table 6.3) to justify the improved quality through the use of local ingredients. Finally, the distribution assessment of the discounted cash flows for each menu item showed that the underlying variance functions were non-linear. Non-linear variance functions suggest that the variance of the variable of interest is not directly proportional to its mean. In application, this would make it harder for decision-makers to accurately predict the expected changes in the variable of interest. In our context, the outcome variable was discounted cash flows, or the expected financial performance of the product improvement strategy, using locally sourced foods. In other words, at least in this sample of menu items and with the stated revenue and cost constraints, it would be difficult for decision-makers (restaurant management) to accurately predict the financial outcome of using locally grown ingredients using historical data and/or simple linear models. This would have implications on how effectively management could predict the performance of product improvement strategies that inherently involved stochastic variables such as those analyzed in this study. The sensitivity analysis of Monte Carlo simulations with all normally distributed stochastic variables did not change any of our conclusions based on DCF magnitudes and DCF distribution fits.

6.6 DISCUSSIONS

While this analysis is based on a limited dataset and restrictive sample of menu items, it does however, demonstrate the benefits of restaurants analyzing product improvement strategies in a systematic and explicit manner. In fact, we propose that restaurants consider other types of strategies that would appropriately fit the product improvement construct, as used in this study. For instance, improved taste through recipe changes, enhanced nutritional value, food safety improvements (Delcour et al., 2012), and others. The framework we propose in this paper could be used for such and other similar product improvement strategies.

Results of our analysis propose several features of evaluating product improvement strategies in restaurants and potentially other foodservice establishments. First, we propose using micro-data on individual menu items within the incremental DCF to conduct a CBA of product improvement strategy. Traditionally, DCF has been applied to firm-level data, that is, at the establishment or restaurant level. However, if product improvement decisions relate to specific menu items then using discounted cash flow to assess viability of individual menu items should be encouraged. Second, we demonstrate that a broader cost–benefit framework can be more inclusive than using a traditional DCF. In the framework, we propose incremental costs can be more effectively included. For instance, in our framework, we were able to incorporate incremental employee time costs. However, in the traditional discounted cash flow approach employee costs would by default be estimated by employee wages or salaries. Third, we conduct a stochastic analysis by using Monte Carlo simulation in the cost–benefit and discounted cash flow framework. As we demonstrate, there were several variables in even our simplistic analysis that were non-deterministic or stochastic. Therefore, simulating the data could allow the decision-makers to better understand the possible impact of these nondeterministic variables on the performance measure.

Finally, we demonstrate that even in such simplistic analyses, there is a high likelihood (2 of the 3 menu items) that the performance measure (discounted cash flows) could be characterized by a non-linear system. Nonlinear systems possess several characteristics that differentiate them from linear systems. For instance, nonlinear systems may be deterministic within a certain range but could behave in a chaotic manner, diverging in an unstable manner (Linstone, 1999). Most importantly, using historical data to predict non-linear system could result in unreliable forecasts.

6.7 IMPLICATIONS

Through the analysis in this paper, we argue that restaurants decision-making could be enhanced by the use of micro-data (at the individual menu item level), in financial analysis models (such as discounted cash flow analysis). Incremental analysis could be broadened by the use of cost-benefit framework, where variables of importance could be emphasized. Furthermore, complexity could be introduced by simulating variables that may not be deterministic. In our analysis, we show several variables that were non-deterministic. Finally, our analysis emphasizes the importance of considering non-linearity in performance measures. Linear analysis has been the norm in decision-making models in restaurants (Hare et al., 2009). Understanding the impact of non-linear dynamics on performance measures could improve the information decision-makers have to make better strategic choices.

6.8 LIMITATIONS

While CBA provides a comprehensive analysis of costs and benefits associated with an investment decision, it also has certain limitations. The estimation process can lead to inaccuracies. Even though the sensitivity analysis we used in this paper could control for these inaccuracies, we still note the sources of these inaccuracies as follows:

(1) Overreliance on data: As in this paper, CBA often utilizes data from past projects. Therefore, in general, there could be an over-reliance of data from these past projects. Certain obvious assumptions are inherent in this process: that these previous projects were conducted with appropriate methods, and that the researchers were well trained to conduct the projects. We control this source of inaccuracies by using published studies of the previous projects, and by obtaining raw data directly from the authors of the previously conducted studies.

(2) Subjective impressions: The CBA process may involve subjective impressions of the researchers. Subjective impressions in this study particularly included the specification of probability distributions of stochastic variables. We tried to address this limitation by conducting a baseline scenario specifying all stochastic of normally distributed variables. Future studies could investigate the nature and characteristics of uncertainty in different types of restaurant operational costs.

In addition, this study was based on a small sample of restaurants, and selected menu items. We compared different types of restaurants to compensate for the small sample sizes. However, this limitation was largely due to challenges in collecting reliable micro menu-level data from independent restaurants. Future studies could consider novel collaborations with industry suppliers of point of sale systems to more easily obtain these datasets.

APPENDIX FOR REFEREES USE

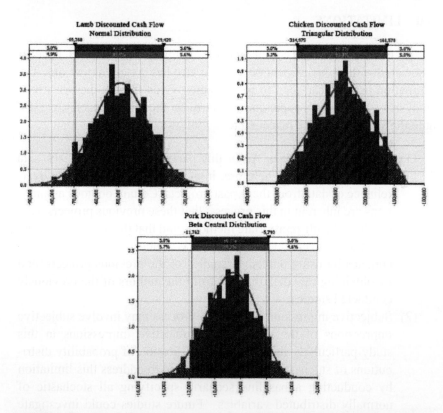

FIGURE 6.A1　(See color insert.) Probability distribution fit for discounted cash flow outputs: (1) lamb; (2) chicken; (3) Pork.

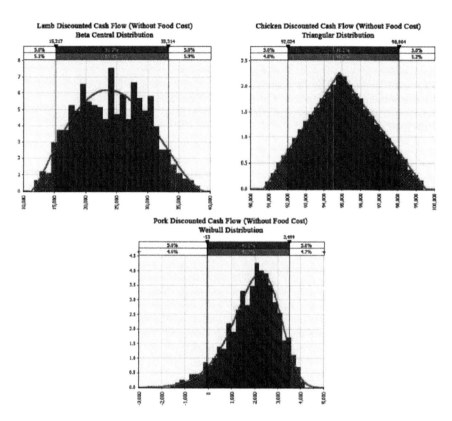

FIGURE 6.A2 (See color insert.) Probability distribution fit for discounted cash flow outputs (no food cost): (1) lamb; (2) chicken; (3) Pork.

KEYWORDS

- local food
- cost–benefit analysis
- financial management
- restaurants
- product improvement

REFERENCES

Agrawal, S. Resort Economy and Direct Economic Linkages. *Ann. Tour. Res.* **2012**, *39*, (3), 1470–1494.

Alfnes, F.; Rickertsen, K. European Consumers' Willingness to Pay for U.S. Beef in Experimental Auction Markets. *Amer. J. Agric. Econ.* **2003**, *85* (2), 396–405.

Altman, M. The Second Generation: Return to Main Stream. *Eur. Herit. Econ. Soc. Sci.* **2011**, *8* (2), 117–133.

Arbel, A. Higher Energy Cost and the Demand for Restaurant Services—A Time-series Analysis. *Int. J. Hosp. Manag.* **1983**, *2* (2), 83–87.

Awad, I. Using Econometric Analysis of Willingness-to-pay to Investigate Economic Efficiency and Equity of Domestic Water Services in the West Bank. *J. Socio-Econ.* **2012**, *41* (5), 485–494.

Brien, B. *Cost Benefit Analysis, Willingness to Pay*; Encyclopedia of Biostatistics. Wiley Online library, 2005.

Bureau of Statistics Consumer Price Indices, 2005. Retrieved on January 4, 2012.

Center for Sustainable Systems (CSS). *U.S. Food Fact Sheet;* University of Michigan, 2006. Retrieved on Jan 24, 2006. http://css.snre.umich.edu/css_doc/CSS01-06.pdf.

Chan, W.; Au, N. Profit Measurement of the Menu Items in Hong Kong's Chinese Restaurants. *Cornell Hotel Rest. Admin. Q.* **1998**, *39* (2), 70–75.

Cohen, E.; Cukierman, G. E.; Schwartz, Z. Cutting Costs on Hazard Analysis Critical Control Points Systems in Food Catering: Sampling Frequency and the Rate of Misclassification. *J. Rest. Foodserv. Market.* **2000**, *4* (1), 19–29.

Delcour, J.; Rouau, X.; Courtin, C.; Poutanen, K.; Ranieri, R. Technologies for Enhanced Exploitation of the Health-Promoting Potential of Cereals. *Trends Food Sci. Technol.* **2012**, *25* (2), 78–86.

Dittman, D.; Hesford, J. A Simulation-Based Optimization Approach for Investment Decisions: A Case Study of Pure Allergy-Friendly Rooms. *Cornell Hotel Rest. Admin. Q.* **2007**, *48* (1), 88–100.

Feinstein, A.; Park, S. The Use of Simulation in Hospitality as an Analytic Tool and Instructional System: A Review of Literature. *J. Hosp. Tour. Manag.* **2002**, *26* (4), 396–421.

Food Channel. *Top Ten Food Trend For 2011*, 2011. Retrieved From: http://www.foodchannel.com/articles/article/top-ten-food-trends-2011/

Gentle, J. *Monte Carlo Method*; Encyclopedia of Statistical Science, 2006.

Gilbert, Richard J.; Riordan, Michael H. Product Improvement and Technological Tying in a Winner-Take-All Market; Competition Policy Center: UC Berkeley, 2005. Retrieved from: http://escholarship.org/uc/item/3v04b2rx.

Gilg, A.; Battershill, M. Quality Farm Food in Europe: A Possible Alternative to the Industrialized Food Market and to Current Agri-Enviromental Policies: Lessons From France. *Food Policy* **1998**, *23* (1), 25–40.

Go, F.; Pyo, S.; Uysal, M.; Mihalik, B. Decision Criteria for Transitional Hotel Expansion. *Tour. Manag.* **1990**, *11* (4), 297–304.

Goebel, J. Enhancing the Local Economic Development Impacts of Large-Scale Residential Estates in South Africa, 1990. *papers.ssrn.com*

Guericke, S.; Koberstein, A.; Schwartz, F.; Vob, S. A Stochastic Model for the Implementation of Postponement Strategies in Global Distribution Networks. *Dec. Supp. Syst.* **2012,** *53* (2), 294–305.

Guiding, C.; Lamminmaki, D. Benchmarking Hotel Capital Budgeting Practices to Practices Applied Non-Hotel Companies. *J. Hosp. Tour. Res.* **2007,** *31* (4), 486–405.

Hare, T.; Camerer, C.; Rangel, A. Self-Control in Decision-Making Involves Modulation of The VMPFC Valuation System, 2009; Vol. 324, pp 646–648.

Harris, P.; Brown, J. Research and Development in Hospitality Accounting and Financial Management. *Int. J. Hosp. Manag.* **1998,** *17* (2), 161–182.

Holt, G.; Amilien, V. Introduction: From Local Food to Localised Food. *Anthropology of Food*, 2007. Retrieved Online On Sep 19, 2007. URL: http://aof.revues.org/document405.html. consulté le 19 septembre 2007.

Huang, R.; Ritter, J. Testing Theories of Capital Structure and Estimating the Speed of Adjustment. *J. Finan. Quant. Anal.* **2009,** *44,* 237–271.

IBM Specifying Distributions. Websphere Business Modeler, Version 6.1, 2012. Retrieved on Oct 15, 2012. http://publib.boulder.ibm.com/.

Jang, S; Park, K. Hospitality Finance Research During Recent Two Decades: Subject, Methodology, and Citations. *Int. J. Contemp. Manag.* **2010,** *23* (4), 479–497.

Kwansa, F. A. Prospects of Financing a Minority-Owned Small Restaurant or Motel. *Int. J. Hosp. Manag.* **1994,** *13* (2), 89–94.

Lin, J. Real Estate Investment in Seismically Active Regions: Feasibility Assessment and Decision Making. *Afr. J. Bus. Manag.* **2012,** *6* (3), 898–907.

Lohmann, L. Toward a Different Debate in Environmental Accounting: The Cases of Carbon and Cost–Benefit. *Account. Organ. Soc.* **2008,** *34* (3), 499–534.

Knychalska, I.; Shaw, M. A Perspective on Marketing Planning and its Essentiality for the Entrepreneurial Restaurateur. *J. Foodserv. Bus. Res.* **2008,** *5* (1), 101–117.

Mantei, M.; Teorey, T. Cost/Benefit Analysis for Incorporating Human Factors in the Software Life Cycle. *Commun. ACM* **1988,** *31* (4), 428–439.

Malk, M.; Schmidgall, R. S. Analyzing Food Operations. *Bottomline* **1995,** *10* (3), 23–27.

Marowsky, M.; Wagner, R. From Scholarly Idea to Budgetary Institution: The Emergence of Cost-Benefit Analysis. *Const. Polit. Econ.* **2009,** *20* (1), 57–70.

Meyn, S.; Tweedie, R. *Markov Chains and Stochastic Stability*; Springer Verlag, 1993.

National Restaurant Association (NRA) *NRA Survey of Chefs Reveals Top Food Trends Heating up Restaurant Menus*, 2007. Retrieved on Jan 25, 2006. http://www.restaurant.org/news/story.cfm?id=545.

National Restaurant Association (NRA). *NRA Survey of Chefs Reveals Top Food Trends Heating up Restaurant Menus*, 2012. Retrieved on Jan 10, 2012. http://www.restaurant.org/news/story.cfm?id=545.

New York University (NYU) Cost of Capital by Sector, 2012. Retrieved on Jan 10, 2012. http://w4.stern.nyu.edu/~adamodar/new_home_page/datafile/wacc.htm.

Newton, A.; Hodder, K.; Catarello, K.; Perrella, L.; Birch, J.; Robins, J.; Douglas, S.; Moody, C.; Cordingley, J. Cost–Benefit Analysis of Ecological Networks Assessed Through Spatial Analysis of Ecosystem Services. *J. Appl. Ecol.* **2012,** *49* (3), 571–580.

Nilsson, M. Toward a Valuation Framework for Hotels as Business Entities. *Int. J. Contemp. Hosp. Manag.* **2001,** *13* (1), 6–12.

Özer, B. An Investment Analysis Model for Small Hospitality Operations. *Int. J. Contemp. Hosp. Manag.* **1996,** *8* (5), 20–24.

Pavesic, D. V. Indirect Cost Factors in Menu Pricing. *Bottomline* **1990,** *5* (5), 22–26.

Raab, C.; Mayer, K. J. Exploring the Use of Activity Based Costing in the Restaurant Industry. *Int. J. Hosp. Tour. Admin.* **2003,** *4* (2), 79–96.

Raab, C.; Mayer, K. Menu Engineering and Activity-Based Costing—Can They Work Together in a Restaurant? *Int. J. Contemp. Hosp. Manag.* **2007,** *19* (1), 43–52.

Rosacker, K.; Olson, D. An Empirical Assessment of IT Project Selection and Evaluation Methods in State Government. *Proj. Manag. J.* **2008,** *39* (1), 49–58.

Rushmore, S. *Hotels and Motels: A Guide to Market Analysis, Investment Analysis, and Valuations*; Appraisal Institute, 1992.

Scott, J. Cost-Benefit Analysis for Global Public–Private Partnerships: An Evaluation of the Desirability of Intergovernmental Organizations Entering into Public–Private Partnerships. *J. Technol. Transf.* **2009,** *34* (6), 525–559.

Scott, R. *Cost-Benefit Analysis, Chemical Leasing Goes Global*; Springer, 2008; 163–175.

Smith, D. A Baker's Dozen: Thirteen Principles for a Successful Restaurant. *Cornell Hotel Rest. Admin. Q.* **1996,** *37* (2), 42–46.

Sharma, A. Economic Impact and Institutional Dynamics of Small Hotels and Restaurants in Tanzania. *J. Hosp. Tour. Res.* **2006,** *30* (1), 76–94.

Sharma, A.; Gregoire, M.; Strohbehn, C. Assessing Costs of Using Local Food in Independent Restaurant. *J. Foodserv. Bus. Res.* **2009,** *12* (1), 55–71.

Steur, H.; Gellynk, X.; Feng, S.; Rutsaert, P.; Verbeke, W. Estimation of Benefits Within CBA can also be Conducted Comprehensively by Accounting for Intangibles. Usually This is Achieved by Obtaining Willingness to Pay Estimates. *Food Q. Pref.* **2012,** *25* (2), 87–94.

Stipanuk, D. M. Energy Management in 2001 and Beyond: Operational Options That Reduce Use and Cost. *Cornell Hotel Rest. Admin. Q.* **2001,** *42* (3), 57–70.

Strohbehn, C. H.; Gregoire, M. *Institutional and Commercial Foodservice Buyers' Perceptions of Benefits and Obstacles to Purchase of Locally Grown and Processed Foods*. Final Report; Iowa State University, Leopold Center For Sustainable Agriculture: Ames, Iowa. Available at: http://www.extension.iastate.edu/hrim/localfoods/

Sullivan, J. Making Profit From Food. *Hotel Cater. Rev.* **2003,** *36* (12), 48–50.

Thompson, G. M. Optimizing a Restaurant's Seating Capacity: Use Dedicated or Combinable Tables? *Cornell Hotel Rest. Admin. Q.* **2002,** *43* (4), 48.

Yin, X.; Jazac, E. The Strategy/Governance Structure Fit Relationship: Theory and Evidence in Franchising Arrangements. *Strat. Manag. J.* **2004,** *25* (4), 365–383.

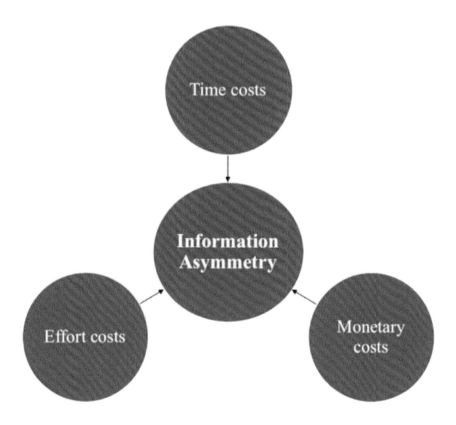

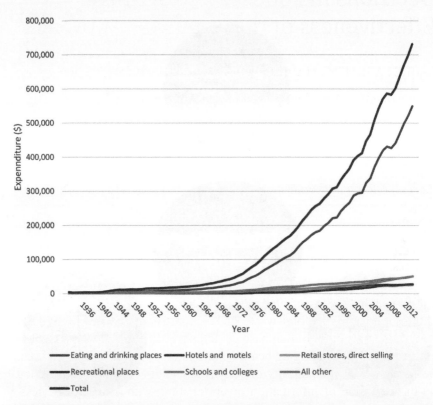

FIGURE 2.1   Total expenditures on food away from home (1929–2014): Dollar (in billions).
Source: Calculated by the Economic Research Service, USDA, from various data sets from the U.S. Census Bureau and the Bureau of Labor Statistics.

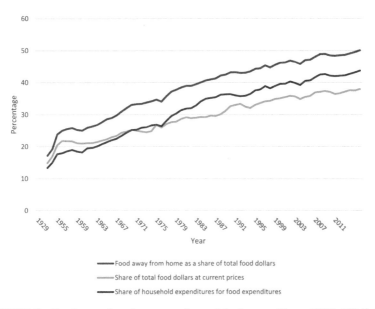

FIGURE 2.2   Food away from home as a share of food expenditures (1929–2014). Share (Percentage).
Source: Calculated by the Economic Research Service, USDA, from various data sets from the U.S. Census Bureau and the Bureau of Labor Statistics.

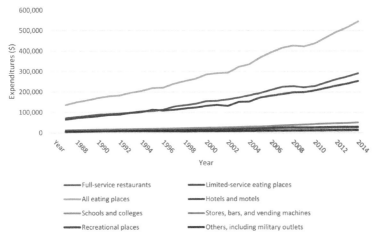

FIGURE 2.3   Sales of meals and snacks away from home by type of outlet (1987–2014). Dollar (in billions).
Source: Calculated by the Economic Research Service, USDA, from various data sets from the U.S. Census Bureau and the Bureau of Labor Statistics

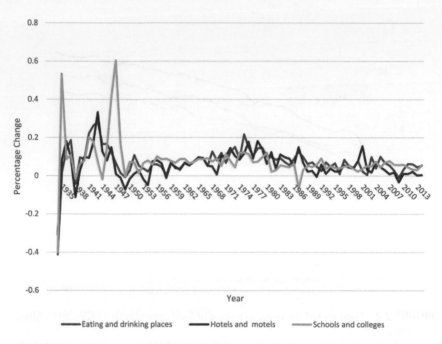

FIGURE 2.4   Percentage changes in expenditures on food away from home by type of outlet (1929–2014). Dollar (in billions).

Source: Calculated by the Economic Research Service, USDA, from various data sets from the U.S. Census Bureau and the Bureau of Labor Statistics.

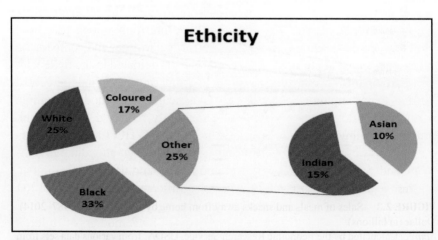

FIGURE 3.2   Ethnicity.

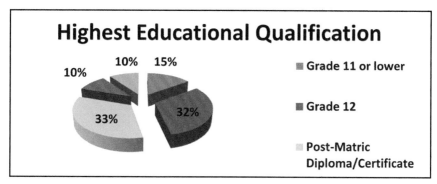

FIGURE 3.3   Highest level of education qualification.

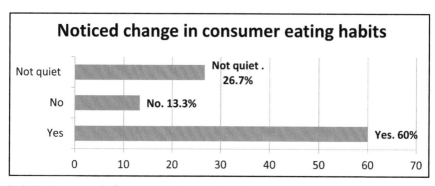

FIGURE 3.4   Level of awareness with regards to changes in consumer eating out habits.

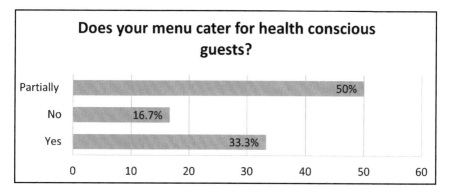

FIGURE 3.5   Restaurant menus cater for health-conscious guests.

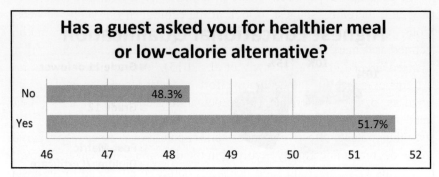

FIGURE 3.6   Waiters requested by guests to assist with healthy alternative meals.

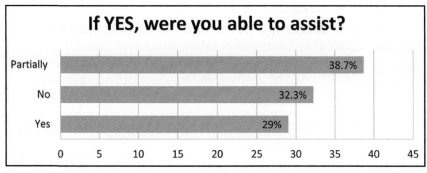

FIGURE 3.7   Ability of waiters to assist with healthy alternatives.

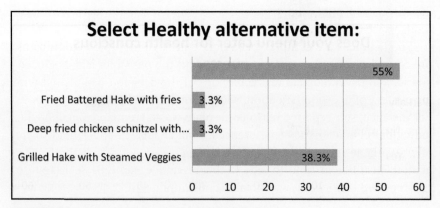

FIGURE 3.8   Meal selected as the healthiest alternative.

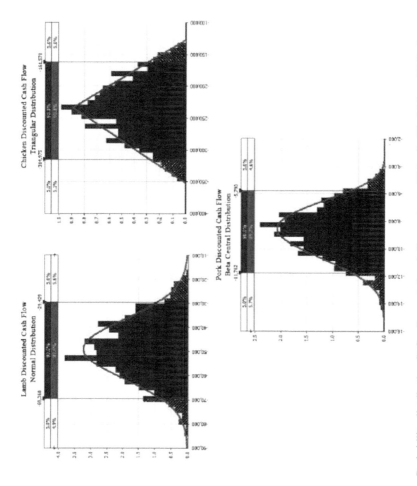

FIGURE 6.A1   Probability distribution fit for discounted cash flow outputs: (1) lamb; (2) chicken; (3) Pork.

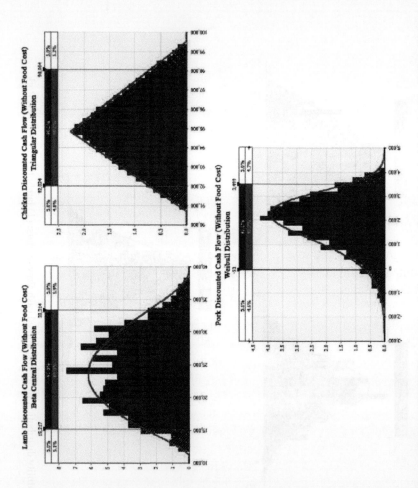

FIGURE 6.A2 Probability distribution fit for discounted cash flow outputs (no food cost): (1) lamb; (2) chicken; (3) Pork.

CHAPTER 7

The Impact of Farm-to-School and Local Food Expenditures on School Foodservice Revenues

VICTOR MOTTA

Sao Paulo School of Business Administration, Fundação Getúlio Vargas

Corresponding author. E-mail: victor.motta@fgv.br

ABSTRACT

Locally grown foods, through Farm to School (FTS) activities, may be a key component to balancing foodservice budgets and alleviating financial constraints in school districts. Therefore, using data from the 2013 United States Department of Agriculture (USDA) Farm to School Census, the purpose of this study is to examine the impact of local food expenditures on school foodservice revenues and earnings. Although the results initially showed a negative impact of local milk and non-milk expenditures on foodservice revenues from food sales, when combined with revenues from the federal government, the impact is positive. In addition, the positive effect of local milk and non-milk items seem to hold when adding foodservice revenues from both food sales and federal funds. The study found a similar pattern for foodservice earnings. This may indicate that competitive foods are still widely prefer in school districts, and as a result, FTS local food-related activities and educating students and parents are an ongoing effort in order to increase participation in local food consumption. In addition, revenues from the federal government is pivotal to maintain FTS activities viable to students and community members although, on average, the federal funds combined with food sales may not cover total foodservice expenditures.

7.1   INTRODUCTION

Farm to school (FTS) programs are among the several efforts dedicated to improve the quality of school meals in U.S. public schools. These programs include a variety of activities design to connect students with local agriculture, such as field trips to farms and taste tests, as an effort to integrate locally grown food into school meals, attempting to connect schools and farms in a mutually beneficial relationship. FTS programs also have the potential of enhancing local economic development, broadly defined as a process of improving both economic and social well-being, measured by the flow of money, goods and services over time, as well as building capacity for creating infrastructure, sustainability, citizen involvement and providing access to employment and quality public goods such as freedom from crime and greater access to education (Pigg, 1999).

FTS programs are responsible for linking farmers and school districts with the primary purposes of contributing to nutritious meals for students and better incomes to farmers in local markets. Awareness for the benefits associated with local foods has also been growing in public schools, as teachers and foodservice administrators are increasingly advocating for fresh, locally produced foods served as school meals and promoting nutritional and experiential education for students (Vallianatos et al., 2004). Foodservice directors are also increasingly getting interested in purchasing more locally grown foods as they realize the various socio-economic benefits for promoting relationship building with small farmers and advocating for alternative agricultural practices.

However, school foodservice directors perceive several financial obstacles to purchasing locally grown foods. Among them, the main perceived financial issues were related to budget constraints that led to the low prioritizing of health initiatives making it more difficult to integrate healthier food components into school meals due to both reductions in foodservice staff and added food costs (Lucarelli et al., 2014). Another financial challenge reflects the greater availability of competitive foods, broadly defined as broadly defined as foods and beverages sold in foodservice areas in addition to, or at the same time as the reimbursable meals of the federal school meals programs, such as the National School Lunch Program (Fox et al., 2008).

Although school districts currently face financial constraints and foodservice administrators may be willing to prefer competitive foods to more nutritious choices since competitive foods generate substantial revenue to school districts, most recent evidence suggests that reducing the availability of competitive foods in school districts results in positive or neutral effects on school foodservice financial measures, such as revenues and profits (Laroche et al., 2017; Peterson, 2011b; Terry-McElrath et al., 2014). As a result, sales of locally grown food in school districts may have a positive impact on school foodservice revenue and profitability.

The purpose of this study is to examine the impact of purchasing locally grown foods on school foodservice revenues and earnings. We anticipate that local food expenditures will have a positive impact on both foodservice revenues and earnings. In this specific case, earnings is equal to foodservice revenue minus foodservice costs. Although public school districts are nonprofit, any annual surplus in earnings remain in foodservice budgets to be used in following years, or may be also used for foodservice improvements, such as equipment and the hiring of additional staff (Bartlett et al., 2008). As a result, the contribution of this study is twofold. First, locally grown foods may be a key component to balancing foodservice budgets and alleviating financial constraints in school districts. According to the latest USDA, Farm to School Census (2015), FTS operations reach nearly 23 million students in the United States, and purchase nearly 800 million dollars in local foods from farmers, potentially leading to over a billion dollars in local economic activity. Several studies estimate that buying local foods has a multiplier effect of 1.4–2.6 throughout the local economy (Hardesty, 2014; Hodges et al., 2014; Pinchot, 2014; Schmit et al., 2016). In other words, for every dollar spent locally, another 40 cents to 1.60 dollars of economic activity is generated.

As a second contribution, there is a lack of evidence demonstrating the impact of purchasing local foods on financial outcomes in foodservice operations of school districts. Schools with balanced budgets are more likely to innovate and create value for students, having positive effects on academic outcomes (Lucarelli et al., 2014). In addition, the potential positive effect on locally grown foods on school district finances is likely to have positive nonfinancial outcomes, such as preventing obesity, achieving higher educational outcomes and integrating students, other school members and farmers in the community.

7.2   BACKGROUND AND LITERATURE

In this section, we review the literature on the development of farm to school programs. We also discuss the main financial concerns of foodservice operations in school districts, and using local foods revenues as a substitute for competitive foods sales.

7.2.1   Farm to School Programs

FTS programs are dedicated to enhance local economic development. These programs include a variety of activities design to connect students with local agriculture, such as field trips to farms and taste tests, as an effort to integrate locally grown food into school meals, attempting to connect schools and farms in a mutually beneficial relationship, providing farmers with a sustainable income. Based on the premise that small and medium-sized farms can benefit from local foods sales to schools (Allen and Guthman, 2006), FTS programs are responsible for linking farmers and school districts with the primary purposes of contributing to nutritious meals for students and better incomes to farmers in local markets. Engaging in direct relationships with school districts, farmers can gain access to a stable market that is likely to guarantee a fair price for their products (Azuma and Fisher, 2001).

Another major component of FTS programs is to improve the quality of school meals in U.S. public schools as they have long been identified as a key setting for promoting childhood health due to their unique positioning to foster healthful eating through meal programs (Wechsler et al., 2001). Fresh food procurement from local farmers has the potential to enhance students diets without posing an additional burden on school foodservice budgets, through increased access of fruits and vegetables. As a result, in light of an epidemic of childhood obesity, attention has been refocused on the pivotal role that school districts play in health promotion.

The National School Lunch Program (NSLP) and the School Breakfast Program (SBP), authorized by the United States Department of Agriculture (USDA) Food and Nutrition Services (FNS), provide affordable meals for over 32 million children each day in the United States approximately. Students who participate in the school breakfast and lunch programs consume are found to consume more than half of their caloric intake in school environment (Briefel et al., 2009). The Healthy, Hunger-Free Kids Act of 2010 (HHKA) required school districts participating in both the NSLP and the SBP to make significant changes to meals served to students. These new guidelines provided the number of required servings in each food group, limiting the amount of sodium, fat, and calories for each meal (Gordon et al., 2009).

Although the nutritional quality of school meals has improved substantially over the past decade, researchers say the overall school food environments that promote healthier food choices continue to be a challenge for school districts (O'Toole et al., 2007). More specifically, budget pressures have complicated the effort of school districts to provide students with quality school meals. In the United States, school foodservice is funded primarily by federal subsidies based on the number of meals served, and since participation in school meals is not required, school districts need to maximize their volume of meals served in order to generate revenues and avoid greater financial constraints. The severe budget constraint of school foodservice operations has led many school districts to serve popular but nutritionally inferior food items that are appealing to students' preferences in order to maximize revenue levels. Among these food items, competitive foods, such as a la carte offerings and vending machine food items, may cover the existing revenue gap (Story et al., 2006). Therefore, schools may remain reluctant to modify their competitive food offerings because of the potential impact nutritional changes could have on school foodservice revenues (Wharton et al., 2008).

7.2.2   Financial Concerns of Foodservice Operations

Many state and federal food policies are being implemented in the school foodservice environment to curtail the increasing rates of childhood obesity and facilitate the promotion of FTS in school districts. A concerned reported by foodservice directors is that the increase in the number of food policies is producing a negative impact on school revenues (French et al., 2001). School foodservices currently face financial constraints, and therefore, the reluctance from school officials to choose competitive foods to more nutritious choices may be understandable if the revenue of such foods is perceived to be critical for school finance. In addition, participation rates and school mean revenues may be also affected by the availability of competitive foods (i.e., foods sold in vending machines, a la carte and in school stores) that students may substitute for school meals. For instance, Fox et al. (2009) investigated the financial contribution of competitive foods have reported that competitive foods generate substantial revenue for schools (Gordon and Fox, 2007). Similar results were also found by the United States General Accounting Office (United States General Accounting Office, 2003; United States Government Accountability Office, 2005).

However, recent evidence indicates that revenue losses due to decreases in the sales of competitive food may be unfounded, at least for the long term. Cohen et al. (2016) suggest that schools may experience short-term losses due to the combined implementation of healthier school means and competitive food policies, but potentially minimal impacts on longer-term overall revenues. Schools struggling school meal revenues or participation rates from school meal standards may benefit from the new guideline standards. The study found that school districts with higher school meal revenues had the lowest competitive food revenues, and similarly, school districts with higher competitive food revenues had the lowest school meal revenues. This finding supports the growing evidence indicating the substitution effect between school meal and competitive food revenues (Long et al., 2013; Peterson, 2011b).

In addition, a recent qualitative analysis of interviews with school foodservice professionals identified several obstacles to promoting increased FTS access in schools, including budgetary constraints, low priority for health initiatives, unhealthy foods available outside school and the availability of unhealthy competitive foods in schools (Lucarelli et al., 2014). The main perceived financial challenges were related to budget cuts leading to reductions in foodservice staff, foodservice budget constraints, making it more difficult to integrate healthier food components into meals due to added food costs, and the greater availability of competitive foods to supplement budget deficits.

Improving the health quality of school meals may reduce participation in the program if students purchase competitive foods or bring food from outside school. However, creating rigorous new competitive food nutrition standards could both support the improvement of meal program standards and remove unhealthy choices to the meal program from school environments. A number of studies found that reducing the availability of unhealthy competitive foods resulted in increased meal program participation and limited impact on overall foodservice revenue (Wharton et al., 2008). The study found that fears of net negative financial impact due to changes in competitive food choices and overall school nutrition are unfounded, since the available data suggest that most school districts do not experience any overall losses of revenue. In some schools, the NSLP participation increased, which might either increase levels of school food revenue, or compensate for potential revenue losses in competitive food sales. While these fruits sometimes include fruits and vegetables, they are more likely to be snacks high in fat, sugar, and salt, such as cookies, potato chips and ice cream (Kann et al., 2005).

Increasing competitive food prices may also increase the demand for healthier options. Laroche et al. (2017) examined student responses to healthy changes made to food items in terms of satisfaction and reported purchases. The results showed that students were price sensitive for competitive food items such as granola bars and trail mix, where a 1% increase in price resulted in a 5% decrease in demand, and an increase in preference for healthier local food items. The results are consistent with previous evidence indicating improved sales of healthy items after price increases of competitive foods (French et al., 2001).

Terry-McElrath et al. (2014) found that district profits were associated with decreased low-nutrient, energy-dense (LNED) food availability and increase fruit and vegetable availability. Although some studies have shown that schools can limit the number or size of LNED food items, or increase the number of low-fat snack options without negatively affecting the overall revenue (French et al., 2001), other studies indicate that revenue loss may accompany improved food vending nutrition standards (Han-markey et al., 2012).

Trevino et al. (2012) have examined changes in revenue and expenses after providing healthier food options in schools. The main results indicate that proving healthier options is affordable and does not compromise school food revenues. In addition, Nollen et al. (2011) found that school districts with nutritionally poor a la carte items had lower a la carte sales. For each $0.10 increase in lunch price, districts were 1.2 times more likely to have low a la carte sales, suggesting that strategies to increase lunch price may be important in reducing a la carte and creating healthier school environments. This finding suggests that students may be interested in purchasing healthier a la cart items and is consistent with the literature showing that restricting a la carte to healthy items improves foodservice revenue through increased participation in school meals (Wharton et al., 2008; Wojcicki and Heyman, 2006).

In addition, there is a lack of evidence demonstrating improvements in school profitability caused by increased in competitive foods revenues. Peterson (2011a) provided evidence that competitive foods revenues are associated with a negative effect on school foodservice finances. The findings suggest that reducing the availability of unhealthy competitive foods in schools results in either positive or neutral effects on foodservice finance, in part by increasing revenue from the school meal programs (NSLP). The results indicate that school officials should examine competitive food profits, not revenue, to assess the financial contribution of competitive foods.

Locally grown foods may be a key component to balancing foodservice budgets and alleviating financial constraints in school districts. Therefore, the purpose of this study is to examine the impact of purchasing locally grown foods on school foodservice revenues and earnings. We anticipate that local food costs will have a positive impact on both foodservice revenues and earnings.

7.3   DATA AND METHODS

A Farm to School Census among public–private schools was conducted in 2013 and 2015 by the United States Department of Agriculture (USDA). The Census questionnaire primarily asked all U.S. public school districts about their farm to school activities during both 2011–2012 and 2013–2014 school years, respectively. The Census prioritized obtaining procurement data related to local sourcing, and included the types and frequency of local products purchased, the percentage of overall food budget spent on local foods and the degree to which the purchasing of locally grown foods is expected to increase, stay the same, or decrease.

The dataset used school districts as the unit of analysis, and consisted of identifying whether school districts participate in farm to school activities, main benefits and problems in procuring local products, number of schools in school district participating in farm to school activities, having school gardens and salad bars, direct and intermediary distributors types of products purchased from local producers and frequency of purchase as well as local food costs, including and excluding locally purchased milk.

The dataset also contains information from the National Center for Education Statistics' Common Core Data (NCES CCD) of public schools, such as the percentage of students eligible for free and reduced-price meals, proportion of minority students and a set of financial variables, including foodservice revenue food sales and the federal government, foodservice benefits, and salary expenditures as well as nonlabor foodservice expenditures (food and supplies) and total school system expenditure. Since financial data was only available for Farm to School Census 2013, we investigate the impact of local foods on school district finances from a cross-sectional rather than panel data perspective.

From a total of 13,133 public school districts in the target list frame, 9896 school districts completed usable responses for a total response rate of over 75%. Of these, 8719 usable responses were collected from March to July 2013 and another 1177 usable responses from October to November 2013. From the sample of 9896 school districts in the United States, nearly 40% of school districts have started FTS activities in the fiscal year 2011–2012. Using only the 3891 schools participating in FTS programs, we performed OLS regression analysis with robust standard errors in order to minimize the potential impact of heteroscedasticity on the explanatory variables.

We specified the general regression equation by:

$$sales = \beta_1 + \beta_2 \left(local\ food\ costs \right) + \beta_2 \left(School\ District\ Characteristics \right) + \varepsilon,$$

where local food costs are segmented into local milk and local nonmilk products, and school district characteristics is a vector comprising racial composition, number of students, number of schools in the district, and the percentage of students that are eligible for free and reduced meal prices. Next, we describe the variables used in the study.

7.3.1 Outcome Variables: Foodservice Sales and Earnings

As a measure of revenue, we have included the foodservice revenue from food sales, foodservice revenue from federal funds and the summation of both. Due to the non-normality of data, these three variables were transformed using the natural logarithm term. In addition, we also calculated earnings by simply measuring the difference between revenues and total food expenditure. Since the distribution of the earnings presented high leptokurtic kurtosis, including very large negative and positive values, a symmetric transformation that pulls in extreme values can be useful. As a result, we have used the cubic root transformation $sign(\blacksquare) \times abs(\blacksquare)^{\frac{1}{3}}$, where the argument is given by the difference of earnings and the median value of earnings. Previous research indicates this as an appropriate transformation in case of leptokurtosis (Cox, 2011; Miles et al., 2013; Whittaker et al., 2005).

7.3.2   Explanatory Variables: Local Milk and Local Nonmilk Expenditures

The two main explanatory variables are the dollar estimates spent on locally grown foods, including and excluding local fluid milk. Both variables were log-transformed due to data skewness. The differences between local milk and local nonmilk foods are important since aggregate local food expenditures for the 2013–2014 year were equal to $789 million, comprising 11% of the value of total food expenditure, among which fluid milk accounted for 61% of the value of local school food expenditures (O'Hara and Benson, 2017).

7.3.3   Control Variables: School District Characteristics

The estimated econometric models a number of control variables to take into account school district characteristics, such as the number of students in the school district and the percentage of students eligible for free and reduced meal prices. Finally, we control for school racial profile as taking into account the percentage of minority (nonwhite) students, such as Hispanic, Asian, Native American, Pacific Islander, and Black students. In addition, we control for school location using a dummy variable for rural area. Previous research indicates these control variables as important determinants of local school food expenditures (Beets et al., 2014; Nicholson et al., 2014; Turner et al., 2016).

7.4   RESULTS

Overall, the average foodservice revenue from both food sales and federal government funding was US$553,687.10 and US$960,260, respectively, while the summation of both revenues was US$1,513,947 on average. On average, school districts incurred negative foodservice profits taking into account the revenues from food sales, federal money and a summation of both minus the total foodservice expenditure (including salary, benefits, and nonlabor expenditures). The mean negative values were minus (US$1,017,615), (US$611,000.40), and (US$57,355.29) respectively. The average total food expenditure was $1,571,302, whereas the mean values for local food expenditures were USUS135,886.80 including local milk and US$67,440.85 excluding local milk, respectively. The total local food expenditure amounted, on average, to US$ 882,426 per school district.

In addition, school districts have, on average, 3892 students (mean of 27% of students belonging to minority ethnic groups), and are comprised of seven schools (including elementary, middle and high schools). Nearly 50% of the students, on average, qualify for free and reduced meal prices.

Table 7.1 lists the OLS results to measure the impact of local milk and nonmilk expenditures on foodservice revenues. We found a negative impact between local milk expenditures (column 1a) and local nonmilk expenditures (column 1b) on foodservice revenue. Local milk expenditures were statistically significant at the 1% level, whereas the negative relationship between nonmilk expenditures and foodservice revenue from food sales was not statistically significant. Both the percentage of students eligible for free and reduced meal prices and nonwhite student proportion had a statistical negative relationship with foodservice revenue from food sales, whereas the number of students and the rural location of school districts showed a positive and statistically significant relationship with foodservice revenue.

Unlike revenues from food sales, local milk and local nonmilk expenditures were found to have a positive impact in the foodservice revenue from the federal government. However, only the local nonmilk expenditure was statistically significant. In addition, all the control variables were found to have a statistically significant positive effect on foodservice revenues from the federal government. Like the previous result, in addition, we found significant results indicating that both local milk and local non-milk expenditures had a positive impact in the total foodservice revenue. The

TABLE 7.1 OLS Models—School Foodservice Revenue.

	Revenue from food sales		Revenue from federal funds		Total foodservice revenue	
Local expenditure (including milk)	−0.00631*		0.00468		0.00515*	
	(0.00333)		(0.00358)		(0.00277)	
Local expenditure (excluding milk)		−0.00367		0.0114***		0.00849***
		(0.00360)		(0.00412)		(0.00308)
No. of students	1.034***	1.031***	0.956***	0.951***	0.973***	0.972***
	(0.0118)	(0.0121)	(0.0116)	(0.0122)	(0.00768)	(0.00822)
Reduced meal	−0.00882***	−0.00844***	0.0227***	0.0225***	0.00637***	0.00620***
	(0.000731)	(0.000735)	(0.000907)	(0.000897)	(0.000542)	(0.000552)
Minority	−0.00985***	−0.0102***	0.00243***	0.00251***	0.00000289	−0.0000421
	(0.000840)	(0.000822)	(0.000795)	(0.000807)	(0.000528)	(0.000531)
Rural area	0.0625***	0.0507**	0.0574**	0.0585**	0.0438***	0.0433***
	(0.0227)	(0.0228)	(0.0234)	(0.0233)	(0.0167)	(0.0168)
Cons	5.450***	5.444***	4.491***	4.482***	5.828***	5.818***
	(0.0887)	(0.0890)	(0.102)	(0.102)	(0.0638)	(0.0651)
N	2291	2328	2298	2334	2322	2360
r2	0.888	0.888	0.886	0.881	0.939	0.935

$*p < 0.10$, $**p < 0.05$, $***p < 0.01$.
(Robust standard errors in parentheses).

number of students, percentage of free and reduce meal prices, and the rural location of school districts also had a significant positive relationship with total foodservice revenues.

Table 7.2 lists the OLS results in order to measure the impact of both local milk and local nonmilk expenditures on foodservice earnings. When investigating the impact of both local milk and non-milk expenditures on foodservice earnings from food sales, our results show a negative relationship between local food expenditures and food sales profits for both local milk and nonmilk. The results are statistically significant only for nonlocal milk. The percentage of students eligible for free and reduced-price meals, the percentage of nonwhite students and schools located in rural settings were also found to have a significant negative relationship with foodservice profits from food sales.

TABLE 7.2 OLS Models—School Foodservice Earnings.

	Earnings from food sales		Earnings from federal funds	
Local expenditure (including milk)	−0.328		0.289	
	(0.205)		(0.201)	
Local expenditure (excluding milk)		−0.544**		0.267
		(0.218)		(0.208)
No. of students	−29.76***	−29.50***	−26.99***	−26.49***
	(0.791)	(0.797)	(0.809)	(0.791)
Reduced meal	−0.604***	−0.611***	0.179***	0.161***
	(0.0360)	(0.0371)	(0.0499)	(0.0502)
Minority	−0.229***	−0.233***	0.282***	0.275***
	(0.0310)	(0.0314)	(0.0534)	(0.0540)
Rural area	−8.711***	−8.759***	−7.584***	−7.382***
	(1.035)	(1.130)	(1.346)	(1.304)
Cons	180.1***	180.5***	114.4***	111.7***
	(6.436)	(6.415)	(6.537)	(6.445)
N	2329	2367	2329	2367
r2	0.758	0.748	0.560	0.553

*$p < 0.10$, **$p < 0.05$, ***$p < 0.01$.

(Robust standard errors in parentheses).

By only taking into account foodservice earnings from the federal government, our results suggest a positive relationship between local milk and nonmilk expenditures and revenue from revenue funds. However, our results are not statistically significant. Our findings yield similar significant results regarding the negative relationship of the impact of the number of students and rural settings on the foodservice profitability from federal funds. However, contrary to columns 1 and 2, the percentage of eligible students to reduced and free meal prices and the proportion of nonwhite students were found to have positive effects on foodservice profitability from the federal government.

7.5   DISCUSSION AND IMPLICATIONS

The purpose of this study was to examine the impact of purchasing locally grown foods on school foodservice revenues and profits. We anticipated positive impact of local food expenditures on both foodservice revenues and earnings. Although our results initially showed a negative impact of local milk and nonmilk expenditures on foodservice revenues from food sales, when combined with revenues from the federal government, the impact is positive. Since local and competitive foods are substitute goods, a higher proportion of local food availability may imply lower accessibility to competitive food items (Fox et al., 2009). As a result, schools with higher levels of local food expenditure may have lower foodservice revenues from food sales as students may choose not to participate in school lunch. The negative impact of local food expenditures on food sales may also be partially explain by students' preferences. Although public schools have been raising awareness about the various benefits of local foods, competitive foods may be a major source of revenue for school districts as students may strictly prefer competitive foods over healthier options (Fleischhacker, 2007; Goslineret al., 2011; Terry-Mcelrath et al., 2014).

As a result, financial incentives from the federal government for schools to purchase locally grown food items are critical to increasing foodservice revenue in school districts. Our results confirm the importance of foodservice revenue from federal funds by showing a positive impact of both local milk and local nonmilk expenditures on federal fund revenues. These findings indicate that school districts with higher local food expenditures may have access to higher foodservice revenues from the federal government, and consequently, increase the multiplier effect in the local economy (Hodges et al., 2014).

In addition, the positive effect of local milk and nonmilk items seem to hold when adding foodservice revenues from both food sales and federal funds. In agreement with previous evidence indicating a negative relationship between competitive foods and revenues (Long et al., 2013; Peterson, 2011b; Terry-Mcelrath et al., 2014), our findings suggest that there is a positive association between local food expenditures and total foodservice revenue, highlighting the importance of federal funds to public school districts as a means to purchase locally grown food items. Confirming previous evidence (Bontrager Yoder et al., 2015a; Chang et al., 2016; Vo and Holcomb, 2011), our study also sheds light and confirm the impact of certain school characteristics, such as the percentage of eligible students for free and reduced meal, rural location, and school composition in terms of proportion of nonwhite students in foodservice revenues from food sales and the federal government.

Our study found a similar pattern for foodservice earnings. While we found a negative impact of both local milk and local nonmilk expenditure on the foodservice profits from food sale only, a positive relationship was found when considering foodservice profits from federal government funds. It is important to note that mean and median values of foodservice profits from food sales, the federal government and total foodservice profits are negative, implying that both federal funds and food sales may not be sufficient to cover the foodservice costs, such as labor costs (benefits, salaries, etc.), food costs, and expenditures in fixed assets.

The findings of this study shed light to the importance of foodservice revenues from federal government funds in order to maintain FTS programs, and direct policymaking to potential changes in behavioral practices that may encourage students to substitute competitive foods to locally grown food items. As several studies suggest, farm to school activities, such as conducting edible gardens and taste-tests, having farmers visit the school, hosting FTS related community events, and conducting student field trips to farms, among several other activities, may encourage students to change their eating habits (Benson, 2014; Bontrager Yoder et al., 2015b; Johnson et al., 2015; Moss et al., 2013).

Another potential policy implication to consider is the regulation of competitive foods in public schools, as evidence suggests that locally grown food items expenditures is greater for public schools in states where the legal framework regulates unhealthy foods in public schools, encouraging the creation of farm to school laws that facilitate the purchase of local foods (Long et al., 2013; Nicholson et al., 2014; Schneider et al., 2012).

7.6 CONCLUSIONS

FTS programs are among the several efforts dedicated to improve the quality of school meals in U.S. public schools. According to the latest USDA Farm to School Census (2015), FTS operations reach nearly 23 million students in the United States, and purchase nearly 800 million dollars in local foods from farmers, potentially leading to over a billion dollars in local economic activity. Several studies estimate that buying local foods has a multiplier effect of 1.4–2.6 throughout the local economy (Hardesty, 2014; Hodges et al., 2014; Pinchot, 2014; Schmit et al., 2016).

The purpose of this study was to examine the impact of purchasing locally grown foods on school foodservice revenues and earnings. We hypothesized a positive effect of that local food expenditures on both foodservice revenues and profits. In agreement with our expectation, our overall results indicate a positive impact of expenditures in local foods and foodservice revenues from food sales and federal funds. However, revenues from both food sales and the federal government seem not sufficient to cover all the costs incurred by foodservice operations in school districts.

Therefore, contrary to our anticipation, we found a negative relationship between local food expenditures and overall profits. This may indicate that competitive foods are still widely preferred in school districts, and as a result, FTS local food-related activities and educating students and parents are an ongoing effort in order to increase participation in local food consumption. In addition, revenues from the federal government are pivotal to maintain FTS activities viable to students and community members although, on average, the federal funds combined with food sales may not cover total foodservice expenditures.

7.7   AREAS FOR FUTURE RESEARCH

There is a clear and urgent need to understand the impact of local food expenditures on schools' foodservice financial management. A second FTS Census was released in 2015, and there are plans for a third Census in 2019 (USDA, 2015). However, unlike the 2013 Census, the 2015 Census did not contain relevant financial data from the National Center for Education Statistics, such as labor and nonlabor foodservice expenditures and foodservice revenues from food sales and the federal government, due to the unavailability of data after fiscal-year 2011–2012. Financial data for further years are critical not only to detecting changes in school foodservice finances, but financial data may assist key stakeholders involved with FTS programs to both enhance the reach of local food-related activities to a higher number of school districts and understand the local foods non participation of school districts.

As a natural segue for this study, another potential study could examine the impact of local food expenditures on key foodservice financial ratios, such as both food and labor cost percentage as separate proportions of total revenue, as well as per meal costs, meals per paid labor hour and other productivity measures. In addition, other studies could investigate the relationship between school food service financial operations and supply chain issues, such as local food transactions through intermediary sources or directly through local farmers and producers, farmers markets, Community Supported Agriculture (CSA), and cooperatives.

KEYWORDS

- **farm-to-school**
- **local food systems**
- **food expenditure**
- **foodservice revenue**
- **public schools**

REFERENCES

Allen, P.; Guthman, J. From "Old School" to "Farm-to-School": Neoliberalization From the Ground up. *Agric. Human Values* **2006,** *23* (4), 401–415. http://doi.org/10.1007/s10460-006-9019-z.

Azuma, A. M.; Fisher, A. *Healthy Farms, Healthy Kids: Evaluating the Barriers and Opportunities for Farm-to-School Programs*; Community Food Security Coalition: Venice, CA, July 2015; pp 1–62. Retrieved from http://foodsecurity.org/pub/HealthyFarmsHealthyKids.pdf%5Cn http://www.foodsecurity.org/healthy.html.

Bartlett, S.; Glantz, F.; Logan, C. *School Lunch and Breakfast Cost Study. Final Report*, 2008. Retrieved from http://search.proquest.com/docview/62638179?accountid=1304 2%5Cnhttp://oxfordsfx.hosted.exlibrisgroup.com/oxford?url_ver=Z39.88-2004&rft_val_fmt=info:ofi/fmt:kev:mtx:book&genre=report&sid=ProQ:ERIC&atitle=&title=School+Lunch+and+Breakfast+Cost+Study.+Final.

Beets, M. W.; Tilley, F.; Turner-McGrievy, G.; Weaver, R. G.; Jones, S. Community Partnership to Address Snack Quality and Cost in After-school Programs. *J. School Health* **2014,** *84* (8), 543–548. http://doi.org/10.1111/josh.12175.

Benson, M. Exploring Extension Involvement in Farm to School Program Activities. *J. Ext.* **2014,** *52* (4), 1–12. Retrieved from http://www.joe.org/joe/2014august/a4.php.

Bontrager Yoder, A. B.; Foecke, L. L.; Schoeller, D. A. Factors Affecting Fruit and Vegetable School Lunch Waste in Wisconsin Elementary Schools Participating in Farm to School Programmes. *Public Health Nutr.* **2015a,** *18* (15), 2855–2863. http://doi.org/10.1017/S1368980015000385.

Bontrager Yoder, A. B.; Foecke, L. L.; Schoeller, D. A. Factors Affecting Fruit and Vegetable School Lunch Waste in Wisconsin Elementary Schools Participating in Farm to School Programmes. *Public Health Nutr.* **2015b,** *18* (15), 2855–2863. http://doi.org/10.1017/S1368980015000385.

Briefel, R. R.; Crepinsek, M. K.; Cabili, C.; Wilson, A.; Gleason, P. M. School Food Environments and Practices Affect Dietary Behaviors of US Public School Children. *J. Amer. Dietetic Assoc.* **2009,** *109* (2), S91–S107. http://doi.org/10.1016/j.jada.2008.10.059.

Chang, Y.; Carithers, T.; Leeke, S.; Chin, F. Geographic Disparity in Funding for School Nutrition Environments: Evidence from Mississippi Schools. *J. School Health* **2016,** *86* (2), 121–128. http://doi.org/10.1111/josh.12361.

Cohen, J. F. W.; Gorski, M. T.; Hoffman, J. A.; Rosenfeld, L.; Chaffee, R.; Smith, L.; Rimm, E. B. Healthier Standards for School Meals and Snacks. *Amer. J. Preven. Med.* **2016,** *51* (4), 485–492. http://doi.org/10.1016/j.amepre.2016.02.031.

Cox, N. Cube Roots. *Stata J.* **2011,** *11* (1), 149–154. http://doi.org/The Stata Journal.

Fleischhacker, S. Food Fight: The Battle Over Redefining Competitive Foods. *J. School Health* **2007,** *77* (3), 147–152. http://doi.org/10.1111/j.1746-1561.2007.00184.x.

Fox, M. K.; Gordon, A.; Nogales, R.; Wilson, A. Availability and Consumption of Competitive Foods in US Public Schools. *J. Amer. Dietetic Assoc.* **2009,** *109* (2), S57–S66. http://doi.org/10.1016/j.jada.2008.10.063.

French, S. A.; Jeffery, R. W.; Story, M.; Breitlow, K. K.; Baxter, J. S.; Hannan, P.; Snyder, M. P. Pricing and Promotion Effects on Low-Fat Vending Snack Purchases: the CHIPS Study. *Am. J. Public Health* **2001**, *91* (1), 112–117.

Gordon, A. R.; Crepinsek, M. K.; Briefel, R. R.; Clark, M. A.; Fox, M. K. The Third School Nutrition Dietary Assessment Study: Summary and Implications. *J. Amer. Dietetic Assoc.* **2009**, *109* (2), S129–S135. http://doi.org/10.1016/j.jada.2008.10.066.

Gosliner, W.; Madsen, K. A.; Woodward-Lopez, G.; Crawford, P. B. Would Students Prefer to Eat Healthier Foods at School? *J. School Health* **2011**, *81* (3), 146–51. http://doi.org/10.1111/j.1746-1561.2010.00573.x.

Han-markey, T. L.; Wang, L.; Schlotterbeck, S.; Jackson, E. A.; Gurm, R.; Leidal, A.; Eagle, K. A Public School District's Vending Machine Policy and Changes Over a 4-year Period: Implementation of a National Wellness Policy. *Public Health* **2012**, *126* (4), 335–337. http://doi.org/10.1016/j.puhe.2012.01.007.

Hardesty, S. Values-Based Supply Chains: Supporting Regional Food and Farms. *Econ. Dev. Q.* **2014**, *28*, 17–27. http://doi.org/10.1177/0891242413507103.

Hodges, A. W.; Stevens, T. J.; Wysocki, A. F. Local and Regional Food Systems in Florida: Values and Economic Impacts. *J. Agric. Appl. Econ.* **2014**, *2* (May), 285–298. http://doi.org/10.1017/S1074070800000791.

Johnson, S.; Berning, J.; Colson, G.; Smith, T. In *Impact of Farm to School Programs on Students' Consumption of Healthful Foods: An Empirical Analysis in Georgia.* 2015 Agricultural & Applied Economics Association and Western Agricultural Economics Association Annual Meeting, 2015. Retrieved from http://ageconsearch.umn.edu/bitstream/205430/2/AAEA 2015 Farm to School Empirical Analysis GA.pdf.

Kann, L.; Grunbaum, J.; McKenna, M. L.; Wechsler, H.; Galuska, D. A. Competitive Foods and Beverages Available for Purchase in Secondary Schools—Selected Sites, United States, 2004. *J. School Health* **2005**, *75* (10), 370–374. http://doi.org/10.1111/j.1746-1561.2005.00058.x.

Laroche, H. H.; Hradek, C.; Hansen, K.; Hanks, A. S.; Just, D. R.; Wansink, B. Healthy Concessions: High School Students' Responses to Healthy Concession Stand Changes. *J. School Health* **2017**, *87* (2), 98–105. http://doi.org/10.1111/josh.12472.

Long, M. W.; Luedicke, J.; Dorsey, M.; Fiore, S. S.; Henderson, K. E. Impact of Connecticut Legislation Incentivizing Elimination of Unhealthy Competitive Foods on National School Lunch Program Participation. *Amer. J. Public Health* **2013**, *103* (7), 59–66. http://doi.org/10.2105/AJPH.2013.301331.

Lucarelli, J.; Alaimo, K.; Mang, E. Facilitators to Promoting Health in Schools: Is School Health Climate the Key? *J. School Health* **2014**, *84* (2), 133–140. http://doi.org/10.1111/josh.12123.

Miles, B. W. J.; Stokes, C. R.; Vieli, A.; Cox, N. J. Rapid, Climate-driven Changes in Outlet Glaciers on the Pacific Coast of East Antarctica. *Nature* **2013**, *500* (7464), 563–566. http://doi.org/10.1038/nature12382.

Moss, A.; Smith, S.; Null, D.; Long Roth, S.; Tragoudas, U. Farm to School and Nutrition Education: Positively Affecting Elementary School-Aged Children's Nutrition Knowledge and Consumption Behavior. *Childhood Obes.* **2013**, *9* (1), 51–56. http://doi.org/10.1089/chi.2012.0056.

Nicholson, L.; Turner, L.; Schneider, L.; Chriqui, J.; Chaloupka, F. State Farm-to-school Laws Influence the Availability of Fruits and Vegetables in School Lunches at US Public

Elementary Schools. *J. School Health* **2014,** *84* (5), 310–316. http://doi.org/10.1111/josh.12151.

Nollen, N. L.; Kimminau, K. S.; Nazir, N. Demographic and Financial Characteristics of School Districts with Low and High à la Carte Sales in Rural Kansas Public Schools. *YJADA* **2011,** *111* (6), 879–883. http://doi.org/10.1016/j.jada.2011.03.017.

O'Hara, J.; Benson, M. *Local Food Production and Farm to School Expenditures*, 2017.

O'Toole, T. P.; Anderson, S.; Miller, C.; Guthrie, J. Nutrition Services and Foods and Beverages Available at School: Results From the School Health Policies and Programs Study 2006. *J. School Health* **2007,** *77* (8), 500–521. http://doi.org/10.1111/j.1746-1561.2007.00232.x.

Peterson, C. A Rotten Deal for Schools? An Assessment of States' Success with the National School Lunch Program's in-kind Food Benefit. *Food Policy* **2011a,** *36* (5), 588–596. http://doi.org/10.1016/j.foodpol.2011.07.006.

Peterson, C. Competitive Foods Sales are Associated with a Negative Effect on School Finances. *J. Amer. Dietetic Assoc.* **2011b,** *111* (6), 851–857. http://doi.org/10.1016/j.jada.2011.03.021.

Pigg, K. E. Community Leadership and Community Theory: A Practical Synthesis. *Commun. Dev. Soc. J.* **1999,** *30* (2), 196–212. http://doi.org/10.1080/15575339909489721.

Pinchot, A. The Economics of Local Food Systems, 2014.

Schmit, T. M.; Jablonski, B. B. R.; Mansury, Y. Assessing the Economic Impacts of Local Food System Producers by Scale: A Case Study From New York. *Econ. Dev. Q.* **2016,** *30* (4), 316–328. http://doi.org/10.1177/0891242416657156.

Schneider, L.; Chriqui, J.; Nicholson, L.; Turner, L.; Gourdet, C.; Chaloupka, F. Are Farm-to-school Programs More Common in States with Farm-to-school-related Laws? *J. School Health* **2012,** *82* (5), 210–216. http://doi.org/10.1111/j.1746-1561.2012.00689.x.

Story, M.; Kaphingst, K. M.; French, S. A. The Role of Schools in Preventing Childhood Obesity. *Fut. Children* **2006,** *16* (1), 109–142. http://doi.org/10.1016/S0140-6736(02)09678-2.

Terry-Mcelrath, Y. M.; Hood, N. E.; Colabianchi, N.; O'Malley, P. M.; Johnston, L. D. Profits, Commercial Food Supplier Involvement, and School Vending Machine Snack Food Availability: Implications for Implementing the New Competitive Foods Rule. *J. School Health* **2014,** *84* (7), 451–458. http://doi.org/10.1111/josh.12165.

Terry-McElrath, Y. M.; O'Malley, P. M.; Johnston, L. D. Accessibility Over Availability: Associations Between the School Food Environment and Student Fruit and Green Vegetable Consumption. *Childhood Obes.* **2014,** *10* (3), 241–50. http://doi.org/10.1089/chi.2014.0011.

Treviño, R. P.; Pham, T.; Mobley, C.; Hartstein, J.; El Ghormli, L.; Songer, T. HEALTHY Study School Foodservice Revenue and Expense Report. *J. School Health* **2012,** *82* (9), 417–23. http://doi.org/10.1111/j.1746-1561.2012.00717.x.

Turner, L.; Eliason, M.; Sandoval, A.; Chaloupka, F. J. Increasing Prevalence of US Elementary School Gardens, but Disparities Reduce Opportunities for Disadvantaged Students. *J. School Health* **2016,** *86* (12), 906–912. http://doi.org/10.1111/josh.12460.

United States General Accounting Office SCHOOL MEAL Revenue and Expense Information from Selected States, May, 2003, 2272.

United States Government Accountability Office. Competitive Foods Are Widely Available and Generate Substantial Revenues for Schools, August, 2005.

Vallianatos, M.; Gottlieb, R.; Haase, M. A. Farm-to-School: Strategies for Urban Health, Combating Sprawl, and Establishing a Community Food Systems Approach. *J. Plan. Educ. Res.* **2004,** *23* (4), 414–423. http://doi.org/10.1177/0739456X04264765.

Vo, A.; Holcomb, R. B. Impacts of School District Characteristics on Farm-to-School Program Participation: The Case for Oklahoma. *J. Food Distrib. Res.* **2011,** *42* (3), 43–60. http://doi.org/10.1353/jhr.2009.0021.

Wechsler, H.; Brener, N. D.; Kuester, S.; Miller, C. Health Services: Results From the School Health Policies and Programs Study 2000. *J. School Health* **2001,** *71* (7), 294–304. http://doi.org/10.1111/j.1746-1561.2001.tb03509.x.

Wharton, C. M.; Long, M.; Schwartz, M. B. Changing Nutrition Standards in Schools: The Emerging Impact on School Revenue. *J. School Health* **2008,** *78* (5), 245–51. http://doi.org/10.1111/j.1746-1561.2008.00296.x.

Whittaker, J.; Whitehead, C.; Somers, M. The Neglog Transformation and Quantile Regression for the Analysis of a Large Credit Scoring Database. *Appl. Stat.* **2005,** *54* (5), 863–878. http://doi.org/10.1111/j.1467-9876.2005.00520.x.

Wojcicki, J. M.; Heyman, M. B. Healthier Choices and Increased Participation in a Middle School Lunch Program: Effects of Nutrition Policy Changes in San Francisco. *Amer. J. Public Health* **2006,** *96* (9), 1542–1547. http://doi.org/10.2105/AJPH.2005.070946.

PART III

Foodservice Behaviors

CHAPTER 8

Food Safety: Integrating Behavior Change and Motivation Design

KEVIN R. ROBERTS* and NAIQING LIN

Department of Hospitality Management, Kansas State University, Manhattan, USA

Corresponding author. E-mail: kevrob@ksu.edu

ABSTRACT

Food safety is a concern in the entire food industry, and even more so for individual foodservice operations, whose employees are tasked with serving wholesome, safe food to the consumer. No other issue can have such a devastating economic impact on a foodservice operation as a single foodborne illness outbreak. Despite various food safety educational efforts, foodborne illness remains a challenge in the industry. Food safety training has been established as an effective means to increase knowledge about the topic. However, research has shown that even when employees are trained in food safety, knowledge does not always translate into improved practices on the job. To effectively convert experiences that result in behavior change, researchers and trainers need to have a practical understanding of current behavioral theories and the underlining psychology that draws from the individual's primary food safety beliefs and situational cues. Therefore, this chapter focuses on discussing the behavior modeling theories that have roots in attentional, retention, reproduction, and motivational processes. Although these models can develop useful persuasive arguments to change food safety beliefs, resulting in behavior change, it is worth noting that empirical experiments related to food safety is still lacking. Thus, future research is discussed.

The foodservice manager has a plethora of responsibility, from human resource management to managing costs, and ensuring the guest has a positive experience in your operation. For many of these tasks, managers rely on their employees to ensure that they are completed and done correctly. Perhaps the single greatest challenge of a foodservice operator is to ensure that food served to the guest is wholesome and safe. No other issue within the operation can have as much of an impact on the business and revenue generated than a single foodborne illness outbreak.

The Centers for Disease Control and Prevention (2016a) estimates that one in every six Americans will fall ill from a foodborne illness each year. Among these, 128,000 are hospitalized and 3000 will die. The cost to an individual operator for a foodborne outbreak is difficult to quantify. Buzby et al. (2001) noted that jury verdicts from 1988 to 1997 ranged from $2256 to greater than $2 million, with a median award of $25,560 (equivalent to $37,858 in 2016). However, these costs do not include the legal fees incurred by the restaurateur to defend themselves in the lawsuit, the increased cost of insurance premiums, nor the negative media exposure and lost business. Often, the increased financial burden of a foodborne outbreak forces the operation to close (Cochran-Yantis et al., 1996).

According to the Centers for Disease Control and Prevention Foodborne (2016b) Outbreak Online Database, there were 656 outbreaks involving foodservice operations in 2015. Of these outbreaks, 9555 individuals were sickened, resulting in 432 individuals who required hospitalization and one death. Thirteen of these outbreaks involved 100 or more victims, resulting in 1949 illnesses, 136 requiring hospitalizations.

Consumers are increasingly aware of foodborne illnesses and proper food handling. Moreover, with the emerging risks and issues related to food safety, widespread attention has been focused on the food industry and regulators (Belasco, 2014; Lofstedt, 2013). In 2016, consumers will spend almost $0.46 of every dollar in a foodservice or other retail operation (US Department of Agriculture, Economic Research Service, 2016). Dining out or purchasing food-to-go has become a common part of life for every American. The increased role that restaurants play in the everyday lives of all Americans, coupled with media coverage of foodborne outbreaks and the influence of social media, has increased consumer awareness of foodborne illness and proper food handling.

Worsfold (2006) noted that 99% of respondents in a survey indicated that hygiene standards were either "very important" or "important" to them when deciding where to dine. In a more recent study, 98% of customers surveyed considered employee hygiene as very important or important consideration when dining at fast-casual restaurants (Trendsource, 2016). Worsfold (2006) noted that employee hygienic practices were found to be more important than the type of food, service, location, and price. The Trendsource Report (2016) noted that 39% of consumers indicate that they would not return to a quick-service operation if it were involved in a foodborne outbreak; 42% reported they would complain on social media if they observed food safety concerns in a restaurant. Only 72% of the public stated that the restaurant industry would be able to protect consumers from foodborne illness, which represented a dramatic increase from the 2007 level of 43% (Food Marketing Institute Research, 2007, 2015). While currently at 72%, given the amount of meals served in restaurant establishments, there is considerable room for improvement in the confidence of the public in the ability of those in the restaurant industry to protect consumers.

Food safety training has been established as an effective means to increase knowledge about the topic. However, the preponderance of research has shown that even when employees are trained in food safety, that knowledge does not always translate into improved practices on the job. Food safety training involves teaching employees the details of tasks or duties assigned to them. Food safety training has evolved in both scope and the amount of money invested by the government and industry (Blume et al., 2010; Riggins et al., 2005; Sivaramalingam et al., 2015). However, sending employees to a training program does not guarantee they will apply what they learned in their actual work (Howells et al., 2008; Roberts et al., 2008).

When the effectiveness of a sanitation training course on sanitation evaluations after the sanitation course was completed, Casey and Cook (1979) discovered that food safety exam scores were not a significant predictor of postexam sanitation scores. Wright and Feun (1986) evaluated inspection scores after a foodservice manager certification exam. While they found that there was a significant increase in attitudes about regulations and inspectors, no significant improvements in knowledge were noted. Similar results were noted by Mathias et al. (1995) and Powell et al. (1997).

Roberts et al. (2008) explored food safety knowledge and practices among independent and chain restaurant operations. When comparing composite scores of cross-contamination, time and temperature abuse, and use of thermometers, only knowledge increased significantly for handwashing. Observational data revealed that only the incompliance percentage for handwashing behavior increased significantly between pre- and posttraining behavior.

The simple fact remains that training courses are usually short in duration and the information is only utilized if the employee understands the information presented and is motivated to use it when they return to the operation (Bryan, 1990). Only those employees who have internalized what they have learned, realize the importance of proper food safety practices, and are encouraged to follow proper practices by their employer will be motivated to implement skills learned from the class on-the-job (Cochran-Yantis et al., 1996).

8.1   UNDERSTANDING TRUE BEHAVIOR CHANGE

Despite various food safety educational efforts, foodborne illness remains a challenge to the industry. Frank Yiannas, pastpresident of the International Association for Food Protection noted that as an industry, we must go beyond the traditional food safety training, testing, and inspections to a system focused on managing risks, focusing on true behavior change (Yiannas, 2008). Food safety training and education involve teaching employees the details of tasks or duties assigned to them through demonstration and what employees must do to keep food safe or make it safe.

When designing food safety training, understanding personal beliefs is fundamental to implement behavior change. Both the International Association for Food Protection and the European Centre for Disease Prevention and Control have noted the pressing need to develop effective behavioral-based training programs to improve current food safety education, noting it as one of the most pressing challenges for industry (Bosman et al., 2016; Yiannas, 2008).

To effectively convert experiences that result in behavior change, researchers and trainers need to have a practical understanding of current behavioral theories and the underlining psychology that draws from the individual's primary food safety beliefs and situational cues. Thus, behavior modeling in the workplace has become popular within educational training as a systematic way for researchers and trainers to think about the psychological constructs and behavioral factors that underlie behavior change and focuses on persuasion (McKenzie and Woodruff, 2013).

The behavior modeling approach has its research roots in attentional, retention, reproduction, and motivational process which is the fundamental of behavior change. The attentional process relates to a trainees' observing stimuli (e.g., observing food safety behavior), and the extent to which the processes being modeled are internalized by the trainee. The internalization of the behavior is influenced by (1) the attributes of the learner; (2) the characteristics of the action or model; (3) the value of the behavior to the learner; and (4) the complexity of the behavior (Decker and Nathan, 1985; Fox, 2009).

Although attentional processes are well suited for short-term memory and behavior, retention processes are necessary for long-term memory processing. Retention processes focus on the trainee's organized behavior and facilitate storage and retrieval of those behaviors (Decker and Nathan, 1985).

Reproduction and motivational processes allow trainees to practice the skills previously presented through training and education, then apply them to the posttraining/learning environment. Behavior rehearsal, which includes collaborative communication between trainees and trainers, serve as a correctional mechanism to help trainees perform desired behavior successfully. The motivational process facilitated the transfer of training/learning by allowing constant reinforcement of observing stimuli within the posttraining/learning environment.

A typical sequence of training design with behavior modeling involves a list of steps that should happen in order. While studies might approach one or more of these components, behavior modeling training has emphasized the importance of including them all. These steps, as identified by Taylor et al. (2005), include:

(1) describing a set of well-defined behaviors/skills to be trained or learned,
(2) providing a module or models displaying the desired training behaviors and effective use of competencies,
(3) providing opportunities to practice the identified behaviors,
(4) providing feedback and social reinforcement to follow future practices, and

(5) taking steps to maximize the transfer of training and learning-to-job behaviors.

There are three main categories of theories that guide researchers in the realm of behavior modeling and motivation design. First, attitudinal theories focus on an individuals' attitude in an attempt to adjust their attitude. Two theories which have been utilized in training programs are the Theory of Planned Behavior (Ajzen, 2011), and its precursor, the Theory of Reasoned Action (Fishbein, 1979). Second, decision making and processing theories describe the different ways of processing stimuli in training and learning environment. One of the most widely used theories in this category is the Elaboration Likelihood Model (Petty and Cacioppo, 1986). Third, the motivational design has been used to identify benefits, barriers, engagement, and feedbacks during training to help improve the level of self-efficacy among trainees and to encourage them to devote more resources toward their goals (Ryan and Deci, 2000). A widely used example that has been used in this area to improve existing learning design is the self-regulation theory (SRL) (Schunk and Zimmerman, 1994).

Although the attitudinal, retentional, and motivational process can be used with different methods for behavioral changes, interventions with existing education and training programs are still the primary methods utilized to improve food safety behavior. Food safety trainers and educators are applying behavioral modeling theories to empirical interventions to improve food safety training programs (Arendt et al., 2014; Howells et al., 2008; Pilling et al., 2008; Roberts et al, 2008).

8.2   ATTITUDINAL PROCESSING THEORIES

An attitude is a relatively enduring set of beliefs, feelings, and behavioral tendencies toward an object, group, or event (Hogg and Vaughan, 2005). Ajzen (2011) defines it as a favorable or unfavorable evaluation of behavior. Attitudes can positively or negatively affect a person's behavior, regardless of whether the individual is aware of the effects (Ajzen, 2011).

In the food safety arena, attitudes toward food safety training programs have been the focus of several research studies. Howes et al. (1996) noted that attitude would have a significant impact on the success of food safety programs and the decrease in foodborne illness outbreaks. Cochran-Yantis et al. (1996) reported that managers who viewed food safety training favorable were more likely to score higher on inspection scores than those with a less favorable attitude.

The determinants of specific behaviors are guided largely by the assumption that and individual's behavior follows reasonably from their beliefs, attitudes, and intentions. Research concerning the influence of these attitudes on behavior is primarily conducted within this conceptual framework. Ajzen has pioneered this research and helped to develop two prominent theoretical approaches, the theory of reasoned action and the theory of planned behavior. Both theories explain the link between attitude and behavior as a controlled and planned process.

8.2.1   Theory of Reasoned Action

The theory of reasoned action (TRA) is a classic persuasion model of psychology. First developed by Fishbein (1967) it was directly descended from previous research on attitude formation. The TRA suggests that attitudes are a function of beliefs, using behavioral intention to mediate the function of two factors, behavioral beliefs and subjective norms (Ajzen and Fishbein, 1977, 1980, 1988). Behavioral beliefs are those beliefs that motivate a person's attitude toward the behavior. While subjective norms refer to the social pressure to perform or not to perform the behavior.

Medeiros et al. (2004) used food safety knowledge and attitude scales guided by the TRA to understand and improve consumer food handling behavior and related educational programs. The researchers used the theory to develop food safety knowledge and attitude scales based on food-handling guidelines. Utilizing a pretest/posttest design to measure both knowledge and attitudes among participants in low-income nutrition education programs and college students, the researchers were able to determine that the individual's attitude was predictive of the participant's behavior.

Clayton et al. (2003) utilized beliefs, attitudes, and knowledge among consumers to determine the underlying factors influencing consumers' implementation of specific food safety practices in the home. Their results suggest that measures of perceived barriers risk may provide developers of food safety intervention materials with more useful information compared with measures of knowledge or intention alone.

8.2.2 Theory of Planned Behavior

The theory of planned behavior (TPB) was based on the TRA, the difference between the two theories is the inclusion of perceived behavioral control in the TPB (Ajzen, 1985). Perceived behavioral control refers to people's perceptions of how difficult it would be to perform or not to perform a given behavior. Barriers exist because behaviors generally require prerequisite knowledge, resources, and/or cooperation of others (Gilbert et al., 1998). The TRA would reasonably explain behavioral intention for any behavior not requiring prerequisite knowledge, resources, or social cooperation. However, some behaviors may require these to fully perform the behavior (Liska, 1984). For example, in the food safety context, if an employee intends to use a thermometer to check the end-point cooking temperatures of a food item, but the management of the operation does not purchase thermometers, the employee would not be able to complete the behavior. According to the TPB, if people evaluate the suggested behavior as positive in attitude, and they received social pressure to perform the behavior from significant others (families or peers), and they do not perceive a high degree of behavioral control, they are more than likely to complete the behavior. A strong correlation of attitudes, subjective norms, and perceived behavioral control toward behavioral intention has been confirmed in many studies (McEachan et al., 2011).

Roberts et al. (2008) utilized the theory of planned behavior to study food safety training and foodservice employee's knowledge and behavior to assess the effect of training on food safety knowledge and behavior. Their sample consisted of 31 restaurants in three Midwestern states. Their sample consisted of 402 employees (242 pretraining and 160 posttraining). Their results indicated that knowledge alone was not sufficient to bring about changes in behavior. They noted that increasing knowledge does not ensure that behaviors will change, as demonstrated by the high scores on knowledge and low percentages on corresponding behaviors.

York et al. (2009) used the TPB framework to guide a focus group and survey to eliciting restaurant employees' beliefs about performing three critical food safety behaviors (handwashing, using thermometers, cleaning, and sanitizing work surfaces). The results indicated restaurant employees understood that customers, employees, managers, and health inspectors care about them practicing proper food safety behaviors. The employees recognized the advantages of proper food safety include fewer illnesses, reduced cross-contamination, and improved employee hygiene and environment. In addition, the employees recognized that following proper food safety practices would help improve food quality and enhance customer satisfaction. The disadvantages to identified include taking time away from other tasks and just being an inconvenience, in general.

8.3 DECISION-MAKING AND PROCESSING THEORIES

Decision making and processing theories propose models to help select and sequence content in a way that will optimize attainment of training and learning goals, by simplifying the content or task. This simplification also recognizes different guidelines may be needed for various instructional situations. This also shifts the instruction from teacher-centered and content-centered to learner-centered, creating new ways to sequence instruction and training. By organizing contents from general and broader ideas to detailed and narrower ideas, the effectiveness of instruction will increase. It is intended for medium to complex types of cognitive and psychomotor learning (Reigeluth, 1999).

There are three main methods to achieve a gradual reduction in ideas, conceptual elaboration sequence, theoretical elaboration sequence, and simplifying conditions sequence (Reigeluth, 2013). These models help assist instructors to achieve cognitive and psychomotor learning, similar to what would occur within a food safety training. One of the common methods used in this approach includes the elaboration likelihood model (ELM), also known as the due processing theory of persuasion (Chen and Chaiken, 1999).

8.3.1 Elaboration Likelihood Model

The ELM is a dual process theory describing the change of attitudes. Originally developed by Petty and Cacioppo (1986), the model aims to explain different ways of processing stimuli and how they impact attitude changes. The authors proposed a dual-process approach to persuasion, the central route, and the peripheral route. The central route generally results from a learner's careful and thoughtful consideration of the true merits of the information presented in support of an argument. The peripheral route induces behavioral change without the learner's careful consideration of the true merits of the information presented. In empirical testing, the central route has proven to be more consistent, accessible, enduring, and resistant than the peripheral route (O'Keefe, 2008). The greater the accessibility of attitudes and attitude-relevant information, whether it is through central or the peripheral route, the greater that learners report the same attitude over time, thus they are more inclined to act on their attitudes and beliefs.

Advantages of the ELM include the integration of scope and sequence into a coherent design, facilitating prototyping in the instructional process, and empowering learners and trainees to make scope and sequence decisions during the training and learning process. Limitations of elaboration models include the fact that often, the instruction does not address the learners' prior knowledge. In addition, the structure is focused on conceptual, procedural, and theoretical design, thus it does not accommodate a "real-life" learning environment.

Several authors have suggested the use of elaboration likelihood models to communicate to those at higher risk for foodborne disease the microbiological hazards and nutrition risks through a central, information-processing route (Buffer et al., 2012; Medeiros and Buffer, 2012). Fischer et al. (2005) proposed a transdisciplinary approach, like the elaboration likelihood models to analyze food risk, through the integration of social and natural sciences to provide the most effective way to improve the consumer health associated with foodborne illnesses. Frewer (2000) has raised the need to communicate to the public and consumers about food safety risks effectively.

Abbot et al. (2012) developed campaign materials for a university campus-based food safety program for young adults. Guided by the ELM, the researchers tailored salient messages for college students, and implemented and evaluated students on eight university campuses. Results indicated that the campaign significantly increased self-ratings of food safety knowledge and skill, food safety self-efficacy, food handling, and reported handwashing behaviors. The authors argued that developing media messaging specifically for unique populations is key to ensuring success of communication to target audiences.

Medeiros and Buffer (2012) assessed 327 registered dietitians' current food safety knowledge by measuring general and pathogen knowledge, food safety training, and information channels. Using the dual processing theory to help develop the survey, results indicated pathogen knowledge differed between those who taught and those who did not teach patients food safety, and food safety information was not in-depth enough to fully understand the implications. Kim and Paek (2009) also explored how individuals process messages in the context of genetically modified foods to change their attitudes and how the persuasion process varies across types of motives. Guided by the dual processing theory, the researchers identified the respondents through either the heuristic or the systematic mode and argued the attitude toward the genetically modified food message may be applied to various risk management and communication methods in the food safety context.

8.4   THE ELEMENTS OF MOTIVATION

The traditional motivation design integrates well with food safety training and instructional design processes. Teachers and trainers frequently use motivation models to integrate motivational tactics into their instruction, incorporating educational psychological approached. For example, self-regulation theory that provides a simple, straightforward, heuristic approach to increase the motivation and effectiveness of food safety training programs. The SLR also provides a practical framework, which can be expanded and generalized to a range of foodservice entities. These theories help teachers and training designers incorporate motivational objectives, simulate reproduction identification and tactics, and develop effective evaluations to test the effectiveness of the training (Reiser and Dempsey, 2007).

Motivational design outlines four principle strategies to improve instruction and training: (1) attention elements used to arouse and sustain curiosity and interest during the training, (2) relevance elements that link to the trainees' needs, interests, and motives, (3) confidence elements that help the trainee develop a positive expectation for successful achievement, and (4) satisfaction elements that provide extrinsic and intrinsic reinforcement of the reproduction endeavor. Some of the obvious advantages of incorporating these theories include the selection and application of motivation strategies and selections. Some of the weakness include the effectiveness of the motivation messaging, the process is time consuming, and avoidance behavior sometimes exhibited by trainees (Greenwald, 1968; Reigeluch, 1999; Reigeluch, 2013).

8.4.1   Self-regulatory Learning

Self-regulatory learning theories describe the process by which one takes control of and evaluates learning and behavior. Originally based on the work of Bandura (1986, 2011), but extensively improved by Pintrich (2000) and Zimmerman (1990, 2000), self-regulatory learning theories emphasize self-direction and control by the learner (Paris and Paris, 2001). These theories elaborate on the forethought, performance, and reflection phases of learning. Zimmerman (2000) notes that as learning conditions are consistently changing, the performance control and feedback mechanisms provide trainees feedback to adjust their efforts.

In the food safety context, York et al. (2009) showed that the lack of self-regulatory processes and managerial reinforcement was crucial to ensuring food safety regulations are followed. One contributing factor appears to be a lack of dedication to food safety. Restaurant managers also indicate that they would be more likely to institute food safety policies if they had more time, money, and employee interest (Roberts and Sneed, 2003).

Kivela and Kivela (2005) studied the self-regulatory and self-directed learning skills in a traditional undergraduate teaching curriculum including food safety and hygiene among Hong Kong students. Results suggest that most students appreciate a self-directed approach to learning, indicating significant perceptual differences between the preintervention and postintervention scores.

8.5   BEHAVIOR CHANGE AND FOOD SAFETY TRAINING EVALUATION

Education and training are the focus of many food safety intervention and programs. However, research suggests that the impacts of food handler training programs are inconsistent, and program evaluation is rarely conducted (Almanza and Nesmith, 2004; Roberts et al., 2008). Furthermore, the current instruction targeting only knowledge results in little changes to actual practices. Yiannas (2016) states that the limitations of focusing entirely on training knowledge and lecture suggest that it is just one factor of a good organization. Instead, conscientious administrators provide training on food safety with proper evaluation tools, remove barriers during instruction, and are mindful that the most important reason to educate and train food safety is to influence behavior.

Food safety behavior and training are consistently being evaluated during the training process. For effective instruction and training to occur, a learned or trained skill has to be transferable to relevant situations and to be maintained over time. Otherwise, the original instruction or training has failed. Transfer of food safety knowledge and generalization of the learned behavior will allow the learned skill or principle to be applied in these new situations.

In order for food safety training and behavior change to be successful, instructors must focus on key elements when designing food safety training and reinforce these elements during the evaluation process. Behavior change theories and intervention design have a considerable impact on a comprehensive training program, such as how training and models are presented, how theories are used in food safety education, how training transfer to the outcomes of job behavior, and what current evaluation criterions are adopted and implemented.

KEYWORDS

- food safety
- motivation
- behavior change
- training
- decision-making
- attitude
- norms
- behavioral control

REFERENCES

Abbot, J. M.; Policastro, P.; Bruhn, C.; Schaffner, D. W.; Byrd-Bredbenner, C. Development and Evaluation of a University Campus–Based Food Safety Media Campaign for Young Adults. *J. Food Prot.* **2012,** *75* (6), 1117–1124.

Ajzen, I. *From Intentions to Actions: A Theory of Planned Behavior;* Springer: Heidelberg, Berlin, 1985, pp 11–39.

Ajzen, I. Theory of Planned Behavior. *Handbook Theory of Social Psychology;* Sage: Thousand Oaks, CA, 2011; Vol. 1, p 438.

Ajzen, I,; Fishbein, M. Attitude-behavior Relations: A Theoretical Analysis and Review of Empirical Research. *Psychological Bulletin* **1977,** *84,* 888–918.

Ajzen, I.; Fishbein, M. *Understanding Attitudes and Predicting Social Behavior;* Prentice Hall: Englewood Cliffs, NJ, 1980.

Ajzen, I.; Fishbein, M. *Theory of Reasoned Action - Theory of Planned Behavior;* University of South Florida: Tampa, FL, 1988.

Almanza, B. A.; Nesmith, M. S. Food Safety Certification Regulations in the United States. *J. Environ. Health* **2004,** *66* (9), 10.

Arendt, S. W.; Roberts, K. R.; Strohbehn, C.; Arroyo, P. P.; Ellis, J.; Meyer, J. Motivating Foodservice Employees to Follow Safe Food Handling Practices: Perspectives from a Multigenerational Workforce. *J. Human Res. Hosp. Tourism* 2014; *13* (4), 323–349. DOI: 10.1080/15332845.2014.888505.

Bandura, A. *Social Foundations of Thought and Action: A Social Cognitive Theory;* Prentice-Hall: Upper Saddle River, NJ, 1986.

Bandura, A. Social Cognitive Theory. *Handbook of Social Psychological Theories;* Sage Publications: Thousand Oaks, CA, 2011; pp 349–373

Belasco, W. J. *Appetite for Change: How the Counterculture Took on the Food Industry;* Cornell University Press: Ithaca, NY, 2014.

Blume, B. D.; Ford, J. K.; Baldwin, T. T.; Huang, J. L. Transfer of Training: A Meta-analytic Review. *J. Manag.* 2010, *36* (4), 1065–1105.

Bosman, A.; Brent, P.; Cocconcelli, P. S.; Conole, G.; Gombert, D.; Hensel, A.; Zilliacus, J. Expertise for the Future: Learning and Training in the Area of Food Safety Risk Assessment. *Eur. Food Safety Authority J.* **2016,** *14* (S1), 10. DOI:10.2903/j.efsa.2016. s0503.

Buffer, J. L.; Medeiros, L. C.; Kendall, P.; Schroeder, M.; Sofos, J. Health Professionals' Knowledge and Understanding about Listeria Monocytogenes Indicates a Need for Improved Professional Training. *J. Food Prot.* **2012,** *75* (7), 1310–1316.

Buzby, J. C.; Frenzen, P. D.; Rasco, B. Product Liability and Microbial Foodborne Illness. *Agricultural Economic.* **2001,** 799. Retrieved from: http://ageconsearch.umn.edu/ bitstream/34059/1/ae010799.pdf

Bryan, F. L. Hazard Analysis Critical Control Point (HACCP) Systems for Retail Food and Restaurant Operations. *J. Food Prot.* **1990,** *53,* 978–983.

Casey, R., Cook, C. Assessment of a Foodservice Management Sanitation Course. *J. Environ. Health* 1979, *41* (5), 281–284.

Centers for Disease Control and Prevention. *Estimates of Foodborne Illness in the United States;* 2016a. Retrieved from: https://www.cdc.gov/foodborneburden/estimates-overview.html

Centers for Disease Control and Prevention. Foodborne Outbreak Online Database (FOOD tool) 2016b. Retrieved from: http://wwwn.cdc.gov/foodborneoutbreaks/

Chen, S.; Chaiken, S. (1999). The Heuristic-systematic Model in its Broader Context. *Dual-process Theories Soc. Psychol.* **1999,** *15,* 73–96.

Clayton, D. A.; Griffith, C. J.; Price, P. An Investigation of the Factors Underlying Consumers' Implementation of Specific Food Safety Practices. *Br. Food J.* **2003**, *105* (7), 434–453.

Cochran-Yantis, D.; Belo, P.; Giampaoli, J.; McProud, L.; Everly, V.; Gans, J. Attitudes and Knowledge of Food Safety Among Santa Clara County, California Restaurant Operators. *J. Foodserv. Syst.* **1996**, *9*, 117–128.

Decker, P. J.; Nathan, B. R. *Behavior Modeling Training: Principles and applications;* Praeger: New York, NY, 1985.

Fischer, A. R.; De Jong, A. E.; De Jonge, R.; Frewer, L. J.; Nauta, M. J. Improving Food Safety in the Domestic Environment: The Need for a Transdisciplinary Approach. *Risk Anal.* **2005**, *25* (3), 503–517.

Fishbein, M. A Consideration of Beliefs and their Role in Attitude Measurement. *Readings in Attitude Theory and Measurement;* New York, NY: Wiley, 1967, pp 257–266.

Fishbein M. A Theory of Reasoned Action: Some Applications and Implications. *Nebraska Symposium on Motivation. Nebraska Symposium on Motivation,* 1979, Vol. *27*, pp 65–116.

Food Marketing Institute Research. *U.S. Grocery Shopper Trends 2015: Executive Summary.* Crystal City, VA: Author, 2015. Retrieved from: http://www.fmi.org/docs/default-source/document-share/fmitrends15-exec-summ-06-02-15.pdf

Fox. W. M. *Behavior Modeling Training for Developing Supervisory Skills;* Information Age: Charlotte, NC, 2009.

Frewer, L. Risk Perception and Risk Communication About Food Safety Issues. *Nutrition Bulletin* **2000**, *25* (1), 31–33.

Gilbert, D. T.; Fiske, S. T.; Lindzey, G., Eds.; *The Handbook of Social Psychology;* 4th ed; McGraw Hill: New York, 1998.

Greenwald, A. G. Cognitive Learning, Cognitive Response to Persuasion, and Attitude Change. In *Psychological Foundations of Attitudes;* Greenwald, A. G., Brock, T. C., Ostrom, T. M., Eds; Academic Press: New York, 1968.

Hogg, M. A.; Vaughan, G. M. *Social Psychology;* Person: Harlow, England, 2005.

Howells, A. D.; Roberts, K. R.; Shanklin, C. W.; Pilling, V. K.; Brannon, L. A.; Barrett, B. B. Restaurant Employees' Perceptions of Barriers to Three Food Safety Practices. *J. Am. Diet. Assoc.* **2008**, *108* (8), 1345–1349. DOI: 10.1016/j.jada.2008.05.010.

Howes, M.; McEwen, S.; Griffiths, M.; Harris, L. Food Handler Certification by Home Study: Measuring Changes in Knowledge and Behavior. *Dairy, Food Environ. Sanit.* **1996**, *16* (11), 737–744.

Kim, J.; Paek, H. J. Information Processing of Genetically Modified Food Messages Under Different Motives: An Adaptation of the Multiple-Motive Heuristic-Systematic Model. *Risk Anal.* **2009**, *29* (12), 1793–1806.

Kivela, J.; Kivela, R. J. Student Perceptions of an Embedded Problem-based Learning Instructional Approach in a Hospitality Undergraduate Programme. *Int. J. Hosp. Manag.* **2005**, *24* (3), 437–464.

Liska, A. E. A Critical Examination of the Causal Structure of the Fishbein/Ajzen Attitude-Behavior Model. *Soc. Psychol. Q.* **1984**, *47* (1) 61–74.

Lofstedt, R. Communicating Food Risks in an Era of Growing Public Distrust: Three Case Studies. *Risk Anal.* **2013**, *33* (2), 192–202.

McEachan, R. R. C.; Conner, M.; Taylor, N. J.; Lawton, R. J. Prospective Prediction of Health-related Behaviours with the Theory of Planned Behaviour: A meta-analysis. *Health Psychol. Rev.* **2011**, *5* (2), 97–144.

McKenzie, D.; Woodruff, C. What Are We Learning from Business Training and Entrepreneurship Evaluations around the Developing World? *The World Bank Res. Obs.* **2013**, *29* (1), 48–82. Doi: 10.1093/wbro/lkt007

Mathias, R. G.; Sizio, R.; Hazelwood, A.; Cocksedge, W. The Effects of Inspection Frequency and Food Handler Education on Restaurant Inspection Violations. *Canadian J. Public Health* **1995**, *86* (1), 46–50.

Medeiros, L. C.; Buffer, J. Current Food Safety Knowledge of Registered Dietitians. *Food Protect. Trends* 2012, *32* (11), 688–696.

Medeiros, L. C.; Hillers, V. N.; Chen, G.; Bergmann, V.; Kendall, P.; Schroeder, M. Design and Development of Food Safety Knowledge and Attitude Scales for Consumer Food Safety Education. *J. Am. Diet. Assoc.* **2004**, *104* (11), 1671–1677.

O'Keefe, D. J. Elaboration Likelihood Model. *Int. EncyclopediaCommun.* **2008**, *4*, 1475–1480.

Paris, S.; Paris, A. Classroom Applications of Research on Self-regulated Learning. *Edu. Psychol.* **2001**, *36* (2), 89–101.

Petty, R. E.; Cacioppo, J. T. *The Elaboration Likelihood Model of Persuasion;* New York, NY: Springer, 1986; pp 1–24.

Pintrich, P. R. Multiple Goals, Multiple Pathways: The Role of Goal Orientation in Learning and Achievement. *J. Edu. Psychol.* **2000**, *92* (3), 544.

Pilling, V. K.; Brannon, L. A.; Shanklin, C. W.; Howells, A. D.; Roberts, K. R. Identifying Specific Beliefs to Target to Improve Restaurant Employees' Intentions for Performing Three Important Food Safety Behaviors. *J. American Diet. Assoc.* **2008**, *108* (6), 991–997. DOI: 10.1016/j.jada.2008.03.014.

Powell, S. C.; Attwell, R. W.; Massey, S. H. The Impact of Training on Knowledge and Standards of Food Hygiene: A Pilot Study. *Int. J. Environ. Health Res.* **1997**, *7*, 329–334.

Reigeluth, C. M. What is Instructional-design Theory and How is it Changing. *Instructional-Design Theories and Models: A New Paradigm of Instructional Theory;* Lawrence Erlbaum Associates: Mahwah, NJ, 1999; Vol. 2, 5–29.

Reigeluth, C. M. *Instructional-design Theories and Models: A New Paradigm of Instructional Theory;* Abingdon, UK: Routledge, 2013; Vol. 2.

Reiser, R. A.; Dempsey, J. V. *Trends and Issues in Instructional Technology and Design.* Pearson: Upper Saddle River, NJ, 2007.

Riggins, L. D.; Roberts, K. R.; Barrett E. B. Status of Prerequisite and HACCP Programs Implementation. *J. Foodserv. Manag. Res.* **2005**, *1* (1). Retrieved from: http://fsmec.org/wp-content/uploads/2011/09/RigginsRobertsBarrett2005.pdf

Roberts, K. R.; Barrett, B. B.; Howells, A. D.; Shanklin, C. W.; Pilling, V. K.; Brannon, L. A. Food Safety Training and Foodservice Employees' Knowledge and Behavior. *Food Protect. Trends* **2008**, *28* (4), 252–260.

Roberts, K. R.; Sneed, P. J. An Assessment of the Status of Prerequisite and HACCP Programs in Iowa Restaurants. *Food Protect. Trends* **2003**, *23* (10), 808–816.

Ryan, R. M.; Deci, E. L. Self-determination Theory and the Facilitation of Intrinsic Motivation, Social Development, and Well-being. *Am. Psychol.* **2000**, *55* (1), 68.

Schunk, D. H.; Zimmerman, B. J. *Self-regulation of Learning and Performance: Issues and Educational Applications;* Routledge: New York, NY, 1994.

Sivaramalingam, B.; Young, I.; Pham, M. T.; Waddell, L.; Greig, J.; Mascarenhas, M.; Papadopoulos, A. Scoping Review of Research on the Effectiveness of Food-Safety Education Interventions Directed at Consumers. *Foodborne Pathog Dis* **2015,** *12* (7), 561–570.

Taylor, P. J.; Russ-Eft, D. F.; Chan, D. W. A Meta-analytic Review of Behavior Modeling Training. *J. Appl. Psychol.* **2005,** *90* (4), 692

Trendsource. 2016 Food Safety in Fast Casual Restaurants. *TrendSource* 2016. Retrieved from: http://trustedinsight.trendsource.com/consumerinsightstudy/2016-consumer-study-food-safety-in-fast-casual-restaurants

U.S. Department of Agriculture, Economic Research Service (2016, November). *Food Prices and Spending.* Retrieved from: http://www.ers.usda.gov/data-products/ag-and-food-statistics-charting-the-essentials/food-prices-and-spending/

Worsfold, D. Eating out: Consumer Perceptions of Food Safety *Int. J. Environ. Health Res.* **2006,** *16* (3), 219–229.

Wright, J.; Feun, L. Foodservice Manager Certification: An Evaluation of its Impact. *J. Environ. Health* **1986,** *49* (1), 12–15.

Yiannas, F. *Food Safety Culture: Creating a Behavior-based Food Safety Management System.* Springer Science & Business Media: New York, NY, 2008.

Yiannas, F. *The Evolution of Food Safety Culture.* In International Association for Food Protection 2016 Annual Meeting. International Association for Food Protection: Des Moines, IA, 2016.

York, V. K.; Brannon, L. A.; Roberts, K. R.; Shanklin, C. W.; Howells, A. D. Using the Theory of Planned Behavior to Elicit Restaurant Employee Beliefs About Food Safety: Using Surveys Versus Focus Groups. *J. Foodserv. Business Res.* **2009,** *12* (2), 180–197.

York, V. K.; Brannon, L. A.; Shanklin, C. W.; Roberts, K. R.; Howells, A. D.; Barrett, E. B. Foodservice Employees Benefit from Interventions Targeting Barriers to Food Safety. *J. Am. Diet. Assoc.* **2009,** *109* (9), 1576–1581. DOI: 10.1016/j.jada.2009.06.370.

Zimmerman, B. J. Self-regulated Learning and Academic Achievement: An Overview. *Edu. Psychol.* **1990,** *25* (1), 3–17.

Zimmerman, M. A. Empowerment Theory. In *Handbook of Community Psychology;* Springer: New York, NY, 2000; pp 43–63.

CHAPTER 9

Consumer Agency and the Ethical Obligations of Foodservice Providers in an Era of Cheap Food, Racial Inequality, and Neoliberal Governance

ROBERT M. CHILES

Pennsylvania State University

*Corresponding author. E-mail: rchiles@psu.edu

ABSTRACT

Political-economic and racial inequalities have systematically disadvantaged the ability of many groups and individuals to participate as equals in the foodservice marketplace. Moreover, the absence of public oversight over the food system has not heralded the disappearance of governance and an upsurge in personal liberty; rather, it has ushered in an era of corporate governance. In drawing attention to each of these issues, I seek to situate the ethical decision-making of policymakers, hospitality managers, and foodservice professionals in social context.

9.1 INTRODUCTION

The modern food system is beset with pressing social issues and challenges: rural development, sustainability, labor conditions, and ethical obligations toward animals, food safety, public health, and social justice, to name a few. What are the ethical responsibilities for foodservice providers and hospitality managers? For Jayson Lusk (2013:78–80), Professor of Agricultural Economics at Oklahoma State University, the answer is clear: their duty is to abide by the law and compete for profit.

Profit-seeking often has a negative connotation, but a surefire way for firms to make profits is to give consumers what they want. Detractors of profit-seeking falsely envision an evil monopolist at work, but the reality is that firms are in fierce competition for business-especially restaurants, which routinely go bust when they cannot supply what the customer wants at a price he is willing to pay... Yes, this kind of world might require more willpower and self-control, but the alternative world of the paternalistic food police would deprive us of the noble act of making a choice when we had the freedom to do otherwise.

In addition to celebrating the principle of consumer sovereignty, Lusk (2013:186–190) moreover argues that the modern food system is liberating, efficient, practical, and cost-effective and that government attempts to meddle with it are both paternalistic and ineffective:

The truth is that we all have different preferences and unique knowledge that cannot be rationally subsumed in a grand food plan. Markets decentralize power and let us each satisfy our desires in unique ways... It is not a perfect system but it is one that has led to the greatest prosperity ever witnessed in human history and has allowed us to feed the world.

While Lusk is certainly correct that there are numerous upsides and advantages to the modern food system as compared to traditional food systems, there are two significant limitations in this view. First, it does not account for how political–economic and racial inequalities have systematically disadvantaged the ability of many groups and individuals to participate as equals in the marketplace. A logical starting point for this discussion concerns two interrelated phenomena which ushered in deep-seated changes with respect to how Americans live, work, and eat: the industrialization of agriculture, the deindustrialization of the workforce, and racial inequality. These historical trends have resulted in a food system that works better for some than it does for others. Second, an absence of public oversight over the food system has not heralded the disappearance of governance and an upsurge in personal liberty; rather, it has ushered in an era of *corporate* governance. In what follows, we examine each of these important historical shifts in turn. We conclude by reflecting upon the ethical implications of these shifts for policymakers, hospitality managers, and foodservice professionals.

9.2 THE INDUSTRIALIZATION OF AGRICULTURE, THE DEINDUSTRIALIZATION OF THE WORKFORCE, AND RACIAL INEQUALITY: SITUATING THE FOODSERVICE AND HOSPITALITY INDUSTRY IN POLITICAL, ECONOMIC, AND HISTORICAL CONTEXT

Traditional food systems can be characterized as small scale, locally based, noncommercial, dependent upon seasons, punctuated by shortages, and reliant upon most members of the population for labor. The industrial revolution would change all of these features. With the acceleration of industrialization came increasing demands for food to feed growing cities, and simultaneous advances in transportation and storage technology gave producers the ability to deliver (Beardsworth and Keil, 1997). Moreover, after agricultural production capacity outstripped demand in the aftermath of World War I, the ensuing "farm crisis" compelled lenders, business leaders, local bankers, and politicians to advocate for rationalist/Fordist modes of agricultural production (Fitzgerald, 2003). Ownership and management of farms would be shifted further and further away from farmers over the coming decades, beginning with corporate monopolies over farmer access to rail transport. The provision of cheap food for urban populations, the decline of smallholder farm viability, and the lure of city life all contributed to a massive demographic transition from rural to urban areas during the 20th century.

Urbanization was also fueled by the "Great Migration" of black families from the rural south to large cities in the North (1916–1970). In order to escape Jim Crow segregation, underemployment, and the economic dead-end of sharecropping, blacks began looking for factory work in Northern cities. This influx would sow the seeds of the black ghetto, a racial institution marked by social isolation and economic vulnerability, where poverty is more concentrated and social and commercial institutions are scarce (Desmond and Emirbayer, 2010).

While many initially did find manufacturing work in the cities, since the 1970s, career opportunities in the service sector have expanded while blue-collar, agricultural, manufacturing, transportation, and construction jobs have disappeared—a phenomenon known as "deindustrialization" (Desmond and Emirbayer; Wilson, 2011). Deindustrialization made the conditions of poverty worse, particularly in the Northeast and Midwest, and America dedicates a smaller percentage of its wealth to antipoverty programs than any other developed country besides Japan (Desmond and Emirbayer, 2010). Deindustrialization was particularly hard on blacks and Puerto Ricans, who were disadvantaged by both institutional as well as interpersonal racism in the service sector labor market (Desmond and Emirbayer, 2010).

Government policy further contributed to the deterioration of the inner city. During this era, the federal government withheld mortgage capital and made it difficult for people in urban areas to purchase their own homes, particularly people in black and European immigrant neighborhoods. Also, federal transportation highway policy subsidized suburban living while dividing urban neighborhoods. Urban force migration also hurt black communities, as did segregated housing projects (Wilson, 2011).

Arguably, the primary cause of continued racial segregation is white preference for racially homogenous neighborhoods and a lack of tolerance (Farley and Squires, 2005). This has profound consequences for people living in the inner cities. Racial segregation concentrates poverty in black neighborhoods, and the addition of class segregation concentrates poverty primarily in poor black neighborhoods (Massey and Denton, 1993). Banks are more likely to offer credit to whites than nonwhites, nonwhites who get mortgage loans often pay higher interest rates, and homes in nonwhite neighborhoods do not accrue as much value as homes in white neighborhoods (Desmond and Emirbayer, 2010). Audit studies indicate the blacks and Hispanics encounter discrimination in one out of every five contacts with a real estate or rental agent (Farley and Squires, 2005). Segregation also has a negative impact on schools, jobs, healthcare, public services, private amenities, wealth, and property values. The cultural impact of these challenges is the perpetuation of prejudice, stereotypes, and racial tension (Farley and Squires, 2005).

The industrialization of agriculture and the deindustrialization of the workforce had major impacts on both the types of foods that people ate, who ate them, how they ate them, and where they ate them. The 20th century witnessed dramatic changes in the time of meals, the availability and number of meals of the day, meal composition, meal temperature, and the availability of substitutes for mass markets. Food took less time to cook at home, and convenience food was now found in multiple places outside the home: fast food restaurants, snack corners, cafeterias (Mennell et al., 1992). Beardsworth and Keil (1997:40) thus observe that "the scientific revolution and its application to the manufacture of new foods sometimes worsened rather than improved the diet of the poor." As further noted by Nestle (2013:19), "Societal changes easily explain why nearly half of all meals are consumed outside the home, a quarter of them as fast food, and the practice of snacking nearly doubled from the mid-1980s to the mid-1990s."

As children eat more and more meals with other caregivers, meals away from home, and processed meals, the influence of marketing and advertising has become increasingly important. According to survey data, the amount of time that children spend watching television correlates with the number of reported requests and purchases of the foods which were advertised (Taras et al., 1989). Experimental data also suggest that when 3–5-year-old children were confronted with otherwise identically prepared foods, they preferred the taste of the foods with a "McDonalds" label to those with a generic label (Robinson et al., 2007)." In a study of top-rated television programming for 12–17 year olds, Powell et al. (2007) noted that food-related ads accounted for 26% of all advertising exposure, with fast food being the most frequently advertised food (23% of food ads). Lastly, in studying 16 hours of children's television, which featured 353 product commercials, Gamble and Cotugna (1999) observed that 27.4% of these commercials were for fast food restaurants.

All of these societal changes have had a particularly marked impact on African American neighborhoods, foodways, and health outcomes, for several reasons. First, low socioeconomic neighborhoods have been associated with a lack of physical activity facilities, a limited access to healthy and affordable food, a decreased likelihood of residents seeking adequate and preventive health care, and potential exposure to environ-mental hazards (Merkin et al., 2007).

Moreover, as observed by Zenk (2007:204), "health risks and resources are spatially and socially structured and African–Americans disproportionately live in economically disadvantaged neighborhoods." Zenk (2007:206) further notes that "Among the most impoverished neighborhoods, distance to the nearest supermarket varied considerably by percentage African–American." Fast food restaurants are especially concentrated in neighborhoods inhabited by minority populations, and race is a bigger predictor of fast food restaurant preferences than age, gender, and income (Wong, 2013). Black audiences are also uniquely targeted by food advertisers. Compared with general market TV programs, black programming showcases more advertising for food products (Powell et al., 2007). Moreover, black programming is more likely to feature advertisements for fast food, meat, candy, and soda, and less likely to feature advertisements for whole grains, fruits and vegetables, and "light and lean" products (Henderson and Kelly, 2005).

Not only do economic arrangements shape the availability and accessibility of different foods, but they also shape historicized narratives of race and class. As noted by Williams-Forson (2007), narratives which articulate blackness as being associated with chicken can be traced back to the days of slavery (when slaves would sell chickens to help make ends meet). Stereotypes of blacks as being passive, loyal, happy-go-lucky "chicken-lovers" became particularly widespread in the aftermath of reconstruction, when white Southerners experienced an economic and cultural identity crisis. Unfortunately, contemporary presentations of blackness frequently (and unwittingly) perpetuate old-time stereotypical narratives by making implicit reference to cultural signifiers.

This raises important ethical questions for food and hospitality service providers. As noted by Nestle (2013:195), "food companies have enormously increased the burden on caretakers to control television viewing, resist requests for food purchases, and teach critical thinking to children whose analytical abilities are not yet developed... marketers depend on caretakers to be too busy to want to deny requests for fast-food meals or snack foods." This problem is compounded by the contextual circumstances of urban life (e.g., racial segregation and poverty), which reinforce and advance health discrepancies through exposure to hazards and maladaptive methods of response (Barondess, 2008). A lack of different menu options in various social settings can potentially sap consumers' sense of efficacy. In short, not only do marginalized populations have more obstacles to overcome, but repeated failures to surmount these obstacles result in a reduced sense of control, fatalism, mistrust, and alienation— thus making it even harder for the marginalized to use what resources they do have—a phenomenon that Ross and Mirkowsky (2003:210) refer to as "the multiplication of despair."

When deciding upon what to eat, consumers face what Fischler (1980:948) has described as "gastro-anomy"—a state of confusion whereby there are no clear-cut social norms and rules for people to follow. Arguably, gastro-anomy is an indirect consequence of a neoliberal governance structure whereby farmers, processors, retailers, foodservice providers, and consumers are largely left to fend for themselves in the marketplace. Given the historical economic challenges and disparities that hospitality providers and customers are facing, several ethical questions demand further exploration. What is the role of the state versus the private sector with respect to producing and providing food in a just and sustainable way? What is the role of the company versus the role of the individual? Ultimately, these questions revolve around issues of governance.

9.3 GOVERNING FOODSERVICE: WHERE DOES ETHICAL RESPONSIBILITY RESIDE?

Drawing on the work of Rose (1999), Guthman (2007) observes that governance involves "the employment of tools that indirectly encourage subjects to act in particular ways, rather than through 'command and control' or so-called coercive forms of regulation." As noted by Guthman, there is thus a key distinction between *government* ("the power and role of the state") and *governance* ("non-state mechanisms of regulation"). Governance scholarship has come into increasing prominence with the emergence of multiple historical and political–economic trends. With these changes, a growing chorus of scholars has increasingly sought to problematize the boundaries and internal mechanisms that define state and market in increasingly globalized societies. Relevant trends include the consolidation of corporate ownership of the food system, globalization of supply chains, the shift in power from producers to retailers, the transition from Fordist consumption (as based on quantity, standardization, and cost) to post-Fordist consumption (as based on quality and differentiated/niche markets), and public concerns about food system oversight following repeated food safety scares (Marsden, 2000; Konefal et al., 2005; Guthman, 2007; Busch, 2011; Fuchs et al., 2011).

Corporate takeover of the food system has involved the "emergence of entirely new sectors of production, new ways of providing financial services, new markets, and above all, greatly intensified rates of commercial, technological, and organizational innovation" [Harvey, 1989: 147 as cited by Konefal et al. (2005)]. Moreover, the emergence of conventions and standards were essential to the process of globalization, as uniformity is required for mass production (Konefal et al., 2005).

Currently, we live in a *neoliberal* era where the government has relatively weak influence on many different aspects of food system regulation. For McCarthy and Prudham (2004), "neoliberalism stands for a complex assemblage of ideological commitments, discursive representations, and institutional practices, all propagated by highly specific class alliances and organized that multiple geographical scales." For neoliberalism's proponents, growth should be pursued above all else, market logic is real and natural, government ought to be privatized, and opponents of the neoliberal regime ought to be ignored/removed. The initial goal of the neoliberalists was to tear down government regulations, break unions, privatize public spheres, slash government budgets, and "rollback" state intervention in all forms. More recently; however, neoliberalism has sought to more actively construct new state infrastructures and "roll in" multinational institutions of economic governmentality (Peck and Tickell, 2002). In order to further fill the regulatory vacuum in the wake of roll-back neolibralism, "roll-out" neoliberalism involved replacing public governance with voluntary and/ or private governance (as fulfilled by corporations, NGOs, civil society, etc.) (Peck and Tickell, 2002). This meant a new set of rules, regulations, and governing institutions (Peck, 2002; Guthman, 2007; Busch, 2011). As noted by Busch (2011), "neoliberalism is not about deregulation, but about shifting from regulation *of* the market toward regulation for the market." Here, Heynen and Robbins (2005) propose four pillars of neoliberal environmental governance: governance, privatization, enclosure (i.e., excluding certain parties from particular high-quality markets), and valuation. Guthman (2007) also adds devolution (whereby regulatory authority is delegated down to the consumers, who in turn are told stories about what types of qualities and values are most important).

Among the most significant trends in the neoliberal era has been the trend toward private labeling and third-party certification. Given stiff price competition and the natural limits to the total quantity of food that consumers can buy, private standards have been particularly important in helping grocers, foodservice, and hospitality companies to expand their market share by focusing on quality and value-added products (Busch, 2000, 2011; Konefal et al., 2005; Murdoch and Miele, 1999). Perhaps more significantly, private labeling schemes and third-party certification has been used to legitimate private food system governance. Sociologists of food and agriculture have taken particular interest in how private standards and conventions have come to replace the traditional role of the state (as per roll-out neoliberalism).

Can private labeling standards help foodservice providers and consumers to support ethical production and consumption systems? The evidence is mixed. Allen and Kovach (2000) argue that the organic food label can potentially de-fetishize food commodities. Barham (2002) also defends "value-based" labeling and standards as a social movement which brings transparency to neoliberal capitalism while institutionalizing private values. Barham (2003) also argues that labels which indicate place can help to counteract the forces of globalization by protecting regional economies. Busch (2000, 2011) has also acknowledged that private standards and niche marketing have arguably been a boon to consumers, who now have greater options, lower prices, and expanded access to safer and higher quality products (provided that they can afford them).

Critiques of private standards concern the implications of these schemes with respect to neoliberalism, consumer responsibility, small-scale farming, food safety, democratic legitimacy, and sustainability. Guthman (2007:456), for example, is skeptical of the ability of labels to catalyze progressive change. She argues that "these labels not only concede the market as the locus of regulation, but in keeping with neoliberalism's fetish of market mechanisms, they employ tools designed to create markets where none previously existed." Guthman (2007:465) further contends that the "kinder, gentler" roll-out neoliberalism is further enabled by "state-led encouragement of civil society institutions [that] provide erstwhile retracted services and other compensatory mechanisms." Busch (2011) accordingly concludes that many NGOs have placed too much faith in certification schemes, when what is needed is that they demand fundamental institutional change in trade governance and legal frameworks. Fuchs et al. (2011) caution, however, that public governance can potentially be just as bad if citizens continue to be excluded from decision making.)

Guthman (2007) also remains critical of the way in which, through devolution, regulatory control is placed into the hands of consumers at the cash register—not only do labels provide information of questionable quantity and quality to consumers, but consumers vary widely in their background understanding of these types of issues. Konefal et al. (2005) agree, noting that food consumption choices remain firmly linked to social class, consumers are faced against powerful public relations industries, consumers are excluded from the decision-making processes of private standard-setting bodies, standards often lacked transparency, and questions remain as to whether explicitly political consumers are democratically legitimate representatives of the overall population.

Ongoing frustration and disenchantment with mass-produced "alternative" foods have catalyzed interest in the local foods movement, a loosely affiliated conglomeration of farmer's markets, community-supported agriculture (CSA) vendors, farm-to-table initiatives, food activists, and upscale consumers. Among its proponents, a localized food system is more self-reliant, fresher, and does a better job of integrated the market with the local community (Kloppenburg et al., 1996). Unfortunately; however, the local food movement has often focused on market potential, economic outcomes, consumerism, and celebrity to the detriment of community empowerment, citizenship, racial equity, place building, and sustainability (DeLind, 2011).

9.4 CONCLUSIONS

"In an era of stagnant wages, dystopian politics and cultural anomie, eating indulgent if unhealthful food has become a last redoubt of enjoyment for Americans who don't feel they have much control in their lives. Higher incomes and better educations — in the classroom, not on the menu board — will do more to solve the obesity epidemic than mandating the disclosure of calorie counts. Before we blame the poor and the overweight for their inability to manage their budgets or control their appetites, we might want to think not only about the foods they encounter in the supermarket and on television but about a culture that relies ever more on unhealthy foods to breathe meaning and purpose into everyday life."

—Martin Bruegel

Market activity is not steered exclusively by the logic of commerce— it is also guided by history and culture. Moreover, consumer tastes and preferences are shaped and influenced by social limitations (Bordieu, 1984). Lastly, for hospitality managers, there is a big difference between selling food to consumers who have entered into a setting through their own presumed volition and selling to those who clearly have not made any such choice. There are differing levels of consumer choice, intention, and constraint at different types of eating establishments, for example, restaurants, corporate lunchrooms, school cafeterias, hotel offerings, prison dining halls, and military mess halls.

In recent years, consumers have increasingly asserted their demands and desires for different lifestyle choices and identities; the consumer landscape has fragmented, and companies have rushed to offer a multitude of product options. This subsequent "quality turn" has fundamentally transitioned the agri-food system from the all-out mass production of increasingly cheaper goods toward the ever-expanding provision of specialized goods with varying levels of quality. The net result, however, has essentially been the emergence of two food systems—a system which provides a broad array of choices for the wealthy, and a smaller array of choices for the poor.

This raises important ethical questions for policymakers, foodservice professionals, and consumers:

(1) What do people "demand?" Is there an ethical obligation to provide consumers with the food that they appear to want? Is providing the food that people enjoy a prosocial behavior?

(2) What does socially responsible foodservice provision look like? Does it involve more than meeting "demand" and targeting consumer market opportunities?

(3) Do government agencies or private foodservice providers have an ethical obligation to help address historical inequalities in the food and agricultural system? Does that obligation vary according to venue (schools, hospitals, restaurants)?

(4) How can foodservice providers responsibly engage with vulnerable and underserved populations?

Reasoned and lasting solutions to these challenges will require inclusive processes that bring multiple stakeholders to the table. Indeed, given that sustainability and social justice are pathways rather than final destinations, the deliberative process is perhaps the most critical element of the solution.

204 Financial Decision-Making in the Foodservice Industry

KEYWORDS

- sociology
- food ethics
- political economy
- racial inequality
- neoliberalism
- foodservice
- food history

REFERENCES

Allen, P.; Kovach, M. The Capitalist Composition of Organic: The Potential of Markets in Fulfilling the Promise of Organic Agriculture. *Agric. Human Values* **2000,** *17* (3), 221.
Barham, E. Towards a Theory of Values-Based Labeling. *Agric. Human Values* **2002,** *19* (4), 349.
Barondess, J. A. Health Through the Urban Lens. *J. Urban Health* **2008,** *85* (5), 787–801.
Beardsworth, A.; Keil, T. *Sociology on the Menu: An Invitation to the Study of Food and Society*; Routledge: AI&SI, London, 1997.
Bourdieu, P. *Distinction: A Social Critique of the Judgement of Taste*; Harvard University Press: Cambridge, MA, 1984.
Bruegel, M. *The Science of Calorie Information*, Sept 9, 2012. Retrieved from http://www.nytimes.com/2012/09/19/opinion/the-science-of-calorie-information.html
Busch, L. The Moral Economy of Grades and Standards. *J. Rural Stud.* **2000,** *16* (3), 273. DOI: 10.1016/S0743-0167(99)00061-3.
Busch, L. The Private Governance of Food: Equitable Exchange or Bizarre Bazaar? *Agric. Human Values* **2011,** *28* (3), 345–352.
Delind, L. Are Local Food and the Local Food Movement Taking us Where We Want to Go? Or are We Hitching Our Wagons to The Wrong Stars? *Agric. Human Values* **2011,** *28* (2), 273.
Desmond, M.; Emirbayer, M. *Racial Domination, Racial Progress: The Sociology of Race in America*; Mcgraw-Hill: New York, NY, 2010.
Farley, J. E.; Squires, G. D. Fences and Neighbors: Segregation in 21st-Century America. *Contexts,* **2005,** *4* (1), 33–39.
Fischler, C. Food Habits, Social Change and the Nature/Culture Dilemma. *Inf. Int. Soc. Sci. Council.* **1980,** *19* (6), 937–953.
Fitzgerald, D. *Every Farm a Factory: The Industrial Ideal in American Agriculture*;Yale University Press: New Haven, 2003.
Fuchs, D.; Kalfagianni, A.; Havinga, T. Actors in Private Food Governance: The Legitimacy of Retail Standards and Multistakeholder Initiatives with Civil Society Participation. *Agric. Human Values* **2011,** *28* (3), 353–367.

Gamble, M.; Cotugna, N. A Quarter Century of TV Food Advertising Targeted at Children. *Amer. J. Health Behav.* **1999**, *23* (4), 261–267.

Guthman, J. The Polanyian Way? Voluntary Food Labels as Neoliberal Governance. *Antipode* **2007**, *39* (3), 456–478.

Harvey, D. *The Condition of Postmodernity: An Enquiry Into the Origins of Cultural Change*; Basil Blackwell: Oxford, 1989.

Heffernan, W. D. In *Concentration of Ownership and Control in Agriculture*. Hungry for Profit: The Agribusiness Threat to Farmers, Food, and the Environment, 2000; pp 61–76.

Henderson, V. R.; Kelly, B. Food Advertising in the Age of Obesity: Content Analysis of Food Advertising on General Market and African American Television. *J. Nutr. Educ. Behav.* **2005**, *37* (4), 191–196.

Heynen, N.; Robbins, P. The Neoliberalization of Nature: Governance, Privatization, Enclosure and Valuation. *Capital. Nat. Soc.* **2005**, *16* (1), 5–8.

Kloppenburg, J.; Hendrickson, J.; Stevenson, G. W. Coming into the Foodshed. *Agric. Human Values* **1996**, *13* (3), 33–42.

Konefal, J.; Mascarenhas, M.; Hatanaka, M. Governance in the Global Agro-Food System: Backlighting the Role of Transnational Supermarket Chains. *Agric. Human Values* **2005**, *22* (3), 291. DOI:10.1007/S10460-005-6046-0.

Lusk, J. *The Food Police: A Well-Fed Manifesto About the Politics of Your Plate*, 2013.

Marsden, T. Food Matters and the Matter of Food: Towards a New Food Governance? *Sociol. Ruralis* **2000**, *40* (1), 20–29.

Massey, D. S.; Denton, N. A. *American Apartheid: Segregation and the Making of the Underclass*; Harvard University Press, 1993.

Mccarthy, J.; Prudham, S. Neoliberal Nature and the Nature of Neoliberalism. *Geoforum* **2004**, *35* (3), 275–283.

Mennell, S.; Murcott, A.; Van Otterloo, A. H. The Sociology of Food: Eating, Diet and Culture, 1992.

Merkin, S. S.; Roux, A. V. D.; Coresh, J.; Fried, L. F.; Jackson, S. A.; Powe, N. R. Individual and Neighborhood Socioeconomic Status and Progressive Chronic Kidney Disease in an Elderly Population: The Cardiovascular Health Study. *Soc. Sci. Med.* **2007**, *65* (4), 809–821.

Mirowsky, J.; Ross, C. E. *Social Causes of Psychological Distress*; Transaction Publishers, 2003.

Murdoch, J.; Miele, M. 'Back to Nature': Changing 'Worlds of Production' in the Food Sector. *Soc. Ruralis* **1999**, *39* (4), 465.

Nestle, M. *Food Politics: How the Food Industry Influences Nutrition and Health*; University of California Press, 2013; Vol. 3.

Peck, J.; Tickell, A. Neoliberalizing Space. *Antipode* **2002**, *34* (3), 380–404.

Powell, L. M.; Szczypka, G.; Chaloupka, F. J.; Braunschweig, C. L. Nutritional Content of Television Food Advertisements Seen by Children and Adolescents in the United States. *Pediatrics* **2007**, *120* (3), 576–583.

Robinson, T. N.; Borzekowski, D. L.; Matheson, D. M.; Kraemer, H. C. Effects of Fast Food Branding on Young Children's Taste Preferences. *Arch. Pediatrics Adolesc. Med.* **2007**, *161* (8), 792–797.

Rose, N. *Powers of Freedom: Reframing Political Thought*; Cambridge University Press, 1999.

Satalkar, B. *Water Aerobics,* July 15, 2010. Retrieved from http://www.buzzle.com

Taras, H. L.; Sallis, J. F.; Patterson, T. L.; Nader, P. R.; Nelson, J. A. Television's Influence on Children's Diet and Physical Activity. *J. Dev. Behav. Pediatrics* **1989,** *10* (4), 176–180.

Wong, V. *How Fast-Food Eaters Split Along Ethnic Lines,* April 3, 2003. Retrieved from https://www.bloomberg.com/news/articles/2013-05-29/how-fast-food-eaters-split-along-ethnic-lines.

Williams-Forson, Chicken and Chains: Using African American Foodways to Understand Black Identities. *Afr. Amer. Foodways: Exp. History Cult.* **2007,** 148, 126–138.

Wilson, W. J. *When Work Disappears: The World of The New Urban Poor;* Vintage, 2011.

Zenk, Shannon N., Amy J. Schulz, Teretha Hollis-Neely, Richard T. Campbell, Nellie Holmes, Gloria Watkins, Robin Nwankwo, and Angela Odoms-Young. "Fruit and Vegetable Intake in African Americans: Income and Store Characteristics." *Am. J. Prevent. Med.* **2005,** *29* (1), 1–9.

CHAPTER 10

Promoting More Sustainable Consumer Decisions in Foodservice Settings: Effectiveness of the "Nudges" Approach

LAURE SAULAIS[1,2*], MAURICE DOYON[1], and CAMILLE MASSEY[2]

[1]*Department of Agri-food Economics and Consumer Science, Laval University, Québec, Canada*

[2]*Center for Food and Hospitality Research, Institut Paul Bocuse, Ecully, France*

Corresponding author. E-mail: laure.saulais@fsaa.ulaval.ca

ABSTRACT

The growth of away-from-home food consumption worldwide raises concern about the associated negative externalities, with food-related chronic diseases and food waste on the forefront. Changing consumer behaviors at the point of purchase could help reducing the extent of these externalities by encouraging healthier and more sustainable food choices. So far, however, the majority of actions aimed at consumers have relied on the provision of information or on labeling, with low effectiveness. Such strategies rely on the assumption that food choice behaviors result principally from rational decision-making. Behavioral Economics models provide a different approach, integrating bounded rationality in the study of consumers' decisions for food. This chapter discusses these approaches on the basis of recent advances in the public health nutrition field that build on these models to design strategies aiming to encourage healthier eating in foodservice settings. We present and discuss a typology of nudges aimed at food decisions, based on a systematic literature review. We discuss the effectiveness and feasibility of such approaches in foodservice, as well as perspectives to extend them to other types of sustainability-related issues and current research gaps. One of the main challenges is to gain a better understanding of the conditions for the effectiveness of nudges. It is, therefore, crucial to investigate the contextual determinants of food decision-making, particularly at the individual level, in order to develop interventions that are efficient and well targeted.

10.1 INTRODUCTION: SUBOPTIMAL FOOD CHOICES AND THE SUSTAINABILITY OF FOODSERVICE SYSTEMS

Suboptimal food systems generate substantial societal, environmental, and economic costs (FAO, 2016). In the particular case of foodservice systems, these costs may originate from organizational and operational complexity, but also from inadequate consumer choices (Filimonau, 2017). For instance, the choice of excessive quantities may lead to plate waste or overconsumption. Likewise, choosing insufficient quality could lead to micronutrient deficiencies, while preferring products that originate from nonsustainable production systems may have a negative environmental impact.

This raises the question of the responsibility of the foodservice sector in these deleterious consumption behaviors, but also potentially opens new avenues for action, as it implies that the sustainability of foodservice systems could be achieved through the design of "smarter" food offers that foster more sustainable consumption behaviors. The challenge for the foodservice sector henceforth lies in the identification of drivers for action at the interaction between supply and demand that are both efficient in terms of sustainability, feasible in terms of implementation, and not detrimental to the overall value of the offer. Addressing this challenge requires better understanding of the factors that may contribute to unsustainable consumer decisions in foodservice settings.

In the rest of this chapter, we provide an overview of the current approaches and perspectives on these issues from the point of view of behavioral economics. In the first part, we briefly introduce the theoretical frameworks that may be used to analyze decision-making for food. The behavioral change programs that are derived from these models presented in the next part. We then propose a typology of possible actions that illustrate the field implementation of these approaches. Their relevance, efficiency, and possible limits are then discussed. We conclude with some perspectives and remaining research questions.

10.2   BEHAVIORAL ECONOMICS' APPROACHES TO DECISION-MAKING FOR FOOD: THEORETICAL FRAMEWORK

10.2.1   *Food Decisions Theories: From Homo Oeconomicus to Homo Sapiens*

The dominant representation of the food decision-maker has, for a long time, been restricted to that of a rational consumer (sometimes referred to as *Homo Oeconomicus)*, who takes into account all the available information, using unlimited time and cognitive resources in order to make an optimal decision (Schulte-Mecklenbeck, 2013). Inadequate choices—of quantity or of quality—were then explained by a failure of the market to provide the necessary conditions (such as, for instance, information) to make an optimal decision.

However, these assumptions of rationality have been increasingly questioned due to their poor predictive and descriptive capacity. In particular, such models fail to explain the influence of some factors, a priori disconnected from the decision task, but that may have an influence on choice behavior, such as the ambiance at the point of choice (Stroebele and DeCastro, 2004), the size of portions (Wansink, 2004) or the framing of the choice question (Cartwright, 2011). In link with these factors, "mistakes" in the choice of quantities or quality of food may occur, favored by the context, leading to suboptimal consumption. Based on these observations, behavioral economics has attempted to develop an alternative approach that would account for these deviations from rational norm, therefore explaining the decision-making behavior of *Homo Sapiens* rather than that of *Homo Oeconomicus*. These works hypothesize the bounded rationality of decision-makers (Simon, 2000): The idea that in a given choice environment, individuals do not have to make a full analytical assessment of all parameters of the choice task, but rather rely on decisional "shortcuts" to minimize cognitive efforts. These shortcuts are referred to as heuristics (Tversky and Kahneman, 1975; Gigerenzer and Todd, 1999).

10.2.2   Heuristics and Biases in Food Decisions

Within Behavioral Economics, the proponents of the "heuristics and biases" program hypothesize that the use of heuristics is equivalent to a trade-off between effort and accuracy: the idea that lower cognitive effort leads to a "lower quality" of decisions. In this approach, the observed errors of decision are deviations from the norm (that is to say, the decision that would be taken by a fully rational individual) due to a use of less cognitive effort (Kahneman, 2003). This theory is linked with dual-process theories of decision, which hypothesize that decision-making processes rely on two coexisting types of systems, popularized by Kahneman as "slow and fast systems" or "Systems 1 and 2." In this approach, "system 1" corresponds to automatic, emotional, fast processes that require low cognitive effort; and "system 2" covers reflexive, slow, cognitively costly processes (Kahneman, 2011). Food choices that have strong habitual, emotional, and physiological components, are typically hypothesized to rely more strongly on System 1 (Köster, 2003), which would explain the poor predictive value of preferences and attitudes for eating behaviors. Some authors defend the hypothesis that these deviations from the rational norm (or "biases"), are systematic, and can, therefore, be predicted and minimized (Ariely, 2008).

10.2.3   Ecological Rationality and Simple Heuristics Program

However, this view of food decision-making is disputed within behavioral economics (Polonioli, 2013). Advocates of the alternative "Simple Heuristics" program, indeed, question the normative nature and paternalistic implications of the "heuristics and biases" program, which defines as optimal (rational) the logically dominant strategy (Grüne-Yanoff and Hertwig, 2016). While this would hold true regarding decisions under risk, there is no evidence that decisions under uncertainty are poorly accurate when they result from heuristics. The accuracy-effort tradeoff may then be representative of a limited ability to use logic in the choices but would omit to take into account other parameters, such as the motivations and goals of each individual, or the use of social intelligence (Lusk, 2013; Gigerenzer, 2016).

In an adaptive perspective, the proponents of the Simple Heuristics program, therefore, suggest to look at the ecological rationality of decisions in order to assess their accuracy. In other words, choices should be defined as "smart" in terms of their ability to meet *correspondence* rather than *coherence* criteria (Hertwig et al., 2013). In that view, there is no a priori evidence for the accuracy-effort tradeoff: Heuristics could be as good as, or even better than, more demanding cognitive processes that need more information and computation. Ecologically valid heuristics may thus operate effectively under certain conditions, especially relative to the degree of uncertainty involved in the decision (Gigerenzer, 2015).

In this view, errors in food decisions could be attributed to the fast-changing characteristics of the environments of choice. For instance, the Protein Leverage Hypothesis (Simpson and Raubenheimer, 2005) states that food intake in humans might be driven in priority by objectives of protein content rather than energy density. Such an influence on decision-making might be ecologically valid in some natural environments. However, if protein content becomes difficult to infer from sensory cues (as it might be the case in modern, highly processed foods), such a mechanism might induce overconsumption or errors in the choice of quality.

10.2.4   *Implications for Foodservice Decision Research*

The design of foodservice offers that generate less negative impacts, both at the individual and at the collective levels, by fostering more appropriate consumption practices, requires to better understand the factors influencing food decisions, and identify, among these factors, which are the most influential, and which can be impacted, both at the levels of foodservice companies and of public policies.

Food choices are complex behaviors that have multiple determinants, linked with the product characteristics, with the physiological, socioeconomic, and psychological characteristics of the decision-maker, and with the context of decision (situation, socio-economic factors) (Köster, 2009). For instance, self-reported reasons for plate waste are mainly attributed to individual characteristics (preferences, hunger level, budget) and to the offer available (substandard quality, inadequate quantities, lack of information, insufficient time to eat) (Sebbane and Costa, 2015). Likewise, self-reported factors of low vegetable consumption are taste, cost, and lack of preparation time (Appleton et al., 2016). Each of these groups of factors are potential drivers of suboptimal food choices, but not all of them can be impacted easily by foodservice on an operational level. Furthermore, and probably more importantly, there is little point in trying to change these factors if the magnitude of their effect is overruled by that of context.

Therefore, taking into account bounded rationality, and, in particular, trying to better include the mechanisms behind the use of heuristics in foodservice contexts, is a path to explore, in order to better understand how food choice "errors" occur, what are the most influencing factors within the foodservice offer, and what is the amplitude of these influences. Achieving this, however, also requires reconsidering the methodologies of food choice behavior studies. While survey data can provide useful insight on possible choice motivations, there is a risk that these self-reported factors will overly reflect rational decision-making processes, and not accurately so actual behaviors. Observation, especially through controlled and systematic choice experiments, may provide a different perspective on how these factors interact with contextual parameters through the use of heuristics.

Such approaches open new avenues, both for public policymakers and for the private foodservice sector, for the informed design of foodservice offers that can contribute to significantly reduce the negative impacts of food consumption behaviors. The next part of this chapter examines in more detail the possible interventional approaches that may be derived from these implications.

10.3 FROM DECISION-MAKING TO BEHAVIOR CHANGE: NUDGES, BOOSTS, AND ENVIRONMENTAL INTERVENTIONS

10.3.1 Moving Beyond Standard Instruments: Associated Challenges

Traditional interventional approaches in link with the neoclassical normative decision-making models view decision-making "errors" as the result of imperfect markets, and typically propose classical policy instruments (such as information and education campaigns, price interventions, and regulation of the supply system such as labeling standards, restrictions on television advertisement or on the provision of certain types of food in specific foodservice environments) to "correct" those failures and tackle the self-reported reasons for unhealthy or unsustainable consumption (Saulais, 2015).

However, the relatively low success of these attempts to address public health and food-related environmental challenges has prompted a reflection toward new policy approaches. The apparent failure of informational or educational strategies, in particular, has been given as an argument in favor of the use of strategies that consider bounded rationality. Growing evidence of the low effectiveness of standard interventions has thus raised interest in the behavioral economics approaches of individual decision making, and the behavioral change programs that may be derived from them (Hansen & Jespersen, 2013). In particular, these approaches have been extended to the field of public health and environment policies in the food domain, with the aim of promoting more beneficial attitudes, including healthier and more sustainable food choices. This idea has even attracted attention outside the academic circle and into policy actors' agenda, with the UK and US governments setting up "nudge units" (de Ridder, 2014).

However, reflecting the current on-going debate on the principles and theoretical grounds of bounded rationality and its consequences on decision-making and implications for public policy-making, several behavioral change programs are coexisting (Lehner et al., 2015).

10.3.2   Nudges

The dominant approach, labeled "nudges," derives from the heuristics and biases program, and is based on the rationale that some heuristics are mobilized by relying on cues from the choice task parameters: For instance, it has been observed that decision-makers tend to have a bias for the status quo over a change (Samuelson and Zeckhauser, 1988). Therefore, people would overly remain in the option presented in the choice task as their current situation, even when a change of status would appear to be more beneficial. This phenomenon labeled the status quo bias, also referred to as default heuristic (Gigerenzer, 1999), has been observed, for instance on organ donation choices (Johnson and Goldstein, 2003).

The rationale of nudges is that, under the assumption that context induces certain decision-making heuristics or biases, an intervention aiming to redirect the decision-maker's biases in a more beneficial direction could, therefore, help consumers make more optimal decisions. In the case of status quo bias, such a nudge would consist in presenting the most beneficial option as the status quo (Thaler and Sunstein, 2008).

These strategies, described as liberal paternalism, are believed to be more effective and just as coercive measures leaving no freedom of choice. The term "nudge" was coined by Thaler and Sunstein in 2008 in their seminal book *Nudge. Improving Decisions about Health, Wealth and Happiness*. Richard Thaler and Cass Sunstein define nudge as 'any aspect of the choice architecture that alters people's behavior in a predictable way without forbidding any options or significantly changing their economic incentives'. In that respect, nudging is tightly connected to the notion of choice architecture (Johnson et al., 2012) which corresponds to the particular way the choice task is defined and structured.

10.3.3 Boosts

An alternative, less widespread approach to behavioral change, is derived from the simple heuristics program. From an interventional perspective, this approach, labeled "Boosts" (a term coined by Grüne-Yanoff and Hertwig) stems from a more "optimistic" perspective of decision-making errors (Polionioli, 2012). This approach considers that limited rationality is not synonymous with failure of decision-makers, but rather that decision heuristics may be rational strategies in natural environments. Under the assumption that the observation of a "bias" in relation to a rational standard based on logical reasoning has no a priori connection to an adaptive behavior (Gigerenzer and Sturm, 2012), it could be possible to "Boost" decision-makers to make ecologically valid decisions either by modifying the choice environment to include these heuristics, or by enabling them to modify their decision processes and adapt them to the new environments. However, in the food domain especially, this approach remains essentially at the theoretical level and has not yet been sufficiently deployed and tested in the field.

10.3.4   Implications for Foodservice

Is there any potential for choice architecture (whether in the form of "nudge" or of "boost") as an instrument for food policy-makers, or as a strategic tool for private stakeholders, such as foodservice companies, in order to foster healthier or more sustainable food choices?

The debate on the relevance and effectiveness of the coexisting intervention approaches, "nudges" and "boosts," is directly linked to the discussion of the legitimacy of so-called "choice architects" to set up interventions based on nonconscious processes of decision-making. As put by Grüne-Yanoff and Hertwig (2016), nudges "re-bias" individuals, in that they manipulate the environment so that decisional biases (seen as systematic and unavoidable) lead to beneficial, instead of detrimental, outcomes for the decision-maker (in the words of George Loewenstein, "The essence of the approach is to use decision errors that ordinarily hurt people to instead help them." (Downs et al., 2009). Boosts, on the contrary, aim to "un-bias" decision-makers by extending or improving their decision-making competences (Grüne-Yanoff and Hertwig, 2016).

In both cases, one of the points raised is the need for demonstration and evaluation of the efficiency of these approaches. The lack of clear evidence on this topic is partly attributed to a lack of a clear definition and typology of food-related interventions on choice environments, preventing good replicability of the effects observed.

The next part tries to contribute some answers to this specific point, by providing an overview of possible food choice architecture experiments in foodservice settings and proposing a typology to define and evaluate actions. This overview focuses on examples of tests of the "nudge" approach, as to our knowledge, no "boost" intervention in the food choice domain has been evaluated in the peer-reviewed published literature yet.

10.4   NUDGES IN FOODSERVICE: A TYPOLOGY AND SOME ILLUSTRATIONS

The term *nudge* remains somewhat of an umbrella term (Ölander and Thogersen, 2014), referring to a wide range of interventions aiming at behavioral change through minimal variations in the environment where choice is to happen. Those variations are in turn expected to influence individuals' decision making, with or without their knowing (Hansen and Jespersen, 2013). Drawing from Thaler and Sunstein's definition, any intervention that does not rely on regulation, legislation or economic incentive can be seen as a nudge (Hollands et al., 2013), giving way to a vast array of nudge types.

Regarding, more specifically, food choice, a number of nudges were experimented, particularly in the UK and the US, mostly with the aim of promoting healthier choices, although there have also been some works attempting to reduce plate waste. Recent literature reviews have attempted to analyze nudges aimed at public health, either with a broader focus than just nutrition (see for instance Hollands et al., 2013), or with a narrow focus on one type of intervention (see for instance Bucher et al., 2016).

To our knowledge, there has not been, to date, a published literature review looking specifically at nudge interventions in foodservice settings, whether for public health or environmental goals. The present section does not ambition to provide a systematic review of existing interventions, but attempts to provide an overview of possible actions and to illustrate them with recently published examples, with the aim of providing elements to the assessment of the efficiency of various approaches.

In the following sections, we propose a typology of different types of nudges that have been investigated in the food choice domain with the purpose of encouraging behavior change toward healthier or more sustainable eating habits. As a starting point for reflection, we used a framework proposed by Hansen and Jespersen (2014), who distinguish between 'type 1' and 'type 2' nudges. Type 1 and type 2 nudges are direct references to Kahneman's proposed representation of dual-process theory. We coupled this framework with the classification designed by Hollands et al. (2013)/, which focused more closely on the design aspect of the nudges and illustrated each type of nudge with examples from the published literature. The methodology is summarized in Box 1.

BOX 10-1: Literature Review Methodology

Keywords: articles with keywords "nudge", "nudging" or "choice architecture" included in title, abstract, or keywords were retrieved.
Scope: No date restrictions were included.
Exclusion criteria • "Nudging" was conceptualized only recently as a research field (Thaler & Sunstein, 2008). As a result, some previous studies could very well not refer to the term "nudge" or its derivate while investigating elements that could a posteriori be interpreted as nudging (Hollands et al., 2013; Nornberg et al., 2015). However, including these previous studies would considerably broaden the scope of research, resulting in an immense body of literature that would be impossible to analyze properly (Hollands et al., 2013). In order to keep the present review practical, we decided to include only studies explicitly referring to the term 'nudge' and its derivates. • In accordance with Thaler and Sunstein's definition of nudge, we excluded studies that either combined nudge with a financial incentive, or considered financial incentives to be a nudge. • Still following Thaler and Sunstein's approach, we excluded studies that either added or removed options participants could choose from.
Electronic databases searched: Econlit, ABI/INFORM Complete, Web of Science, CINAHL plus, Pubmed, Cochrane library, Social Science Citation Index, Database of abstracts of reviews of effects, NHS EED. Snowball techniques were additionally used.

10.4.1 Type 1 Nudges

10.4.1.1 Definition

Type 1 nudges aim "at influencing the behavior maintained by automatic thinking" (Hansen and Jespersen, 2013, p. 14). As such, they "do not involve deliberation, judgment, and choice" (Hansen and Jespersen, 2013,

p. 15) and the intended result is on behavioral change rather than change in choice. In that sense, "Type 1" nudges refer to the most popularized representation of nudges, those that rely on biases to alter behavior in a way that does not involve awareness of the decision-maker or changing the nature of the choice task. Several types of interventions have been tested that can fall into that category, which we describe using the categories proposed by Hollands et al. (2013) as availability interventions, functional design, and proximity interventions.

10.4.1.2   Availability Interventions

Availability refers to interventions that "alter availability through adding behavioral options, or changing capacity for engagement with behavioral options, providing broadly equivalent options/behaviors from the previous potential behavior set remain available within the microenvironment" (Hollands et al., 2013, p.31).

In the context of foodservice environments, availability is a key lever of action. However, in the current literature, it is yet unclear what type of changes to availability may have a significant impact on choice. The only nudge intervention identified that has been tested and has yielded consistent results so far is an increase of a variety of target products (either healthier or more sustainable). For instance, an experiment increasing the variety of vegetables offered to children on a buffet significantly increased the percentage of energy derived from vegetables amongst participants (Bucher et al., 2014). Similarly, in the context of "bound choice" (where a range of options was available but participants were required to choose one of them), increasing variety led to a significant increase in actual consumption of fruits and vegetables, measured by observation and waste weight data (Hakim and Meissen, 2013). An increasing variety of healthy snacks also had a significant effect on healthy snacks purchase in both lab and field experiment (van Kleef et al., 2012).

10.4.1.3   Functional Design

The functional design consists in altering "the design or (adapting) the physical microenvironment, through changes to equipment or objects" (Hollands et al., 2013), and as such fall into the category of "type 1 nudges". In foodservice settings, such a nudge may involve shrinking plate sizes or removing trays from the cafeteria, insofar as such changes aim at impacting consumers' behavior through a change in consumers' environment. In a controlled lab experiment, Libotte et al. (2014) found that plate size has no significant effect on the total energy of the meal chosen by participants. Yet, participants in the group with larger plates did serve themselves with significantly more vegetables. Thus, plate size could impact meal composition, although this remains understudied to this date (Libotte et al., 2014). When looking at food waste, shrinking plate size was found to be effective at reducing waste (Kallbekken and Sælen, 2013).

10.4.1.4   Proximity Interventions

Proximity is another type of nudge that can be included in "type 1 nudges." It refers to "interventions that facilitate engagement with available behavioral options by making such options more immediately salient or reducing required effort, primarily through altering proximity, but also accessibility or visibility" (Hollands et al., 2013, p. 31).

Rozin et al. (2011) examined whether the number of opportunities to encounter a given food item impacted intake. Specifically, food items were presented either in one large tray in the center of a row of a salad bar or in two small trays at the end of the row. No single relation was found, intake decreasing for chicken and bell peppers, and increasing for cucumbers and eggs. However, none of the results were statistically significant, pointing out that further research is needed.

Proximity includes interventions that impact accessibility, such as the amount of effort required to take hold of the food (Hollands et al., 2013). Results are inconsistent. In their field experiment, Rozin et al. (2011) found that foods made slightly less easy to reach in a salad bar (by placing them in the middle row versus placing them on the edge rows of the bar) were less frequently chosen than when they were easier to reach. However, the decrease was not statistically significant for all food items under study. Namely, chicken, eggs, and tomatoes were not significant while broccoli, shredded cheese, cucumbers, mushrooms, and olives were. This discrepancy was not discussed by the authors. Rozin et al. (2011) also examined whether serving implements impacted product selection in a salad bar. They found that all ingredients under study (tomatoes, artichoke hearts, mandarin oranges, cheddar cheese cubes) were less chosen when served with a pair of tongs compared with spoons. Such difference was statistically significant for all items, except tomatoes. However, van Kleef et al. (2012) found no significant impact of shelf arrangement in the purchase of healthy snacks (which were displayed either on top or bottom shelf of a 89-cm high display).

Proximity also includes interventions that impact visibility. In other words, interventions that increase opportunities for food items to be seen (Hollands et al., 2013), such as products placed at checkout counters for example. Results are inconclusive. Chapman and Ogden (2012) found that, unpredictably, sales of both fruits and confectionary items decreased when placed closer to checkout counters, unlike Kroese et al. (2015) who found a significant increase in purchases of healthy snacks when they were positioned close to checkout counters. Rozin et al. (2011) found that two opportunities to select a food item in a salad bar did not significantly increase purchase. Another example of visibility is the retrofitting of one of two lunch lines in a high school cafeteria to offer only healthier food items (Hanks et al., 2012). Authors found that the number of selected healthy food items significantly increased, as well as the percentage of healthier foods consumed in terms of total grams consumed. However, the quantity of healthy foods consumed by students remained strikingly stable, thus indicating that it is the quantity of unhealthy foods that made a difference, as evidenced by the significant drop (−27.9%) in consumption in this category (Hanks et al., 2012). While such drop is likely to be beneficial overall, these results do indicate that further research is needed regarding the way nudges are in fact effective. Let us also note that the two notions of "availability" and "visibility" somewhat overlap. Indeed, if quantity of product increases, it is likely products will be more visible as well, further complicating the analysis of effectiveness.

One last subcategory deals with ordering, that is to say, the order or rank in which the options are presented. Concerning positions of menu items, results are inconsistent. Dayan and Bar-Hillel (2011) found that items placed either in the top or bottom position in a restaurant menu were chosen significantly more often, Thunstrom and Nordstrom (2013) found no effect in placing healthier meals first. It is possible however that the different amount of options in the two studies (10 vs. 3 entrées) could account for such differences. Campbell-Arvai et al., (2012) observed that making meat-less dishes the default option in a menu (by placing nonvegetarian dishes on a different menu) significantly increased the odds of meat-less dishes selection. In a different implementation of ordering, Wansink and Hanks (2013) found that in all-you-can-eat buffet settings, people are greatly influenced by the order of the foods items they are presented with, with the first three items amounting to about two-thirds of the food they served themselves. As a result, presenting people with healthier items first significantly increased their selection of healthier items, and decreased their selection of less healthy items. Most strikingly, the percentage of participants opting for cheesy eggs in breakfast buffet went from 75.4% when this option was offered first to 28.8% when offered last.

10.4.2   Type 2 Nudges

10.4.2.1   Definition

Type 2 nudges aim "at influencing the attention and premises of (…) reflective thinking (i.e., choices), via influencing the automatic system" (Hansen and Jespersen, 2013, p. 14). Type 2 nudges aim at influencing "behaviors best characterized as actions, the results of deliberation, judgment, and choice" (Hansen and Jespersen, 2013, p. 15). In other words, type 2 nudges aim at impacting the premises of a choice, while the act of choosing itself remains deliberate (even though the use of nudging can remain unknown to the choosing agent) (Hansen and Jespersen, 2013). These interventions are more targeted at the decision process itself by altering the nature of the choice task or the level of cognitive effort required to perform it.

   In foodservice environments, those types of nudges have been quite extensively tested. We refer, once again, to the categories provided by Hollands et al. (2013).

10.4.2.2   Product Presentation

Presentation refers to interventions "alter[ing] the sensory qualities or visual design of the product itself, including that actually consumed and its packaging, but not factors external to that" (Hollands et al., 2013, p. 30). Unlike the category "functional design", the category "presentation" is only concerned with changes with the product itself or its packaging, which include changes in color or shape of the food itself or its packaging.

One article was retrieved regarding presentation nudging (van Kleef et al., 2014). It examined whether shapes of rolls of bread (regular versus fun shapes, such as fish or heart) had an impact on children's choice between white and whole-wheat bread. Results suggest that shape does impact the average number of whole-wheat bread rolls consumed, especially when regular-shaped white rolls were offered versus fun-shaped whole-wheat rolls. However, the effect size was small. Moreover, the shape has no significant impact on the average number of white rolls consumed. It is also unknown whether the effect found is due to the specific shapes selected as experimental factors, or to the general concept of shape as a cognitive category.

10.4.2.3 Prompting

Prompting is another type of type 2 nudges, as individuals are aware that they are given a choice, even though they might not be aware that they are being nudged. Prompting refers to "interventions that contain standardized explicit verbal, visual and/or numeric information intending to promote or raise awareness of, and thus motivation for, a given behavior" (Hollands et al., 2013, p. 32). Wilson, Bogomolova, and Buckley (2015) found no significant effect overall of visual prompting regarding the use of low-fat milk (vs. regular milk) in a kitchen of a research institute in Australia. Although low-fat milk consumption did significantly increase the first two weeks of the study compared with baseline period and compared with regular milk, the effect ran out over the course of the study. What is more, prompting also led to a significant increase in regular milk consumption, the authors concluding that in this case, nudging was not effective for a specific product targeted (Wilson et al., 2015). Similarly, prompting undergraduate students to select meat-less options through information about the environmental effect of meat-consumption proved nonsignificant (Campbell-Arvai et al., 2012). When prompting consumers of a coffee shop through signs displaying caloric content and relative ranking of offered products, Allan et al. (2014) found no significant impact on drinks either. Authors did, however, find a significant decrease in purchases of highly caloric snacks. Verbal prompting proved more effective, significantly increasing sales of the products prompted (orange juice, fruit salad, and pancakes) although to different degrees (Kleef et al., 2015). Another type of prompting has to do with social norms. For example, promoting one behavior by stressing its social acceptability. Kallbekken and Sælen (2013) found that encouraging hotel guests to return several times at a buffet (thereby taking less food each time) allowed to significantly reduce food waste. Such results indicate that the type of prompting used (verbal or visual) could have different impacts. Moreover, impacts could vary depending on the food items involved, a similar design in the same setting yielding different results for drinks and for snacks (Allan et al., 2014).

10.4.2.4   Priming

Priming refers to interventions involving "the placement of incidental cues, objects or stimuli within the microenvironment, or within the material that a person is exposed to, to induce or influence nonconscious behavioral response" (Hollands et al., 2013, p. 32). Priming healthy food choice can, for example, consist in giving new, attractive names to healthy items (Olstad et al., 2014), or in offering free sample testing (Olstad et al., 2014; Tal and Wansink, 2015). Results remain inconclusive. New naming did not significantly increase consumption of healthier items (Olstad et al., 2014). Results are inconsistent regarding product samples, with Olstad et al. (2014) finding no significant effect on healthy items purchases while Tal and Wansink (2015) noticing a marginal effect. Perhaps more interestingly, in another design, Tal and Wansink (2015) found that prompting through healthy item sample offering (apple vs. chocolate chip cookie) significantly increased (hypothetical) purchase of healthier products across categories, and not only of sampled product or closely-related items (fruit in general in case of apple).

10.4.3   Multiple Nudges

This section refers to studies examining different food choice nudge designs simultaneously. Since we cannot exclude an interaction effect, we chose to separate such designs from single nudge studies.

10.4.3.1   Labeling + Proximity (visibility) + Availability (convenience)

Thorndike et al. (2012) found that when bottled water was more readily visible (by being placed at eye level in cafeteria fridges) and accessible (by being placed in several baskets throughout the cafeteria), bottled water purchases largely and significantly increased. Regular soda purchases significantly decreased by 5.9%. It should be noted that this intervention is the second phase of the study, first being labeling of items through color-coding. Effects of intervention remained stable over a two-year period, for regular and less frequent consumers alike (Thorndike et al., 2014).

10.4.3.2   Proximity + Prompting

Cohen et al. (2015) found that placing vegetables at the beginning of the lunch line in schools (proximity), coupled with signage promoting fruit and vegetable consumption (visual prompting) significantly increases the chance of vegetable selection among students. However, it had no impact on consumption (Cohen et al., 2015). Improving the attractiveness of fruits through attractive baskets (presentation) and increasing visibility (proximity) coupled with signage promoting fruit and vegetable consumption (visual prompting) also significantly increases the chance of fruit selection among students while having no significant impact on actual consumption (Cohen et al., 2015).

10.4.3.3   Prompting + Proximity + Functional Design

An array of small changes implemented in a UK school canteen proved effective to increase the selection of fruit, vegetarian alternatives, and sandwiches containing salad (Ensaff et al., 2015). Overall, students were 2.5 times more likely to select one of the designated items during the intervention compared with the initial period. However, the odds ratios greatly differed from one food to another, with whole fruits being 1.15 time more likely to be selected, and sandwiches reaching over 35.

10.4.4   Implications for Foodservice

TABLE 10.1   Summary of Study Examples Presented and Their Results.

	Number of studies examined	Effects in available studies	Main target variables examined
		Type 1	
Availability (increased variety of target options)	3	Increase in selection and consumption of target options	Selection consumption
Functional design (container size /shape)	2	Unclear effect on meal balance: possible impact of plate size on meal composition	Meal composition intake (and plate waste)
		Smaller portion sizes reduce food waste	
Proximity (easiness to reach)	1	Inconsistent effect on selection; depends on type of food	Selection
Proximity (convenience of serving utensil)	1	Significant impact on selection of some items. Some foods not impacted	Selection
Proximity (visibility)	4	Inconsistent results	Selection
		Increased visibility reduces selection in some cases, increases it in others, has no effect in other studies	
Proximity (placing items first; default options)	4	Inconsistent effect:	Selection
		Observed increase in selection for items placed first, except in one study	
		May depend on the number of options	
		Type 2	
Presentation (product shape)	1	Small effect	Consumption
Prompting	8	Overall no effect found, depends on type of prompting and on products	Selection
Priming	3	Inconclusive	Selection

Table 10.1 provides a summary of the studies presented in the previous parts. While this overview did not intend to be systematic or exhaustive, the few examples in each category illustrates the fact that, both on the topic of healthy eating and on the reduction of food waste in foodservice, field evaluation of "nudges" as a general approach is, so far, insufficient to assess their potential to contribute to the emergence of sustainable food practices in foodservice.

For foodservice, another critical point, largely understudied at the moment, is the operational feasibility of the implementation of nudges, which is crucial in the assessment of the relevance of these interventions, especially in the long term (Saulais, 2015).

The high level of heterogeneity in studies about nudges can account in part for the inconsistency found in the results of the studies presented and therefore their low reproducibility (Johnson et al., 2012). While we tried to follow existing typologies of nudges, it is important to note that a single category (proximity, prompting…) or even subcategory of a nudge as presented in our typology (accessibility, visibility…) can encompass very different designs.

More precisely, differences have been noted in the following key points of evaluation:

- Outcome variables: even when the nudge design in itself is the same, outcome variables can be different. When testing the effect of plate size shrinking, main outcome variables used were either caloric intake (Libotte et al., 2014) or food waste (Kallbekken and Sælen, 2013). More importantly, it is usually impossible to determine whether foods purchased/selected are actually consumed (Rozin et al., 2011; Wansink and Hanks, 2013), thus raising questions regarding the impact on food waste and consumer satisfaction of the interventions. For example, investigating the question, Cohen et al. (2015) observed that while choice architecture changes did significantly increase the odds of fruit and vegetable selection, impact on actual consumption was not significant, a trend which was stressed as well by Hanks et al. (2012). The actual consumption of healthier foods (v. selection) is worth further investigating, as increased selection and similar consumption levels can lead to more plate waste (Hanks et al., 2012).

- Target population characteristics: There has been, to our knowledge, no study which has attempted to compare the impact of a specific nudge in different populations. Yet, the literature in decision-making points toward possible differences in the manifestation of heuristics and biases according to population characteristics, for instance, age groups (Kovalchik et al. 2005), or level of expertise (Burmeister and Schade, 2007). These differences could induce different responses to interventions. This is all the more an issue if the behavior targeted by the interventions occurs more frequently in specific populations. In particular, obesity and overweight have a higher prevalence in low-income populations. Yet, the socioeconomic status of populations in intervention studies is often overlooked in the literature.

- Location and time: Studies so far lack consistency in settings and in the configuration of choice tasks. For instance, the studies on the effects of menu presentation use a different range of options, ordering procedure, and types of products. Therefore, these studies as such are not comparable, and not easily transferrable to other settings or operational strategies for foodservice. More systematic, controlled studies of the same effect in *ceteris paribus* conditions would be required to do so.

- The scale of focus and possible side-effects: when testing nudges, it can be tempting to overlook items that are not being nudged. However, there are indications that those items can benefit or suffer from nudge interventions as well. Prompting specific items can thus lead to a significant increase in the selection of unprompted (but related) items, suggesting a "spillover effect" (Ensaff et al., 2015; Tal and Wansink, 2015). Similarly, some food items have strong complementarity between each other (bacon and eggs for example), which can induce a "trigger effect" (Wansink and Hanks, 2013), selecting one food item leading consumers to select another, complimentary item. Taking such potential effects into account seem pertinent for both the design of the study and analysis of data. "Un-nudged" items can also remain unaffected, thus questioning the effectiveness of interventions overall. For example, while altering availability or proximity can significantly increase the purchase of healthy snacks, such interventions have been found to have no impact on purchases of unhealthy snacks (Kroese et al., 2015; van Kleef et al., 2012). It was also found that prompting for skim milk also led to an increase in consumption of regular milk (Wilson et al., 2015). Keeping in mind that nudge interventions aim at improving eating habits, such findings do raise the question of nudges' effectiveness overall.

10.5 PERSPECTIVES AND FURTHER RESEARCH QUESTIONS

Following the new perspective on decision-making brought forward by Behavioral Economics, the advocates of "nudges" and "boosts" ambition, through small changes in the environment of decision, to help individuals minimize the deleterious effects of certain decision biases to which they would be subject. This hypothesis is the subject of increasing interest, particularly in the field of public health related to food, in which these approaches are presented as an alternative to strategies using levers such as nutrition information and education food.

However, despite a growing interest on the part of public policymakers, the evidence of the effectiveness of nudges to correct the "deviations" of eating behaviors from the norm remains both insufficiently demonstrated and insufficiently justified (Hollands et al., 2013; Bucher et al., 2016). The ethical issues behind libertarian paternalism are widely discussed in the economics literature (see for instance Blumenthal-Barby and Burroughs, 2012).

Critics and questions to address are mainly directed at two aspects: first, methodological issues regarding the theoretical grounds on which these behavioral programs are developed; and second, the normative aspects the lack of consensus regarding the existence and definition of the norm that should be the intended target of the interventions. In the case of food decisions, another largely unexplored topic is whether there is a domain-specificity of food that may affect decision-making and thus, in turn, the possible impacts of nudge and boost interventions.

10.5.1 Link Between Theory and Practice

Beyond the issues (discussed in the previous sections) of quality and reproducibility of evidence, there is a more fundamental difficulty to move beyond the accumulation of isolated, reduced-scale case studies. This difficulty has been attributed to the weak theoretical grounds on which these behavioral change programs are based, beyond their initial rationale (Grüne-Yanoff and Hertwig, 2016; Hollands, 2013). In order to move the debate forward, this weak link between the theory of decision-making and implementation must be resolved. This issue appears particularly visible in food decision research, where the conceptualization of food decision-making theory under the assumptions of bounded rationality is still in its early stages, while tests of practical implementations derived from it already flourishes. Therefore, the design and implementation of nudges and choice architecture for food offers, both with public health or private goals, is based mostly on assumptions of cognitive biases that were never consolidated in the specific case of food decisions. The field data from intervention studies do not provide sufficient evidence for the investigation of decision-making due to the heterogeneity of contexts, outcome variable, and populations. This observation calls from more systematic and controlled experiments in which the food decision heuristics can be described and characterized.

10.5.2   Defining the Norm: Risk and Uncertainty, Knowing the Preferences or Reducing Externalities

In food decision-making, one of the more pressing issues within the debate on nudge ethics is its normative aspect—that is to say, the idea that there is a "correct" behavior that decision-makers seem to be deviating from- and which would correspond the one toward which the policies should be oriented (Lehner et al., 2015). A related concern, raised by the proponents of the simple heuristics program, is that the focus of behavioral economics has been placed mostly on individual decisions under risk, and less so on decisions that involve uncertainty (Gigerenzer, 2016). Food decisions typically may involve the assessment of risks (such as sanitary risks), but also a large part of uncertainty (especially regarding future outcomes). This may imply that some observed decisions regarded as deviations from the norm may simply be an ecologically rational way for the decision-maker to deal with uncertain outcomes. In that case, the normative view of decision-making defended by the nudge advocates might be less beneficial.

The debate on the normative aspect of choice architecture interventions refers to a more fundamental debate in Economics, that is to say, whether there exists, beyond the choice behaviors as observed in context, underlying preferences that can be measured and used as a benchmark for the evaluation of public policies. If such is the case, then the systematic identification and investigation of heuristics are required for a better design and evaluation of such interventions (McFadden, 2001). If, however, underlying preferences are unclear, then the use of nudging might call for a different justification of these approaches, such as the reduction of externalities due to decisions (Guala and Mitone, 2015). In the case of food decisions, poor choices may have consequences at the individual level (such as future health outcomes, or loss of money), but also at the societal level (such as health-related costs, misuse of resources, greenhouse-gas emissions). Up until now, as has been shown in the overview presented, the focus in food nudges has been placed mostly on individual outcomes. One of the ways to improve the legitimacy of nudges might be to better integrate the societal impacts of decisions into the intended design.

10.5.2   Taking into Account the Specificities of Food Decisions

Another area that requires further investigation is the potential domain-specificity of decision-making for food. There is currently insufficient investigation of the specific mechanisms of food decisions and of their potential implications for behavioral change programs. Yet food decisions, especially outside the home in foodservice settings, have specific characteristics that may distinguish them from other types of decisions. These characteristics could come to modulate the extent and nature of the heuristics that have been identified and studied in other domains such as insurance choices, financial investments, the choice of medical treatment options or the choice to be an organ donor.

Characteristics, such as the repetitive and habitual nature of food choice, their overall low monetary consequences, and the high uncertainty about environmental and health outcomes in the long term, should be taken into account when modeling such choices. Beyond these aspects, two major specificities of food should be further taken into account within the field of choice architecture.

The first aspect is the impact of the sensory characteristics of food on decisions that account for a major part of decision-making for food. It is still unclear whether, and how, these sensory characteristics could be connected to the manifestation of specific biases or heuristics, or whether they contribute to define boundary conditions for the success of certain nudges.

The second major aspect is the physiological function of food. The link between appetite and decision-making has been studied from the angle of the impact of appetite on future choices (Read and Van Leeuwen, 1998); however, it is unclear whether the efficiency of certain nudge interventions could be modulated by hunger through, for instance, increased impatience leading to reduced time allocated to decision-making, or even through the influence of some hormonal mechanisms such as ghrelin. Other works show an impact of certain food components on economic behavior, in particular, glucose (Orquin et al., 2016). Better knowledge of how these various characteristics may impact or modulate the use of context for decision-making could provide a clearer view on the conditions of effective choice architecture.

10.6   CONCLUSIONS

Responsibility for unsustainable food consumption behaviors is often partly attributed to foodservice systems, through the environments of food choice that these systems provide. A major challenge for the foodservice industry is to identify the relevant and most efficient changes to apply to food choice architecture to foster more beneficial consumption behaviors. These actions must be translated into operational strategies that can contribute to the reduction of the environmental impact of its activities, while promoting a high level of food and service quality, without affecting the economic value of the offer or the consumers' satisfaction.

For this purpose, it is necessary to better understand the mechanisms of consumer choice in reaction to a given foodservice offer as well as the acceptability of so-called "smarter" environments for consumers. Behavioral economics models brought a new perspective on the links between the environments of choice and decision-making processes, prompting, in the recent years, a search for efficient *nudges* - choice architecture tools that may contribute to building "smarter" environments. However, despite a growing literature testing potentially beneficial changes of the choice context, the existing evidence, especially in the foodservice domain, still appears to be overall weak, and the links between decision-making theory and their applied counterpart remain unclear.

While the contribution of behavioral economics to these goals appears to be promising, the derived instruments are probably best considered complementarily to other instruments, such as information and education programs, which may help to address more long-term aims and persistence of behavioral change.

Thus, to advance in the promising way of the provision of environments to choose more favorably to health and sustainable, economic research on dietary behavior must face a number of challenges. First, a closer look should be paid to the identification and characterization of potential sources of deviation from rationality in food choices and to the evaluation of their systematic nature and their societal acceptability. In addition, a better knowledge of decision-making in specific population groups, and across the lifespan, seems instrumental in addressing the current challenges of sustainability in foodservice as a whole.

KEYWORDS

- nudges
- food choice
- sustainable diets
- choice environments
- consumers
- decision-making

REFERENCES

Allan, J. L.; Johnston, M.; Campbell, N. Snack Purchasing is Healthier when the Cognitive Demands of Choice Are Reduced: a Randomized Controlled Trial. *Health Psychol* **2015,** *34* (7), 750.

Appleton, K. M.; Hemingway, A.; Saulais, L.; Dinnella, C.; Monteleone, E.; Depezay, L.; ... Hartwell, H. Increasing Vegetable Intakes: Rationale and Systematic Review of Published Interventions. *Eur. J. Nutr.* **2016,** *55* (3), 869–896.

Ariely, D. *Predictably Irrational* New York: Harper Collins, 2008; p 20.

Blumenthal-Barby, J. S.; Burroughs, H. Seeking Better Health Care Outcomes: The Ethics of Using the "nudge". *Am. J. Bioethics* **2012,** *12* (2), 1–10.

Bucher, T.; Siegrist, M.; van der Horst, K. Vegetable Variety: An Effective Strategy to Increase Vegetable Choice in Children. *Public Health Nutr.* **2014,** *17* (06), 1232–1236.

Bucher, T.; Collins, C.; Rollo, M. E.; McCaffrey, T. A.; De Vlieger, N.; Van der Bend, D.; Perez-Cueto, F. J. Nudging Consumers Towards Healthier Choices: A Systematic Review of Positional Influences on Food Choice. *Br J. Nutr.* **2016,** *115* (12), 2252–2263.

Burmeister, K.; Schade, C. Are Entrepreneurs' Decisions More Biased? An Experimental Investigation of the Susceptibility to Status Quo Bias. *J. Bus. Ventur.* **2007,** *22* (3), 340–362.

Campbell-Arvai, V.; Arvai, J.; Kalof, L. Motivating Sustainable Food Choices: the Role of Nudges, Value Orientation, and Information Provision. *Environ. Behav.* **2014,** *46* (4), 453–475.

Chapman, K.; Ogden, J. Nudging Customers Towards Healthier Choices. An Intervention in the University Canteen. *J. Food Res.* **2012,** *1* (2), 13–21.

Cohen, J. F.; Richardson, S. A.; Cluggish, S. A.; Parker, E.; Catalano, P. J.; Rimm, E. B. Effects of Choice Architecture and Chef-Enhanced Meals on the Selection and Consumption of Healthier School Foods: A Randomized Clinical Trial. *JAMA Pediatrics* **2015,** *169* (5), 431–437.

Dayan, E.; Bar-Hillel, M. Nudge to Nobesity II: Menu Positions Influence Food Orders. *Judgm. Decis. Mak* **2011,** *6* (4), 333–342.

Downs, J. S.; Loewenstein, G.; Wisdom, J. Strategies for Promoting Healthier Food Choices. *Am. Econ. Rev.* **2009,** *99* (2), 159–164.

Ensaff, H.; Homer, M.; Sahota, P.; Braybrook, D.; Coan, S.; McLeod, H. Food Choice Architecture: An Intervention in a Secondary School and its Impact on Students' Plant-based Food Choices. *Nutrients* **2015,** *7* (6), 4426–4437.

Food and Agriculture Organization of the United Nations. The State of Food and Agriculture. Climate Change, agriculture and food security. http://www.fao.org/publications/sofa/2016/en/ (accessed online March 28, 2017)

Filimonau, V.; Lemmer, C.; Marshall, D.; Bejjani, G. `Nudging'as an Architect of More Responsible Consumer Choice in Food Service Provision: the Role of Restaurant Menu Design. *J. Clean. Prod.* **2017,** *144*, 161–170.

Gigerenzer, G.; Todd, P. M.; ABC Research Group, T. *Simple Heuristics that Make us Smart*; Oxford University Press, New York, NY, USA, **1999.**

Gigerenzer, G., Sturm, T. How (far) can Rationality be Naturalized? *Synthese* **2012,** *187* (1), 243–268.

Gigerenzer, G. Introduction: Taking Heuristics Seriously. In *The Behavioral Economics Guide 2016 (with an introduction by Gerd Gigerenzer);* Samson, A., ed; Behavioral Science Solutions Ltd.: London, UK, 2016; pp V–XI.

Grüne-Yanoff, T.; Hertwig, R. Nudge Versus Boost: How Coherent are Policy and Theory? *Minds Mach.* **2016,** *26* (1–2), 149–183.

Guala, F.; Mittone, L. A Political Justification of Nudging. *Rev. Philos. Psychol.* **2015,** *6* (3), 385–395.

Hakim, S. M.; Meissen, G. Increasing Consumption of Fruits and Vegetables in the School Cafeteria: The Influence of Active Choice. *J. Health Care Poor Underserv.* **2013,** *24* (2), 145–157.

Hanks, A. S.; Just, D. R.; Smith, L. E.; Wansink, B. Healthy Convenience: Nudging Students Toward Healthier Choices in the Lunchroom. *J. Public Health* **2012,** *34* (3), 370–376.

Hansen, P. G.; Jespersen, A. M. Nudge and the Manipulation of Choice: a Framework for the Responsible Use of the Nudge Approach to behaviour Change in Public Policy. *Eur. J. Risk Regulat.* **2013**, *4* (1), 3–28.

Hertwig, R.; Hoffrage, U.; The ABC Research Group *Simple Heuristics in a Social World*; Oxford University Press: New York, NY, USA, 2013.

Hollands, G. J.; Shemilt, I.; Marteau, T. M.; Jebb, S. A.; Kelly, M. P.; Nakamura, R.; ... Ogilvie, D. Altering Micro-environments to Change Population Health Behaviour: Towards an Evidence Base for Choice Architecture Interventions. *BMC Public Health* **2013**. *13* (1), 1218.

Johnson, E. J.; Goldstein, D. Do Defaults Save Lives? *Science* **2003**, *302* (5649), 1338–1339.

Johnson, E. J.; Shu, S. B.; Dellaert, B. G.; Fox, C.; Goldstein, D. G.; Häubl, G.; ... Wansink, B. Beyond Nudges: Tools of a Choice Architecture. *Market Lett.* **2012**, *23* (2), 487–504.

Just, D.; Price, J. Default Options, Incentives and Food Choices: Evidence from Elementary-School Children. *Public Health Nutr.* **2013**, *16* (12), 2281–2288.

Kahneman, D. A Perspective on Judgment and Choice: Mapping Bounded Rationality. *Am. Psychol.* **2003**, *58* (9), 697.

Kallbekken, S.; Sælen, H. Nudging' Hotel Guests to Reduce Food Waste as a Win–Win Environmental Measure. *Econ. Lett* **2013**, *119* (3), 325–327.

Köster, E. P. The Psychology of Food Choice: Some Often Encountered Fallacies. *Food Qual. Prefer.* **2003**, *14* (5), 359–373.

Köster, E. P. Diversity in the Determinants of Food Choice: A Psychological Perspective. *Food Qual. Prefer.* **2009**, *20* (2), 70–82.

Kovalchik, S.; Camerer, C. F.; Grether, D. M.; Plott, C. R.; Allman, J. M. Aging and Decision Making: A Comparison Between Neurologically Healthy Elderly and Young Individuals. *J. Econ. Behav. Organ.* **2005**, *58* (1), 79–94.

Kroese, F. M.; Marchiori, D. R.; de Ridder, D. T. Nudging Healthy Food Choices: a Field Experiment at the Train Station. *J. Public Health* **2015**, *38* (2), e133–e137.

Lehner, M.; Mont, O.; Heiskanen, E. Nudging—A Promising Tool for Sustainable Consumption Behaviour? *J. Clean. Prod.* **2015**, *134*, 166–177.

Levy, D. E.; Riis, J.; Sonnenberg, L. M.; Barraclough, S. J.; Thorndike, A. N. Food Choices of Minority and Low-income Employees: A Cafeteria Intervention. *Am. J. Prev. Med.* **2012**, *43* (3), 240–248.

Libotte, E.; Siegrist, M.; Bucher, T. The Influence of Plate Size on Meal Composition. *Liter. Rev. Exp. Appetite* **2014**, 82, 91–96.

Lusk, J. *The Food Police: A well-fed Manifesto about the Politics of your Plate.* Crown Forum: New York, NY, USA. **2013**.

McFadden, D. Economic Choices. *Am. Econ. Rev.* **2001**, *91* (3), 351–378.

Nørnberg, T. R.; Houlby, L.; Skov, L. R.; Peréz-Cueto, F. J. A. Choice Architecture Interventions for Increased Vegetable Intake and Behaviour Change in a School Setting: a Systematic Review. Perspect. *Public Health* **2016**, *136* (3), 132–142.

Ölander, F.; Thøgersen, J. Informing Versus Nudging in Environmental Policy. *J. Consum. Policy* **2014**, *37* (3), 341–356.

Olstad, D. L.; Goonewardene, L. A.; McCargar, L. J.; Raine, K. D. Choosing Healthier Foods in Recreational Sports Settings: A Mixed Methods Investigation of the Impact of Nudging and an Economic Incentive. *Int. J. Behav. Nutr. Phys. Activity* **2014**, *11* (1), 6.

Orquin, J. L.; Kurzban, R. A Meta-analysis of Blood Glucose Effects on Human Decision Making. *Psychol. Bull.* **2016,** *142* (5), 546.

Polonioli, A. (Gigerenzer's 'External Validity Argument' Against the Heuristics and Biases Program: An Assessment. *Mind Soc.* **2012,** *11* (2), 133–148.

Polonioli, A. Re-assessing the Heuristics Debate. *Mind Soc.* **2013,** *12 (2),* 263–271

Read, D.; Van Leeuwen, B. (Predicting Hunger: The Effects of Appetite and Delay on Choice. *Organ. Behav. Hum. Decis. Process.* **1998,** *76* (2), 189–205.

De Ridder, D. Nudging for Beginners. *Eur. Health Psychol.* 2014, *16* (1), 2–6.

Rozin, P.; Scott, S.; Dingley, M.; Urbanek, J. K.; Jiang, H.; Kaltenbach, M. Nudge to Nobesity I: Minor Changes in Accessibility Decrease Food Intake. *Judgm. Decis. Mak.* **2011,** *6* (4), 323–332.

Samuelson, W.; Zeckhauser, R. Status Quo Bias in Decision Making. *J. Risk Uncertain.* **1988,** *1* (1), 7–59.

Saulais, L. Foodservice, Health and Nutrition. Responsibility, Strategies, and Perspectives. In *The Routledge Handbook of Sustainable Food and Gastronomy;* Sloan, P., Legrand, W., Hindley, C. eds; 2015; pp 253–266.

Schulte-Mecklenbeck, M.; Sohn, M.; de Bellis, E.; Martin, N.; Hertwig, R. A Lack of Appetite for Information and Computation. Simple heuristics in Food Choice. *Appetite* **2013,** *71,* 242–251.

Sebbane, M. ; Costa, S. Gaspillage alimentaire en restauration d'entreprise : une analyse qualitative des normes personnelles et sociales. *Working Paper MOISA, 2.* http://prodinra.inra.fr/record/307995

Simon, H. A. Bounded Rationality in Social Science: Today and Tomorrow. *Mind Soc.* **2000,** *1* (1), 25–39.

Simpson, S. J. ; Raubenheimer, D. Obesity: The Protein Leverage Hypothesis. *Obes. Rev.* **2005,** *6* (2), 133–142.

Stroebele, N.; De Castro, J. M. Effect of Ambience on Food Intake and Food Choice. *Nutrition* 2004, *20* (9), 821–838.

Tal, A.; Wansink, B. An Apple a Day Brings More Apples your Way: Healthy Samples Prime Healthier Choices. *Psychol. Market. 32* (5), 575–584.

Thaler, R. H., Sunstein, C. R. Nudge. Improving Decisions About Health, Wealth, and Happiness. Yale University Press: New Haven, CT, 2008.

Thorndike, A. N.; Riis, J.; Sonnenberg, L. M.; Levy, D. E. Traffic-light Labels and Choice Architecture: Promoting Healthy Food Choices. *Am. J. Prevent. Med.* **2014,** *46* (2), 143–149.

Thorndike, A. N.; Sonnenberg, L.; Riis, J.; Barraclough, S.; Levy, D. EA 2-phase Labeling and Choice Architecture Intervention to Improve Healthy Food and Beverage Choices. *Am. J. Public Health* **2012,** *102* (3), 527–533.

Thunstrom, L.; Nordstrom, J. The Impact of Meal Attributes and Nudging on Healthy Meal Consumption—Evidence from a Lunch Restaurant Field Experiment. *Modern Economy* **2013;** *4* (10A), 1–8.

Tversky, A.; Kahneman, D. Judgment Under Uncertainty: Heuristics and Biases. In *Utility, probability, and Human Decision Making;* Springer: Netherlands, 1975; pp 141–162.

van Kleef, E.; van den Broek, O.; van Trijp, H. C. Exploiting the Spur of the Moment to Enhance Healthy Consumption: Verbal Prompting to Increase Fruit Choices in a Self-Service Restaurant. Appl. Psychol. *Health Well-Being* **2015,** *7* (2), 149–166.

van Kleef, E.; Vrijhof, M.; Polet, I. A.; Vingerhoeds, M. H.; de Wijk, R. A. Nudging Children Towards Whole Wheat Bread: A Field Experiment on the Influence of Fun Bread Roll Shape on Breakfast Consumption. *BMC Public Health* **2014**, *14* (1), 906.

van Kleef, E.; Otten, K.; van Trijp, H. C. Healthy Snacks at the Checkout Counter: a Lab and Field Study on the Impact of Shelf Arrangement and Assortment Structure on Consumer Choices. *BMC Public Health* **2012**, *12* (1), 1072.

Wansink, B. Environmental Factors that Increase the Food Intake and Consumption Volume of Unknowing Consumers. *Annu. Rev. Nutr.* **2004**, *24*, 455–479.

Wansink, B.; Hanks, A. S. Slim by Design: Serving Healthy Foods First in Buffet Lines Improves Overall Meal Selection. *PLoS ONE* *8* (10), e77055.

Wilson, A. L.; Bogomolova, S.; Buckley, J. D. Lack of Efficacy of a Salience Nudge for Substituting Selection of Lower-Calorie for Higher-Calorie Milk in the Work Place. *Nutrients* **2015**, *7* (6), 4336–4344.

CHAPTER 11

The Influence of Managerial Traits and Behavior in the Foodservice Industry

KWANGLIM SEO

University of Hawaii, Manoa

E-mail: kwanglim@hawaii.edu

ABSTRACT

Given its unique organizational structure and management style in the foodservice industry, it is especially important to understand the impact of managerial behavior on business decisions and strategies. While abundant anecdotal evidence for the managerial influence exists, it is unclear to what extent existing research has progressed toward clarifying this particular issue in the context of foodservice industry. Therefore, by systematically reviewing the extant literature, we aim to identify managerial behavior and decision-making as an important research topic and describe directions for future research in the fields of hospitality and tourism management. In particular, a behavioral finance approach is used to better understand and explore the financial impacts and implications of managerial behavior in the foodservice industry.

11.1 UNDERSTANDING MANAGERIAL BEHAVIOR IN THE FOODSERVICE INDUSTRY

Research on managerial behavior and decision making in the fields of economics, business management, and finance has rapidly evolved over the past few decades. Many scholars have attempted to understand and explain how managerial behavior and emotions influence their decision-making process. Understanding behavioral aspects of management is also considered particularly important in the foodservice industry. Many commercial foodservice establishments involve an entrepreneurial and autocratic style of leadership, increasing the influence of managerial behavior on important business decisions and strategies (Minett et al., 2009; Reich, 1994). While abundant anecdotal evidence for the managerial influence exists, it is unclear to what extent existing research has progressed toward clarifying this particular issue in the context of foodservice industry. Therefore, by systematically reviewing the extant literature, we aim to identify managerial behavior and decision making as an important research topic and describe directions for future research in the fields of hospitality and tourism management. Specifically, a behavioral finance approach is used to better understand and explore the financial impacts and implications of managerial behavior in the foodservice industry. The behavioral finance approach, integrating psychology and economics into the study of human biases and judgment in decision making under uncertainty (Kahneman and Tversky, 1979; Tversky and Kahneman, 1992) can provide unique and alternative insights, complementary to the conventional economics and finance approaches used in the existing literature.

The study of behavioral finance focuses primarily on how behavioral and psychological factors influence important business decisions and strategies (Kahneman and Tversky, 1979). Using the behavioral finance approach is suitable to explore the role of managerial behavior in the foodservice industry in which human element is considered especially important. The organizational structure of small commercial foodservice businesses in North America is mostly a sole proprietorship or partnership, enhancing the influence of human behaviors and emotions on crucial business decisions (He et al., 2011; Milton, 2003). Findings in hospitality literature provide evidence identifying specific behavioral traits of hospitality business entrepreneurs. For example, while new restaurant entrepreneurs are generally perceived passionate, enthusiastic, goal-oriented, and opportunistic, they have a higher tendency toward risk-taking, optimism, overconfidence, and internal locus of control (Enz and Harrison, 2008; Muller and Inman, 1996; Parsa et al., 2010, 2015). Research further suggests that causes of many business problems result from these behavioral and personality traits of the management (Hambrick and Crozier, 1985; Holmes et al., 2011; Sanders and Hambrick, 2007). The impact of managerial behavior and decision making can be detrimental to a business especially when managers lack the necessary understanding of the fundamental principles of business such as marketing, finance, accounting, information technology management, and human resource management (Haswell and Holms, 1989; Parsa et al., 2015). For instance, Parsa et al. (2005) found that many restaurant businesses often fail because owners and managers lack the necessary knowledge, experience, and business acumen while showing a higher tendency of risk-taking and optimism. Other scholars also found empirical evidence of managerial behavioral influences such as overconfidence on restaurant business failure (Camillo et al., 2008; Enz, 2010). Given its unique organizational structure and management style in the foodservice industry, it is especially important to understand the impact of managerial behavior on business decisions and strategies. In the next section, we discuss financial impacts and implications of managerial behavior in various business decisions.

11.2   CAPITAL STRUCTURE DECISIONS

While various capital sources, such as commercial banks, venture capitalists, corporate partnerships, and private investment groups, are available, acquiring capital is one of the most critical decisions for a new business. Most small start-up restaurants rely primarily on personal financial resources due to their limited access to capital sources (Enz and Harrison, 2008). For example, because lenders and investors are often concerned about low profitability and high risks involved in the restaurant business, they are unwilling to provide financing unless restaurants are fully established and mature with a good business track record (Hudson, 1995). The lack of financing availability combined with high levels of business risks can increase the likelihood of behavioral influences of managers on various capital structure decisions. In particular, a large body of literature discusses the impacts of certain behavioral traits, such as overconfidence and optimism, on firms' financing choices. Malmendier and Tate (2005) show that overly confident executives choose debt financing over equity financing when external financing is required because they believe that their firms are undervalued in the equity market. In addition, overconfident and optimistic managers issue too much debt because they tend to underestimate the probability of financial distress (Fairchild, 2005; Hackbarth, 2009; Heaton, 2002; Sunder et al., 2009).

The relationship between managerial overconfidence and financing decisions has been further examined in relation to the maturity of debt. Several scholars found a positive relationship between overconfidence and short-term debt (Huang et al., 2013; Landier and Thesmar, 2009; Sunder et al., 2009). They argued that overconfident CEOs are more likely to shorten their debt maturities because they underestimate liquidity risk involved in short-term debt maturity. On the other hand, other scholars posit that overconfident executives are more likely to commit to longer debt maturities because they overestimate stability of their firms' profitability and cash flows while underestimating the probability of bankruptcy in the long run (Barros and Silveira, 2007; Ben-David et al., 2007; Malmendier et al., 2011). Research on capital structure decisions is also found in the hospitality literature. In particular, several studies examined the relationships between long-term debt and various firm-level determinants such as firm size, growth opportunities, and profitability (Dalbor and Upneja, 2002; Upneja and Dalbor, 2007; Kim et al., 2011). Kizildag (2015) also investigated factors affecting the variations in financial leverage structure in four hospitality sub-sectors, finding that liquidity is positively related to long-term debt in the restaurant industry. While the findings of these studies are somewhat inconsistent; however, no theoretical or empirical explanation was provided as to why and how certain restaurant firms choose long term debt maturities compared to short term debt maturities.

Using a behavioral approach, a recent study by Seo et al. (2017) investigated the relationship between managerial overconfidence and the determinant of long-term debt used in the U.S. restaurant industry. In particular, by incorporating managerial overconfidence into traditional capital structure theories, they provided alternative insights into why certain restaurant firms prefer longer term debt maturities—overconfident executives pursuing growth and expansion are more likely to borrow long-term because they tend to overestimate (underestimate) future cash flow (financial risk). Their preference for long-term maturity remained relatively consistent regardless of internal cash flow available, suggesting more prominent influence of managerial overconfidence on financing decisions than that of conventional firm-level determinants, such as cash flow and liquidity. The findings of their study provided a new platform for future research, highlighting the importance of considering behavioral traits of managers, such as overconfidence, in understanding complex firm behaviors in the restaurant industry. Nevertheless, the findings of the extant research are somewhat limited as their study samples are mainly constrained to larger, more mature, and established publicly traded restaurant firms (Kizildag, 2015; Nan and Dalbor, 2013). As discussed, however, most restaurant businesses are small and less established firms with limited access to external financing sources. Therefore, future research is needed to determine whether similar managerial influences pertain to smaller foodservice establishments.

11.3   STRATEGIC INVESTMENT DECISIONS

Behavioral finance research attempts to explain corporate investment behavior as a consequence of a series of executives' actions and decisions. Especially, the assumption that executives are not always rational but often biased when making decisions provides a more realistic context to investigate abnormal corporate investment behavior (Kanhneman and Tversky, 1979). Empirical studies have found evidence for the consequences of managerial irrationality on corporate investment decisions, such as value-destroying mergers and acquisitions (Hayward and Hambrick, 1997; Roll, 1986), overinvestments (Baker et al., 2007; Ben-David et al., 2007; Heaton, 2002; Malmendier and Tate, 2005, 2008), and distortions in capital budgeting (Gervais et al., 2011; Hackbarth, 2009). In particular, assuming that executives' risk preferences are displayed through their choice behavior on behalf of a firm, behavioral agency theory argues that changes in their risk preferences in relation to the framing of situations affect corporate investment decisions (March and Shapira, 1987; Wiseman and Gomez-Mejia, 1998). For example, executives frame situations positively when positive acceptable values are expected from available options while framing situations negatively when negative unacceptable values are expected. It is further predicted that positively framed situations will motivate risk-averse choices and negatively framed situations will encourage risk-seeking actions (Wiseman and Gomez-Majia, 1998). Many scholars found evidence for the context-dependent risk preferences among executives and their consequences in a corporate setting (Wiseman and Gomez-Mejia, 1998; Sanders and Hambrick, 2007; Devers et al., 2007; Devers et al., 2008; Lim, 2011). For instance, some executives choose extremely risky investment strategies even when return on investment is expected to be negative.

Findings of the behavioral finance literature provide important implications for the foodservice industry. Many commercial foodservice businesses rely primarily on growth and expansion of their stores to increase sales, requiring constant large capital investments in land, buildings, equipment, as well as facilities (Nan and Dalbor, 2013). However, restaurant firms pursuing growth and expansion may face higher risk of financial failure if overconfident executives engage in value-destroying investment projects based on their biased valuation of future return. While there is a general consensus that overconfidence may be detrimental to firm value, empirical findings are still inconclusive and inconsistent across studies (Gervais et al., 2011; Hirshleifer et al., 2012). Therefore, industry-specific research is needed to explore its influence in the foodservice context where overconfidence is identified as one of the key characteristics of top management (Camillo et al., 2008; Enz, 2010; Muller and Inman, 1996; Parsa et al., 2010, 2015). Adopting behavioral agency theory, Seo et al. (2014) investigated the impact of managerial overconfidence on corporate strategic investments in the U.S. restaurant industry. Consistent with previous studies, findings of their study suggest that overly confident executives are likely to make more risky investments. In particular, overconfidence reinforced the risk-seeking preference among executives under circumstances where risk-aversion is generally perceived as more pervasive. Despite their valuable insights, however, they did not address the consequences of managerial irrationality, suggesting important future research opportunities: How does managerial irrationality, such as overconfidence, impact investment performance? Can we evaluate the performance of investment strategies in relation to specific managerial characteristics? More scholarly attention needs to be devoted to behavioral perspectives on assessing investment performance relative to the foodservice sector.

11.4 MEASURING MANAGERIAL TRAITS

One of the major challenges in behavioral finance research is how to measure behavioral and psychological traits of management. Several different ways have been developed to measure managerial irrationality and biases, such as overconfidence. First, using executives' stock option exercise data, an innovative study by Malmendier and Tate (2005) suggested an effective way to determine whether or not executives are overconfident. Research argues that risk-averse executives would exercise their stock options early in order to hedge against the risk of holding company stock (Heaton, 2002; Gervais et al., 2011; Malmendier and Tate, 2008). However, this logic cannot provide an explanation of why some executives consistently fail to exercise their stock options when the payoff is sufficiently high. Malmendier and Tate (2008) maintain that overly positive prospects about future returns by overconfident CEOs lead them to hold onto their stock options, anticipating that the payoff of their stock options will grow as the prices of underlying stocks will continue to rise. Malmendier and Tate (2005) further developed the rational threshold for exercise based on the Hall and Murphy model (2002). Assuming that shares acquired through exercise are sold immediately, Hall and Murphy (2002) provided a framework for early exercise decisions by executives. Executives exercise their options at the price where they are indifferent between exercising early or holding for another period. Using different pairs of risk aversion and diversification, the Hall and Murphy model predicts this threshold price is lower for more risk-averse and less diversified executives. Based on the model by Hall and Murphy (2002), Malmendier and Tate (2005, 2008) calibrated a range of rational thresholds for stock option exercise. In particular, if the market value of stock option is 67% higher than its granted value during the fifth year, executives must have exercised, if not all, at least some portion of their stock options during or before the fifth year. Therefore, overconfidence is measured as a binary variable that equals one if an executive fails to exercise his/her stock options with a 67% appreciated market value when five years remain before expiration. Although many subsequent studies followed the approach of Malmendier and Tate (2005) to measure managerial overconfidence, however, this approach is relatively limited because it does not allow much variation over time within a firm or an individual. For example, overconfidence measure only indicates if a subject is overconfident but not the degree of overconfidence or variation over time.

Second, a text analysis approach was used to measure managerial traits and beliefs. For instance, Malmendier and Tate (2008) analyzed past articles appeared in prominent business publications, such as the *Wall Street Journal* or *Business Week*, to find words that describe executives to be overconfident. Similarly, Otto (2014) used executives' voluntary earnings forecasts to measure managerial overconfidence. He argued that executives are overconfident if their forecasts turn out to be greater than the realized earnings. With recent advances in data mining and text analytics in academic research, this approach has great potential to improve our understanding of how managerial traits and attitudes influence corporate behavior.

Lastly, other scholars used survey instruments to avoid the limitations of accounting data. Ben-David et al. (2013) measured managerial biases by asking chief financial officers (CFOs) to project one- and ten-year market-wide stock returns to illustrate how confident they are in their predictions. Graham et al. (2103) also measured the psychological traits and attitudes of senior executives by conducting an anonymous psychometric personality test on CEOs and CFOs who subscribed to particular business magazines and attended the World Economic Forum in Davos. The survey-based approach is more flexible as the sample and data are not limited to large publicly traded firms whose data are legally available to public. Given abundant small and medium-sized foodservice establishments with little or no accounting data available, this type of methodology can provide more sophisticated practices in the hospitality and tourism research. This approach will further provide inter-disciplinary research opportunities with scholars in other fields of academic research where survey method has been more widely used and implemented.

11.5 CONCLUSIONS: FUTURE DIRECTIONS

Subsequently less scholarly attention has been devoted to behavioral finance perspectives on firm behavior and decision making in the fields of hospitality and tourism management. Behavioral and psychological traits of management merits consideration because of unique organizational and leadership structures that emphasize the importance of executives to strategic decision making at the firm level in the commercial foodservice industry. This chapter has summarized the important roles of managerial traits in various corporate decisions, methodological issues measuring managerial traits in the extant literature, and provided suggestions for future research in hospitality literature. The discussion here proposes an alternative approach to analyzing one of the key problems of the foodservice establishments, involving human influences and interactions. To the extent that behavioral and psychological traits of management matter, new approaches to better understand their impacts on business decisions are required. Behavioral finance perspectives can provide a more realistic and promising direction for future research. One promising area for future research is to analyze the link between the behavioral biases of the restaurant entrepreneurs and their strategic choices in various decision-making situations. While behavioral finance literature focuses on studying executives' personal characteristics and attitude of large corporates, further study of entrepreneurs of small- and medium-sized businesses could be another interesting area as many foodservice businesses rely on entrepreneurial business model. In addition, several limitations of dominant behavioral measurement addressed earlier suggest that efforts to improve and develop alternative measures may be essential for future research. It is especially important to invest more in building a theoretical and empirical framework that allows us to effectively assess managerial and entrepreneurial actions and behavior. Methodologies permitting in-depth interactions and observations of entrepreneurs will help shape the direction of future research and warrant more interesting findings.

KEYWORDS

- behavioral finance
- foodservice industry
- managerial behavior
- overconfidence
- decision-making

REFERENCES

Baker, M.; Ruback, R. S.; Wurgler. J. Behavioral Corporate Finance. In *Handbook of Corporate Finance: Empirical Corporate Finance*; Espeneckbo, B., Ed.; Amsterdam: North-Holland, 2007; pp. 145–188.

Ben-David, I.; Graham, J. R.; Harvey, C. R. Managerial Overconfidence and Corporate Policies. Working Paper, 2007.

Ben-David, I.; Graham, J. R.; Harvey, C. R. Managerial Miscalibration. *Q. J. Econ.* 2013, *128* (4), 1547–84.

Camillo, A. A.; Connolly, D. J.; Kim, W. G. Critical Success Factors for Independent Restaurants. *Cornell Hosp. Q.* **2008**, *49* (4), 364–380.

Dalbor, M.; Upneja, A. Factors Affecting the Long-term Debt Decision of Restaurant Firms. *J. Hosp. Tour. Res.* **2002**, *26* (4), 422–434.

Devers, C. E., Wiseman, R. M.; Holmes, R. M. The Effects of Endowment and Loss Aversion in Managerial Stock Option Valuation. *Acad. Manag. J.* **2007**, *50* (1), 1–18.

Devers, C. E.; McNamara, G.; Wiseman, R. M.; Arrfelt, M. Moving Closer to the Action: Examining Compensation Design Effects on Firm Risk. *Organ. Sci.* **2008**, *19* (4), 548–566.

Enz, C. *The Cornell School of Hotel Administration Handbook of Applied Hospitality*; SAGE: Los Angeles, 2010.

Enz, C.; Harrison, J. Innovation and Entrepreneurship in the Hospitality Industry. In *The Sage Handbook of Hospitality Management*; Brotherton, B., Wood, Eds.; SAGE, 2008; pp 213–228.

Fairchild, R. Managerial Overconfidence, Moral Hazard, and Financing and Investment Decisions. Working Paper; University of Bath: England, June 2005.

Graham, J. R.; Harvey, C. R.; Puri., M. Managerial Attitudes and Corporate Actions. *J. Financ. Econ.* **2013**, *109* (1), 103–121.

Hackbarth, D. Determinants of Corporate Borrowing: A Behavioral Perspective. *J. Corp. Finan.* **2009**, *15* (4), 389–411.

Hambrick, D.; Crozier, L. Stumblers and Stars in the Management of Rapid Growth. *J. Bus. Ventur.* **1985**, *1* (1), 31–45.

Haswell, S.; Holmes, S. Estimating the Small Business Failure Rate: A Reappraisal. *J. Small Bus. Manag.* **1989**, *27*, 68–74.

Hayward, M. L. A.; Hambrick, D. A. Explaining the Premiums Paid for Large Acquisitions: Evidence of CEO Hubris. *Admin. Sci. Q.* **1997**, *42* (1), 103–127.

Heaton, J. B. Managerial Optimism and Corporate Finance. *Fin. Manag.* **2002**, *31*, 33–45.

Hirshleifer, D.; Low, A.; Teoh, S. H. Are Overconfident CEOs Better Innovators? *J. Finance* **2012**, *67* (4), 1457–1498.

Holmes, R. M.; Bromiley, P.; Devers, C. E.; Holcomb, T. R.; McGuire, J. B. Management Theory Applications of Prospect Theory: Accomplichments, Challenges, and Opportunities. *J. Manag.* **2011**, *37* (4), 1069–1107.

Hudson, B. T. Venture Capital in the Restaurant Industry. *Cornell Hosp. Q.* **1995**, *36* (3), 50–61.

Kim, J.; Kim, H.; Woods, D. Determinants of Corporate Cash-holding Levels: An Empirical Examination of the Restaurant Industry. *Int. J. Hosp.Manag.* **2011**, *30*, 568–574.

Kizildag, M. Financial Leverage Phenomenon in Hospitality Industry Sub-sector Portfolios. *Int. J. Contemp. Hosp. Manag.* **2015**, *27* (8), 1949–1978.

Landier, A.; Thesmar, D. Financial Contracting With Optimistic Entrepreneurs. *R e v . Finan. Stud.* **2009**, *22* (1), 117–150.

Lim, N. K. Loss Aversion or CEO Confidence? Unpacking the Accumulation Effects of CEO Stock-based Incentives on Strategic Risk-taking. Working Paper, 2011.

Malmendier, U.; Tate, G. CEO Overconfidence and Corporate Investment. *J. Finance* **2005**, *60* (6), 2661–2700.

Malmendier, U.; Tate, G. Who Makes Acquisitions? CEO Overconfidence and the Market's Reaction. *J. Finan. Econ.* **2008**, *89*, 20–43.

Malmendier, U.; Tate, G.; Yan, J. Overconfidence and Early-life Experience: The Effect of Managerial Traits on Corporate Financial Policies. *J. Finan.* **2011,** *66* (5), 1687–1733.

March, J. G.; Shapira, Z. Managerial Perspectives on Risk and Risk Taking. *Manag. Sci.* **1987,** *33,* 1404–1418.

Milton, D. Industry Surveys Restaurants. Standard and Poor's, 2003.

Minett, D.; Yaman, H. R.; Denizci, B. Leadership Styles and Ethical Decision-making in Hospitality Management. *Int. J. Hosp. Manag.* **2009,** *28,* 486–493.

Muller, C.; Inman, C. Characteristics and Behavior of Top Chain-restaurant CEOs. *Cornell Hotel Rest. Admin. Q.* **1996,** *37* (3), 64–69.

Nan, H.; Dalbor, M. Evidence of Franchising on Outperformance in the Restaurant Industry: A Long Term Analysis and Perspective. *Int. J. Contemp. Hosp. Manag.* **2013,** *25* (5), 723–739.

Otto, C. A. CEO Optimism and Incentive Compensation. *J. Finan. Econ.* **2014,** *114* (2), 366–404.

Parsa, H. G.; Self, J. T.; Njite, D.; King, T. Why Restaurants Fail. *Cornell Hotel Rest. Admin. Q.* **2005,** *46* (3), 304–322.

Parsa, H. G.; Gregory, A.; Terry, M. Why do Restaurants Fail? Part III: An Analysis of Macro and Micro Factors. *Emerg. Aspects Redef. Tour. Hosp.* **2010,** *1* (1), 16–25.

Parsa, H. G.; van der Rest, J. P. I.; Smith, S. R.; Parsa, R. A.; Bujisic, M. Why Restaurants Fail? Part IV: The Relationship Between Restaurant Failures and Demographic Factors. *Cornell Hosp. Q.* **2015,** *56* (1), 80–90.

Reich, A. Z. Applied Economics of Hospitality Production: Reducing Costs and Improving the Quality of Decisions Through Economic Analysis. *Int. J. Hosp. Manag.* **1994,** *12* (4), 337–352.

Roll, R. The Hubris Hypothesis of Corporate Takeovers. *J. Bus.* **1986,** *59,* 197–216.

Sanders, W. G.; Hambrick, D. C. Swing for the Fences: The Effects of CEO Stock Option on Company Risk-taking and Performance. *Acad. Manag. J.* **2007,** *50* (5), 1055–1078.

Seo, K. L.; Kim, E. E. K.; Sharma, A. Examining the Determinants of Long-term Debt in the U.S. Restaurant Industry: Does CEO Overconfidence Affect Debt Maturity Decisions? *Int. J. Contem. Hosp. Manag.* **2017,** *29* (5), pp. 1501–1520.

Sunder, J.; Sunder, S.; Tan, L. The Role of Managerial Overconfidence in the Design of Debt Covenants. Working paper; University of Arizona, 2009.

Tversky, A.; Kahneman, D. Advances in Prospect Theory: Cumulative Representation of Uncertainty. *J. Risk Uncert.* **1992,** *5* (4), 297–323.

Upneja, A.; Dalbor, M. Agency Costs, Bankruptcy Costs and the Use of Debt in Multinational Restaurant Firms. *Hosp. Rev.* **2007,** *25* (1), 54–59.

Wiseman, R. M.; Gomez-Mejia, L. R. A Behavioral Agency Model of Managerial Risk Taking. *Acad. Manag. Rev.* **1998,** *23,* 133–153.

CHAPTER 12

Processing Fluency: An Approach to Looking for Nudge Interventions

YUXIA OUYANG

School of Hospitality Management, Pennsylvania State University,
University Park, Pennsylvania, USA

E-mail: oriazhuang@gmail.com

ABSTRACT

This study discussed the inherent link between the nudge theory and the theory of processing fluency and how researchers could use the theory of processing fluency to look for interventions to effectively nudge individuals' choices. Related studies and choice experiments are intensively reviewed in this paper.

12.1 INTRODUCTION

In behavior economics, researchers have been attempting to help individuals make wise choices in their daily lives because "people often make poor choices" as said by Thaler and Sunstein (2008). Recall how many times you regretted after indulging in a beefsteak or a large slice of chocolate cake? Like architects, behavior economists construct choices to be presented in a way that nudge people toward behaviors that could lead to personally and socially desirable outcomes. In this process, the careful design of the environment in which people make choices is called choice architecture. Accordingly, a nudge is "any aspect of the choice architecture that alters people's behavior in a predictable way without forbidding any options or significantly changing their economic incentives" (Thaler and Sustein, 2008). The conception of nudge is first labeled by Thaler and Sustein (2008) in the book *Nudge*:

improve decisions about health, wealth, and happiness. Hitherto, the theory, has been largely employed in food economics and successfully "nudged" individuals to healthier choices in empirical studies. However, the results of these studies did not reach agreement. On one hand, it has been justified by numerous experiments that well-designed choices architectures can improve individuals' welfare through compensating for their irrational design-making biases. On the other hand, admitting the theoretically attractive of nudge theory, there has been controversy with the effectiveness of the approach because empirical findings did not consistently support outcome by nudge intervention, nor could any well-designed choice architecture give a robust evidence to change population health behaviors in a long run. As alternative choices become more numerous and more complex on various dimensions, choice architects have to seek for multiple interventions and construct more effective choice designs. The purpose of the paper is to introduce another theory "processing fluency" which inherently associates with the essence of nudge theory as it provides an approach to look for other interventions in addition to the tools that are currently used in the nudge framework.

The theory of processing fluency, first defined by Schwarz (2004), focuses on providing the ease or fluency with which new external information can be processed in an individuals' judgment or decision-making process. Therefore, the fluency in the cognitive process has underlying link with the nudge theory because such fluency can minimize mental effort during information processing. Interventions that are widely used to stimulate mental processing fluency such as familiarity, repetition, congruency, and so on have been found effective in influencing individuals' preferences and favorable selections (Schwarz, 2004). Therefore, this paper by conducting a thorough literature review to introduce the two theories aims to provide the view that processing fluency can be used as an approach to looking for interventions that can help build the choice architecture and further effectively nudge individuals' choices. In addition, the paper will provide suggestions for how to design experiments based on processing fluency theory to nudge individuals' choices and preferences for future studies.

12.2 NUDGE THROUGH CHOICE ARCHITECTURE

Choice architecture should be designed in a way that could make receivers to achieve non-forced compliance at their own discretion. Such process is called nudge, and the construction design of choices is called choice architecture. Two principles are simultaneously observed in the nudge architecture construction: libertarism and paternalism. Libertarism refers to no prohibition on any alternative choices; paternalism indicates that options have to be presented in a manner to favor the behavior actor's optimal outcomes. In the sense, libertarian paternalism is called soft paternalism. Nudges can be implemented through simple, easy, and inexpensive interventions or small and unnoticed environmental changes (Thaler and Sustein, 2008), such as making the optimal choice more convenient to approach by rearranging choices display. Thaler et al. (2014) suggested basic principle to effectively design choice architecture as follows:

(1) Defaults choices are ubiquitously effective as individuals' choices will be determined by doing nothing.
(2) Giving feedback means that the system should inform the actor behaviors whether they are doing well or making mistakes.
(3) Expecting error refers to a system that allows actors' mistakes and acts as forgiving as possible.
(4) Understanding mappings and structuring complex choices both indicate that a good choice architecture has to enable a complex choice set to be understandable to receivers.
(5) Creating incentives reinforces the importance of the standard economic forces and underlines the importance to attract receivers' attention to the designed incentives.

The most applicable tool that has been used in healthy eating context is default choice, or any choice architecture that can lead behavior actors to the optimal choices with the least effort as compared to choosing alternatives. Many experiments have successfully "nudged" individuals to healthier choices using the least effort principle because individuals inherently have decision inertia and want to minimize any cost, in terms of convenience, time, and effort. For example, Rozein et al. (2011) presented a choice design for a pay-by-weight-of-food salad bar. In the experiment, they made a certain food slightly more difficult to reach by adding its proximity by about 10 inches, or by using tongs instead of spoons as the serving utensil. Such deliberate rearrangement of food display reliably reduced total intake of the targeted food by 8–16%. Wansink et al. (2013) applied the principle of convenience and "nudged" children to more apple consumption by simply serving sliced apples in middle schools. Out of six schools that participated in the study, three were randomly assigned in the treatment group and served apples in slices. Since presliced apples were more convenient to consume than whole apple, schools serving apple slices showed increased average daily apple sales by 71% compared to control schools. Additionally, Hanks et al. (2012) designed a convenient line in which serving was faster but only provided healthier food options to nudge individuals' choices. In the field experiment, they opened a fast line that only served healthier food options; while the regular line provided both healthier and unhealthier food options. After 8 weeks manipulation was compared with 8 weeks before the intervention, researchers found that the healthier foods consumed increased by 18% and sales of less healthy foods declined by nearly 28%. Menu positions also influenced the frequency of food orders. Menu experts suggested that the upper right-hand side as the "sweet spot" should be the most selected area (Cohen and Baby, 2012). Dayan and Bar-Hillel (2011) found that items printed at the beginning or the end of the list had advantages to be selected over those that were placed in the center of the list. In addition, multiple nudge strategies were jointly implemented in a choice architecture. Hubbard et al. (2014) created a Smarter Lunchroom in a residential school with students between 11 and 22 years old. The food choice architecture for the special lunchroom applied a combination of interventions simultaneously, including bundling healthy food selections as side dish (default choices), providing smaller portion sizes, making healthy choices more convenient, improving visibility of healthier foods, and utilizing suggestive verbal prompts. Positive results were reported in favor of different types of healthy foods, such as whole -grain selections, vegetable plates, and fruits. Similar to the conception of Smaller Lunchroom, Silver Diner, a regional restaurant chain, redesigned their menu, in which added prevalence of healthy side dishes and bundled healthy dishes with entrees. The new menu was considered an effective tool to promote healthier meals' ordering (Anzman-Frasca et al., 2015).

Salient improvement of healthy food choices was not consistently resulted from nudge interventions, however, some studies failed to support nudge as a compelling way in changing individuals' behaviors and cast doubt on how powerful these small changes in the environment could affect individuals' behaviors. Wilson et al. (2015) placed a sign with the message "Pick me! I'm low fat!" on the low-fat milk selections and recorded sales for different milks for two weeks, and found that such verbal signal failed to notably promote the low-calorie milks. Similarly, Olstad et al. (2014) tried to promote healthier foods by using newly designed attractive names and salient signs for their targeted foods in a recreational sports setting. New names contained descriptive and appealing words, such as changing "Very berry smoothie" to "The purple moo smoothie." Names for the healthy items were also printed double in size on the advertisement board, which was placed as close as possible to the register stand. However, before implementing the price reduction intervention, healthy foods sales were significantly lower than unhealthy food sales. Olstad et al. thus indicated that nudging should be combined with the use of other strategies that had been proven to encourage healthier food choices, such as risk aversion or price promotion after finding small and inconsistent impacts of nudging. Manipulation of portion size did not lead to the healthier eating outcome either. Rolls et al. (2007a), on one hand, suggested that providing large portion sizes significantly caused overconsumption; while on the other hand, they found that it was not equally easy to decrease food consumption when giving participants smaller plates. In a buffet setting, smaller plates only lead participants more trips to get foods (Rolls et al., 2007a). The use of calorie information as a nudging intervention was repeatedly examined but was found to affect only subgroups of participants, such as women (Gerend, 2009) or non-overweight individuals (Wisdom et al., 2010). Finkelstein et al. (2010) compared purchasing behaviors in fast-food restaurants in two towns, one of which implemented mandatory calorie labeling while the other did not. Either purchasing behavior or calorie consumptions varied between the two towns. One explanation for the difficulty to robustly nudge food choices is due to individuals' inherent decision-making mechanism for food. Eating-related decisions are generally driven by fast and spontaneous motives but little conscious thought (Cohen and Farley, 2008). Although individuals may express rational intention to eat healthfully in self-reported context, in practice, they are more often choose foods for immediate reasons, such as taste gratification, limited time, or convenience, without valuing the future health cost (Downs et al., 2009). Therefore, combination of effective nudging strategies is encouraged to use simultaneously because they are likely to result in cumulative effects as suggested by Hubbard et al. (2014), Anzman-frasca et al. (2015), and Velema et al. (2017). In addition, there is no guarantee that the interventions that are proven to be effective for the empirical studies will have long-term effects (Rozin, et al., 2011). Continuously putting the unhealthy meals in a farther corner may eventually drive people to directly head to the indulgent spot. Therefore, it is important to look for additional nudge cues to reinforce the orientation on individuals' optimal choices. One of the theories that potentially can be taken as a way to look for nudge interventions is the view of processing fluency because fluent processing is essentially driven by stimuli that can minimize mental effort during information processing.

12.3   PROCESSING FLUENCY

Processing fluency refers to the ease or difficulty with which new external information is processed when an individual makes judgement or decisions (Schwarz, 2004). Schwarz, who first defined the theory of processing fluency, indicated that "our thought processes are accompanied by metacognitive experiences." Naive theories on which processing fluency is grounded, were introduced in the paper, such as meta-memory theory "the more exemplars exist, the easier it is to bring some to mind," the "My Mind" theory meaning "examples from categories that are well represented in memory are easier to recall" or knowledge-related theories "familiar (previously seen) material is easier to process." When new information was processed, the fluency (ease or difficulty) of certain past knowledge, experience, or memory would be inherently but unconsciously brought to mind and affect preference, judgement or decision making. A classic example could demonstrate the theory: people tend to think a statement true when the words rhyme (McGlone and Tofighbakhsh, 2000). In another case, when participants were shown a list of words at a rapid speed, they tended to perceive the test words more familiar when they were presented in higher clarity (Whittlesea et al., 1990). The underlying mechanism of the theory of processing fluency is that people unconsciously control the effort during mental process thus perceived ease offers a fluent channel for cognitive performance (Schwarz, 2004).

12.4   PERCEPTUAL STIMULI IN PROCESSING FLUENCY

Empirically, fluency can be influenced by a variety of cues that are likely to simplify perceptual patterns and facilitate fast, effortless, and spontaneous decision making. Processing fluency can be measured in both objective (e.g., the speed and accuracy of thought processing) and subjective domains (e.g., the level of liking, impression and preference of the stimulus). Such perceptual cues can be regularity, similarity, clarity, symmetry, familiarity, relatedness, and congruity through stimulating different sensory systems. Olfactory simplicity was shown to facilitate information processing in the objective sense. Herrmann et al. (2013) found that subjects could solve anagrams easier with more accuracy in the presence of an ambient orange scent, which is a simple and fluent aroma, than in no-scent condition or in the environment of complex basil–orange with green tea scent. In the subjective domain, processing fluency theory has been largely applied to impact individuals' preferences and manipulate their choices (Novemsky et al., 2007) through stimulating visual, sounds, olfactory, and taste system. For instance, similar to the olfactory similarity example, visual simplicity was also found to increase participants' likings. When presented with pictures of deli service environment, participants gave significantly higher rating on the level of attractiveness to the pictures showing low-complexity environment with a sparse interior than those showing high-complexity environment with highly irregular store arrangement (Orth and Wirtz, 2014). Labroo et al. (2008) conducted an experiment in which participants were first asked to imagine a scene according to an oral description where the word "frog" was repeated in the story. Then participants were asked to choose between two bottles of wine, one of which was branded as "Frog Wines." The result that participants had higher preference for the Frog branded wine suggested that repetition could increase the ease of information processing. Another field study through stimulating olfactory system investigated if gender-based appropriateness would further information processing. Spangenber et al. (2006) first identified vanilla as the most feminine scent while Maroc rose as the most masculine scent, then diffused both aromas in a department store on different days. Female shoppers were found to spend more money and time in the presence of vanilla; while male shopper was affected in a similar way by Maroc rose. Familiarity is another stimulus to facilitate information processing because past knowledge or experience was brought to mind by the familiar stimulus thus favoring the acquainted choices (Novemsky et al., 2007). In a drink taste test, subjects were invited to taste unfamiliar soft drinks once a week over continuous four weeks. Liking scores increased as participants were exposed more to the drinks, showing that familiarity led to taste processing fluency (Sulmont-Rossé et al., 2008). Lévy et al. (2006) also found favorable results for repeated exposure to similar orange drinks. Relatedness was also suggested to help individuals unconsciously reflect upon past information. In an experiment by Lee and Labroo (2004), prior exposure to a picture of mayonnaise enhanced the favorable attitudes to ketchup, an associatively related product, but did not favor the attitudes to Vitamin. Those examples suggested that the view of processing fluency could provide us a way to look for stimuli to influence individuals' liking, positive evaluation, and favorable choices through multiple sensory dimensions. Similar to the nudge theory, processing fluency lead to the same goal that through an implicit intervention, choice designers aim to subconsciously influence behavioral actors' attitudes, affection, preference, judgment and finally the actual choice of the targeted option over the alternatives. Due to the inherent association and consistent ultimate goal between the two conceptions, we propose that the theory of processing fluency could serve as an approach to seek more interventions to nudge individuals' choices through multiple sensory dimensions.

12.5 STIMULI AS INTERVENTIONS TO NUDGE INDIVIDUALS' FOOD CHOICES

Some studies underpinned on the nudge theory, although not explicitly identified it, have essentially employed certain stimulus to ease information processing. Snack packages with familiar cartoon characteristics (e.g., Dora from Dora the Explorer or SpongeBob from SpongeBob SquarePants) could effectively increase children's liking and purchase intention of fruit up to a level similar to candy (de Droog et al., 2011). However, authors admitted that "we did not find support for the theoretical assumption that for a product, familiar characters can elicit more liking and higher purchase request intent than unfamiliar characters." Additionally, Schwartz (2007) found that a simple verbal promotion "would you like fruit or juice with your lunch?" significantly promoted fruit sales and consumption, but only concluded that "simple intervention of a verbal promotion may have a significant impact on fruit consumption." Furthermore, Papies et al. (2014) distributed recipe flyers that contained health consciousness information in a grocery store and found that such information reduced snack purchase almost 75% as compared to the context without health-related flyers. The authors only noted that the recipe flyers, acting as health priming, could activate the mental processing of the goal and affect subsequent behavior, but did not systematically discuss characteristics of health priming or other possible priming cues. In fact, the underlying mechanism for the studies mentioned above is inherently integrated with the view of information fluency: through stimulus such as visual familiarity, oral reoccurrence, and health-related information repetition. Interventions employed in these studies made the healthier food choices somewhat more related to past experience or the current context, thus enabling mental processing fluent in favor of healthier food choices.

12.6   SUMMARY AND FUTURE STUDIES

By understanding the theoretical logic of the nudge theory and the processing fluency theory, as well as related literature, we can make systematic linkage among the studies and more importantly, look for potential interventions for future work. On one hand, nudge theory aims to design choice architecture, in which simple, inexpensive, and unnoticed interventions or environmental changes are deliberately presented to influence one' choices in order to achieve individually or socially desired outcomes. On the other hand, the processing fluency theory inspires us with a variety of interventions such as regularity, similarity, clarity, symmetry, familiarity, relatedness, and congruity, essentially any cue that is likely to facilitate memory or perceptual ease. Those stimuli can be triggered through multiple sensory dimensions, such as visual, taste, olfactory, and auditory systems. Combining principles of the two conceptions, some possible suggestions could be: post appealing fruit pictures in the cafeteria to stimulate the visual familiarity and favorable emotion, diffuse a certain type of fruit aromas to elicit olfactory congruity, or repeatedly display certain food in different sectors in the cafeteria. Additionally, Spangenber et al. (2005) increased individuals' liking and willingness to purchase by playing Christmas congruent music and Christmas represented scent during Christmas. A similar design for choice orientation could be to print holiday-related pictures or symbols on packages of healthier foods during the holiday season. Sales for the targeted foods are very likely to be raised by such simple manipulation.

Within food economics, researchers have been looking for and testing different interventions to persuade individuals' eating behaviors and lead them to wiser food choices. The nudge theory as a powerful theoretical framework has been successfully used to direct individuals' behaviors and choices to gain personal and social welfare. However, some studies had controversial results and cast doubt on how consistent and effective such small interventions could robustly change individuals' behaviors. Therefore, additional nudging stimuli and interactive nudging interventions are recommended to use for reinforcing the effect of nudging. The theory of processing fluency could provide an approach to look for potential nudging cues because such stimuli would ease information processing thus enhancing the liking of and favorable bias on the target options. Based on the fact that existing studies under nudging theory have applied the view of processing fluency theory, although without clearly identifying it, we shall systematically look into interventions within the framework of processing fluency and apply them into food economics field. Future research has promising potentials to lead people to optimal behaviors.

KEYWORDS

- nudge theory
- processing fluency theory
- choice experiment
- choice architecture design
- sensory stimuli

REFERENCES

Anzman-Frasca, S.; Mueller, M. P.; Lynskey, V. M.; Harelick, L.; Economos, C. D. Orders of Healthier Children's Items Remain High More Than Two Years After Menu Changes at a Regional Restaurant Chain. *Health Aff.* **2015,** *34* (11), 1885–1892.

Bar-Hillel, M. Position Effects in Choice From Simultaneous Displays: A Conundrum Solved. *Persp. Psychol. Sci.* **2015,** *10* (4), 419–433.

Cohen, D. A.; Babey, S. H. Contextual Influences on Eating Behaviours: Heuristic Processing and Dietary Choices. *Obes. Rev.* **2012,** *13* (9), 766–779.

Cohen, D.; Farley, T. A. Peer Reviewed : Eating as an Automatic Behavior. *Prev. Chron. Dis.* **2008,** *5* (1), 1–7.

Dayan, E.; Bar-Hillel, M. Nudge to Nobesity II: Menu Positions Influence Food Orders. *Judg. Dec. Making* **2011,** *6* (4), 333.

De Droog, S. M.; Valkenburg, P. M.; Buijzen, M. Using Brand Characters to Promote Young Children's Liking of and Purchase Requests for Fruit. *J. Health Commun.* **2010,** *16* (1), 79–89.

Downs, J. S.; Loewenstein, G.; Wisdom, J. Strategies for Promoting Healthier Food Choices. *Amer. Econ. Rev.* **2009,** *99* (2), 159–164.

Finkelstein, E. A.; Strombotne, K. L.; Chan, N. L.; Krieger, J. Mandatory Menu Labeling in One Fast-Food Chain in King County, Washington. *Amer. J. Preven. Med.* **2011,** *40* (2), 122–127.

Gerend, M. A. Does Calorie Information Promote Lower Calorie Fast Food Choices Among College Students? *J. Adoles. Health* **2009,** *44* (1), 84–86.

Hanks, A. S.; Just, D. R.; Smith, L. E.; Wansink, B. Healthy Convenience: Nudging Students Toward Healthier Choices in the Lunchroom. *J. Public Health* **2012,** *Fds003.*

Herrmann, A.; Zidansek, M.; Sprott, D. E.; Spangenberg, E. R. The Power of Simplicity: Processing Fluency and the Effects of Olfactory Cues on Retail Sales. *J. Retail.* **2013,** *89* (1), 30–43.

Hubbard, K. L.; Bandini, L. G.; Folta, S. C.; Wansink, B.; Eliasziw, M.; Must, A. Impact of a Smarter Lunchroom Intervention on Food Selection and Consumption Among Adolescents and Young Adults With Intellectual and Developmental Disabilities in a Residential School Setting. *Pub. Health Nutr.* **2015,** *18* (02), 361–371.

Labroo, A. A.; Dhar, R.; Schwarz, N. Of Frog Wines and Frowning Watches: Semantic Priming, Perceptual Fluency, and Brand Evaluation. *J. Consum. Res.* **2008,** *34* (6), 819–831.

Lee, A. Y.; Labroo, A. A. The Effect of Conceptual and Perceptual Fluency on Brand Evaluation. *J. Market. Res.* **2004,** *41* (2), 151–165.

Lévy, C. M.; Macrae, A.; Köster, E. P. Perceived Stimulus Complexity and Food Preference Development. *Acta Psychol.* **2006,** *123* (3), 394–413.

Mcglone, M. S.; Tofighbakhsh, J. Birds of a Feather Flock Conjointly (?): Rhyme as Reason in Aphorisms. *Psychol. Sci.* **2000,** *11* (5), 424–428.

Novemsky, N.; Dhar, R.; Schwarz, N.; Simonson, I. Preference Fluency in Choice. *J. Market. Res.* **2007,** *44* (3), 347–356.

Olstad, D. L.; Goonewardene, L. A.; Mccargar, L. J.; Raine, K. D. Choosing Healthier Foods in Recreational Sports Settings: A Mixed Methods Investigation of the Impact of Nudging and an Economic Incentive. *Int. J. Behav. Nutr. Phys. Activ.* **2014,** *11* (1), 6.

Orth, U. R.; Wirtz, J. Consumer Processing of Interior Service Environments: The Interplay Among Visual Complexity, Processing Fluency, and Attractiveness. *J. Serv. Res.* **2014,** *17* (3), 296–309.

Papies, E. K.; Potjes, I.; Keesman, M.; Schwinghammer, S.; Van Koningsbruggen, G. M. Using Health Primes to Reduce Unhealthy Snack Purchases Among Overweight Consumers in a Grocery Store. *Int. J. Obes.* **2014,** *38* (4), 597–602.

Reber, R.; Schwarz, N. Effects of Perceptual Fluency on Judgments of Truth. *Consc. Cogn.* **1999,** *8* (3), 338–342.

Rolls, B. J.; Roe, L. S.; Meengs, J. S. The Effect of Large Portion Sizes on Energy Intake is Sustained for 11 Days. *Obesity* **2007a,** *15* (6), 1535–1543.

Rolls, B. J.; Roe, L. S.; Halverson, K. H.; Meengs, J. S. Using a Smaller Plate Did Not Reduce Energy Intake at Meals. *Appetite* **2007b**, *49* (3), 652–660.

Rozin, P.; Scott, S.; Dingley, M.; Urbanek, J. K.; Jiang, H.; Kaltenbach, M. Nudge to Nobesity I: Minor Changes in Accessibility Decrease Food Intake. *Judg. Dec. Making* **2011**, *6* (4), 323.

Schwartz, M. B. The Influence of a Verbal Prompt on School Lunch Fruit Consumption: A Pilot Study. *Int. J. Behav. Nutr. Phys. Activ.* **2007**, *4* (1), 6.

Schwarz, N. Metacognitive Experiences in Consumer Judgment and Decision Making. *J. Consum. Psychol.* **2004**, *14* (4), 332–348.

Spangenberg, E. R.; Grohmann, B.; Sprott, D. E. It's Beginning to Smell (and Sound) a Lot Like Christmas: The Interactive Effects of Ambient Scent and Music in a Retail Setting. *J. Bus. Res.* **2005**, *58* (11), 1583–1589.

Spangenberg, E. R.; Sprott, D. E.; Grohmann, B.; Tracy, D. L. Gender-Congruent Ambient Scent Influences on Approach and Avoidance Behaviors in a Retail Store. *J. Bus. Res.* **2006**, *59* (12), 1281–1287.

Sulmont-Rossé, C.; Chabanet, C.; Issanchou, S.; Köster, E. P. Impact of the Arousal Potential of Uncommon Drinks on the Repeated Exposure Effect. *Food Qual. Pref.* **2008**, *19* (4), 412–420.

Thaler, R. H.; Sunstein, C. R. Nudge: Improving Decisions About Health, Wealth, and Happiness, 2008.

Thaler, R. H.; Sunstein, C. R.; Balz, J. P. Choice Architecture, 2014.

Velema, E.; Vyth, E. L.; Steenhuis, I. H. Using Nudging and Social Marketing Techniques to Create Healthy Worksite Cafeterias in the Netherlands: Intervention Development and Study Design. *BMC Pub. Health* **2017**, *17* (1), 63.

Wansink, B.; Just, D. R.; Hanks, A. S.; Smith, L. E. Pre-sliced Fruit in School Cafeterias: Children's Selection and Intake. *Amer. J. Prev. Med.* **2013**, *44* (5), 477–480.

Whittlesea, B. W.; Jacoby, L. L.; Girard, K. Illusions of Immediate Memory: Evidence of an Attributional Basis for Feelings of Familiarity and Perceptual Quality. *J. Memory Lang.* **1990**, *29* (6), 716–732.

Wisdom, J.; Downs, J. S.; Loewenstein, G. Promoting Healthy Choices: Information Versus Convenience. *Amer. Econ. J. Appl. Econ.* **2010**, *2* (2), 164–178.

Index

For Product Safety Concerns and Information please contact our EU
representative GPSR@taylorandfrancis.com Taylor & Francis Verlag GmbH,
Kaufingerstraße 24, 80331 München, Germany

Printed and bound by CPI Group (UK) Ltd, Croydon, CR0 4YY
08/05/2025
01864390-0001